Q & A SERIES
CRIMINAL LAW

FOURTH EDITION

Cavendish
Publishing
Limited

London • Sydney • Portland, Oregon

Q & A SERIES
CRIMINAL LAW
FOURTH EDITION

Norman Baird, BA, BSc

Course Director,
Online LLB,
Semple Piggot Rochez

Cavendish
Publishing
Limited

London • Sydney • Portland, Oregon

Fourth edition first published in Great Britain 2002 by
Cavendish Publishing Limited, The Glass House,
Wharton Street, London WC1X 9PX, United Kingdom
Telephone: + 44 (0)20 7278 8000   Facsimile: + 44 (0)20 7278 8080
Email: info@cavendishpublishing.com
Website: www.cavendishpublishing.com

Published in the United States by Cavendish Publishing
c/o International Specialized Book Services,
5804 NE Hassalo Street, Portland,
Oregon 97213-3644, USA

Published in Australia by Cavendish Publishing (Australia) Pty Ltd
3/303 Barrenjoey Road, Newport, NSW 2106, Australia

© Baird, N	2003
First edition	1993
Second edition	1995
Third edition	1999
Fourth edition	2002
Reprinted with updates	2003

British Library Cataloguing in Publication Data
Baird, Norman
Criminal law – 4th ed – (the Cavendish Q & A series)
1 Criminal law – England   2 Criminal law – Wales
I Title
345.4'2
ISBN 1-85941-628-4

3 5 7 9 10 8 6 4 2

Printed and bound in Great Britain

CONTENTS

INTRODUCTION

The purpose of this book is to assist students in their study of criminal law and it is aimed primarily at those who are studying on degree courses and courses leading to professional examinations. It is not intended to replace standard textbooks, law reports and academic journals but to complement them by providing illustrations of answers to typical examination and course assessment questions. It is anticipated that it will be of most use to the student who has acquired a good knowledge of the relevant rules and principles of criminal law but who still experiences difficulty in expressing that knowledge.

It is often not clear to students what is expected of them when answering questions in criminal law. Common difficulties include tackling problem questions where some of the relevant facts are not disclosed, the treatment of conflicting or ambiguous rules of law, the resolution of problems where there are no adequate authorities, and judging the extent to which it may be necessary to refer to the facts of previous decisions. It is hoped that this book will help to resolve these difficulties.

Where the law is in doubt, reference is occasionally made to the opinions of academics expressed in the standard texts on criminal law.

The questions are modelled on those used in past examination papers. They include 'problem questions', 'essay questions' and 'mixed part questions'. The answers to each question are preceded by an answer plan which explains, in outline, the issues raised by the question.

I hope that this book will assist you to make the best use of your knowledge of criminal law in examinations and course assessments.

I have endeavoured to state the law as at June 2003.

Norman Baird
London
July 2003
www.spr-law.com
www.spr-consilio.com

TABLE OF CASES

TABLE OF STATUTES

CHAPTER 1

GENERAL PRINCIPLES OF CRIMINAL LAW

Introduction

This chapter contains questions concerning some of the fundamental principles of criminal law. Also included are questions regarding the objectives of punishment and the proper scope of the criminal law.

Inevitably, because of the subject matter, the majority of the questions in this chapter are of the essay type.

Checklist

The following topics should be prepared in advance of tackling the questions:

- the competing theories of punishment: why do we punish? What objectives ought we to have in mind? 'Utilitarian' and 'desert' theories of punishment;

- the scope of the criminal law: what types of conduct ought to be subject to criminal sanctions? Should behaviour be subject to the criminal law merely because it is considered 'immoral', or should only 'harmful' conduct be criminalised? Other considerations that the legislature ought to bear in mind when deciding whether to make particular conduct unlawful;

- *mens rea* terms – 'intention' and 'recklessness': the meaning of 'intention'; the meaning of 'recklessness'; '*Caldwell* recklessness' and '*Cunningham* recklessness' – the distinction between 'advertent' and 'inadvertent' recklessness;

- liability for omissions: the circumstances in which criminal liability may be incurred for a failure to act; the duty principle; co-incidence of *actus reus* and *mens rea*;

- strict liability: what is meant by a crime of strict liability? How do the courts determine whether or not an offence requires *mens rea*? What are the justifications for imposing liability on a strict basis?

Question 1

[For a practice to be subject to the criminal sanction] it is not enough in our submission that [it] is ... regarded as immoral. Nor is it enough that it should cause harm. Both of these are minimal conditions for action by means of the criminal law, but they are not sufficient [Clarkson, CMV and Keating, HM, *Criminal Law: Text and Materials*, 1990, p 25].

Discuss.

Answer plan

The quotation expresses the commonly held view that immorality and harmfulness are *necessary but not sufficient* conditions of criminal liability: that the legislator ought to consider further matters when deciding whether to criminalise or legalise particular conduct. The starting point in answering this question is the well known 'debate' in the 1950s and 1960s between Lord Devlin and Professor Hart:

- the 'moral' theory: the Wolfenden Committee and Lord Devlin's response to the Report;
- criticisms of the 'moral' theory – its irrationalism;
- the 'harm' principle;
- the limitations of the 'harm' principle;
- considerations additional to the supposed immorality or harmfulness of the behaviour – the social effects of prohibition and enforcement;
- is immorality a 'necessary' condition?

Answer

In 1959, Lord Devlin delivered the Maccabean Lecture in Jurisprudence of the British Academy under the title 'The enforcement of morals' in which he argued that the legislature is entitled to use the criminal law against behaviour which is generally condemned as immoral.

The catalyst for Lord Devlin's thesis was the *Report of the Wolfenden Committee on Homosexual Offences and Prostitution*, 1957. The Committee had recommended that homosexual behaviour between consenting adults in private should no longer be a criminal offence. The Committee thought it was not the function of the law to intervene in the private lives of citizens or to enforce any particular morality *except* where it is necessary to protect the citizen from what is offensive or injurious and to provide protection against exploitation and corruption.

Lord Devlin contended that these additional criteria were unnecessary. In his opinion, there are no limits to the power of the State to legislate against immoral behaviour – 'immorality' is a necessary and sufficient condition of criminalisation.

Lord Devlin based his argument upon the premise that if morality is not underwritten by the law, social harmony will be jeopardised. According to this view, tolerance of immorality threatens the social fabric and therefore the legislature should criminalise behaviour where it is clear that there is a 'collective judgment' condemning the behaviour in question.[1]

According to Lord Devlin, immorality is what every 'right minded' person considers to be immoral. If the behaviour in question provokes feelings of disgust and indignation in this 'individual', then it should be subject to the criminal sanction. Lord Devlin suggests the judiciary are particularly well placed to express the appropriate standards by virtue of their familiarity with the 'reasonable man in the jury'.

There are a number of different objections to Lord Devlin's thesis, but the principal criticisms relate to its 'overt rejection of rationality'.[2] That is, instead of rational argument and empirical investigation of the likely effects of criminalisation or legalisation, Lord Devlin advocates that we place our reliance upon *presumptions* about the *feelings* of the right minded individual and *assumptions* about the societal effects of liberalisation and tolerance.

Opponents of Devlin's thesis argue that, although the feelings of the community are an important consideration, they cannot be the sole basis for deciding whether behaviour is to be subject to the criminal sanction. And Graham Hughes points out that if the revulsion of the ordinary person is a dangerous basis for criminalisation, then reliance on judicial estimates of that disgust is even more dangerous. Bentham warned us to be suspicious when officials claim that they are acting in the name of 'right minded people'. In many cases, 'popular opinion' is used as a pretext to justify the prejudices of the legislators themselves.[3]

With reference to Lord Devlin's assertion that morality forms a seamless web, Professor Hart claims that there is no evidence that people abandon their moral views about murder, cruelty and dishonesty purely because a practice which they regard as immoral is not punished by law.[4]

Professor Hart argues that the proper approach to determining whether the criminal law should intervene involves full consideration of the social consequences of the conduct in question. To this extent, he is a supporter of the liberal approach which stresses the importance of rational analysis in terms of the possible harmful consequences of the conduct. The principle of democracy may require the legislator to consider the values of the 'moral' majority but the liberal tradition urges that the autonomy of the individual be respected and that individuals have rights that may trump majority will.

The general approach of this tradition was expressed by John Stuart Mill in his essay, *On Liberty*. He maintained that the exercise of force over an individual is justified only if it is done to prevent harm to others. The fact that the behaviour might cause harm to the person who performs it is no justification for criminalisation.[5]

Professor Hart agrees that we must consider whether a practice which is generally regarded as immoral is also harmful before we take the step of criminalising it. He argues that a reasoned assessment of the harmful effects of the behaviour is a far superior approach to the question whether it should be outlawed than simple reliance on the feelings of disgust that the behaviour might cause us to feel.[6]

It might be supposed that harm theorists would be opposed to legislation controlling narcotics or compelling the use of seat belts in motor vehicles, on the basis that legislation of this type involves a violation of the fundamental principle of individual autonomy. The harm theorist is opposed to legislation designed to protect the individual from himself.

In fact, legislation of this type is often supported by modern harm theorists. They point out that the prohibited behaviour *is* potentially harmful to others. Kaplan explains that there are different categories of harm, any one of which may be used to justify the criminalisation of behaviour that at first sight appears only to expose the actor to the risk of harm.[7] The individual who drives without wearing a seat belt or the person who consumes drugs may expose others to a 'public ward harm', that is, he may impose on others the cost of rectifying the damage he causes himself. He may be rendered incapable of discharging economic responsibilities he owes to others ('non-support harm'). Alternatively, a case may be made out that, if the individual is allowed to indulge in certain behaviour, other susceptible individuals may copy or 'model' the behaviour and suffer harm as a consequence.

This reveals one of the limitations of the liberal 'harm' theory. When secondary harms are taken into account, the theory appears to lack precision. As Kaplan points out, if we acknowledge the broad concept of harm, there are few actions that one can perform that threaten harm only to oneself.

Moreover, the prohibition of particular 'harmful' conduct may, in itself, result in harmful consequences. For example, the sale of certain commodities (heroin, alcohol, sugar, petrol, hamburgers, etc) may directly or indirectly cause *physical* harm to consumers. However, prohibiting the sale of those commodities will cause *economic* harm to the business enterprises involved. Thus, we must weigh the harms resulting from tolerance against the harms of prohibition.

Bentham recognised that, in this process, careful consideration should be given to the general effects of prohibition. Even though certain behaviour may be regarded as immoral or harmful, it should not be prohibited if punishment would be inefficacious as a deterrent or the harm caused by prohibition would be greater than that which would be suffered if the behaviour was left unpunished.[8]

For example, it is sometimes argued that, as the demand for certain commodities and services (for example, prostitution, abortion, alcohol and other drugs) is relatively inelastic, there is little point in criminalisation of the behaviour concerned. Indeed, it is suggested that criminalisation may make matters worse. Prior to legalisation, backstreet abortions were carried out in conditions of great risk to the mother. Legalisation permits official control, allowing matters of public health to be addressed.[9]

In addition, the criminalisation of certain types of conduct (for example, the possession of drugs) requires, for reasons of enforcement, intrusive forms of policing, involving, for example, powers of stop and search. There is the danger that these powers might be used in a discriminatory and oppressive manner against particular groups. The outlawing of homosexual behaviour meant that the police were often involved in dubious and degrading practices to catch offenders.[10]

Thus, the fact that behaviour is harmful to others cannot be a sufficient condition of prohibition. The virtue of the harm theory is that, at least, it focuses attention on the empirical issues concerning the social effects of the conduct *and* the effects of legal intervention – issues which the moral principle patently ignores.

The quotation suggests that immorality is a *necessary* condition of criminalisation. Is this correct? What importance should be attached to the moral feelings of a section of the community?

It is sometimes argued that support for the law is stronger where the prohibited conduct is perceived by a significant section of the population to be immoral.[11]

It is submitted, however, that immorality ought not to be regarded as even a necessary condition of prohibition. Much of modern criminal legislation (for example, road traffic laws) is concerned with conduct which would not ordinarily be termed 'immoral', but one would be hard pressed to deny the need for that legislation.

In any case, where behaviour is perceived to be immoral, it is normally supported by empirical claims expressed in terms of the harmful consequences, real or imagined, that will result if the behaviour is tolerated.[12] It is right that the debate should be focused on those empirical claims. It is only by insisting upon arguments articulated in terms of the social consequences of tolerance, on the one hand, and prohibition, on the other, that a rational analysis of the fairness of legal intervention can be conducted.

The fact that a section of the community *feels* that certain behaviour is immoral cannot be either a necessary or a sufficient condition of prohibition. Although it may be prudent *on some occasions* for the legislator to acknowledge the 'feelings' of a section of the community – to ignore those irrational sentiments may result in the harmful consequence of social unrest – he should not *rely* upon the 'stomach of the man in the street'. Disgust or revulsion ought never to replace careful investigation of the social effects of prohibition.[13]

Notes

1 Lord Devlin argued that morality forms a 'seamless web'. By this metaphor, he intended to convey the notion that 'society's morals' form a fragile structure and that, if morality is not generally reinforced by legal means, then 'damage' to the entire structure will follow.

2 Hughes, G, 'Morals and the criminal law', in Summers, R (ed), *Essays in Legal Philosophy*, 1968, p 198.

3 Bentham, J, *Theory of Legislation*, 1876.

4 Hart, HLA, 'Immorality and treason' (1959) 30 The Listener 30.

5 Harm is not to be understood as restricted to 'physical harm'. As Gross points out, 'harm' is caused when any recognised interest is violated (Gross, H, *A Theory of Criminal Justice*, 1979).

6 Professor Hart does suggest, however, that Mill's thesis is, perhaps, too simple. Cruelty to animals, for example, should be outlawed, although there is no harm caused to other people. It might also be argued that legal intervention may be appropriate to restrain young people, for example, from certain activities. This is justified not on the grounds that the behaviour may cause harm to the young person, but on the grounds that such a person is not sufficiently mature to be capable of appreciating the dangers of the behaviour in question.

7 See the extract from Kaplan, J, 'The role of law in drug control', in Clarkson, CMV and Keating, HM, *Criminal Law: Text and Materials*, 4th edn, 1998, p 14.

8 Bentham, J, 'Principles of morals and legislation', in Bentham, J and Mill, JS, *The Utilitarians*, 1961.

9 Similarly, if prostitution were decriminalised, a condition of operating as a licensed or registered prostitute might be periodic health checks.

10 In addition, homosexuals were exposed to the risk of blackmail.

11 Packer, H, *The Limits of the Criminal Sanction*, 1968.

12 For example, Lord Devlin believed that tolerance of homosexuality would result in harm – that is, damage to society at large (see note 1, above). If this hypothesis were testable, and if it were true, it would provide a very good argument in favour of prohibiting homosexuality. (Emperor Justinian believed that homosexual behaviour was the cause of earthquakes. Seismologists do not agree!) On the other hand, the assertion that 'homosexuality should be prohibited *because it is immoral*' cannot be evaluated in the same way.

13 Hughes, G, 'Morals and the criminal law', in Summers, R (ed), *Essays in Legal Philosophy*, 1968, p 206.

Question 2

Assess the modern approaches to the definition of 'intention' in English criminal law.

Answer plan

The principal issues are:

*   the hierarchy of fault elements;
*   intention and recklessness contrasted;
*   foresight and intention.

Principal authorities: *Hyam v DPP* (1975); *Moloney* (1985); *Hancock and Shankland* (1986); *Nedrick* (1986); *Woollin* (1998).

Answer

For a number of offences, the prosecution must prove beyond a reasonable doubt that the accused intended a particular consequence. To secure a conviction for murder, for example, it must be proved that the accused intended either to kill or cause grievous bodily harm. Recklessness will not suffice. Similarly, intention, and intention alone, is the basis of liability for the offence of wounding with intent, contrary to s 18 of the Offences Against the Person Act 1861 and for offences of attempt contrary to s 1(1) of the Criminal Attempts Act 1981.

The meaning of intention itself is not to be found in any statute. Its meaning is to be found in judicial decisions. Unfortunately, there has been a lack of consistency in the approach of the courts to the question of what constitutes intention. Before reviewing these decisions, it is necessary to consider the functional significance of intention in criminal law and the principles which ought to be considered when constructing a definition of the concept.

The fault elements most commonly encountered in the definition of offences – intention and recklessness – reflect different levels or degrees of blameworthiness. A person who kills, intending to kill, is, all other things being equal, more blameworthy than a person who kills recklessly. This is reflected in the fact that the former is guilty of murder and subject to a *mandatory* term of life imprisonment, whereas the latter is guilty of manslaughter which carries, *at the discretion of the court*, a life sentence.[1]

The concepts of intention and recklessness are distinct and stand in a hierarchical relationship one to the other. Thus, the definition of intention should not overlap with the definition of recklessness (the essence of which is unjustified risk taking with respect to a defined consequence) and the boundary between the two concepts should be drawn to reflect the difference in degree of moral blameworthiness.

Furthermore, since the jury will have the task of determining whether the accused did or did not intend the evil consequence in question, the judicial instruction as to the meaning of intention should be clear, intelligible and correspond as closely as possible to the ordinary meaning of the word. If the legal definition of intention deviated significantly from ordinary usage, then the risk of the jury failing to understand the judge's direction would be increased. In addition, it is often argued that the law should reflect ordinary principles concerning the attribution of moral responsibility.

It is generally accepted that the central or core meaning of 'intention' is *aim, objective* or *purpose*. A person intends a consequence if he acts in order to bring it about. This approach to intention was adopted by the Court of Appeal in *Mohan* (1976), in which James LJ defined 'intention' as a decision to bring about a particular consequence, irrespective of whether the defendant desired that consequence.

The latter part of the definition indicates that a person can be said to intend a particular consequence, even though it is not desired, if it is a condition precedent to the desired consequence.

The definition in *Mohan* corresponds to the ordinary meaning of the word,[2] but, on many occasions, the judiciary has accepted a wider definition. Prior to the decision of the House of Lords in *Moloney*, it was generally accepted that a person could be said to have intended a result if he foresaw that the result was *virtually certain* to result from his acts, even if the result was not his aim or purpose.[3]

The point is commonly discussed by reference to the following hypothetical example:

D places a bomb on a plane. The bomb is timed to explode when the plane is in mid-flight. His aim is to collect the insurance money on cargo he has placed on the flight. Although he hopes the passengers and crew will survive the explosion, D knows that it is practically certain that they will die.

Does D intend to kill in these circumstances or is he 'merely' reckless with respect to killing the passengers and crew?

It has been argued that a consequence is intended only where its non-occurrence would be regarded as a failure and thus, as D would not regard the survival of the passengers and crew as marking the failure of his plan, he does not intend to kill.[4]

On the other hand, it has been suggested that, despite the fact that it is not D's purpose to kill the passengers, there is no moral distinction between D and the purposeful killer, and D ought to be categorised as an intentional killer and convicted of murder if the plan is carried out and death results. Intention, it is said, ought to be defined to include foresight of virtual certainty.[5]

Until the 1980s, there had been some judicial recognition of an even broader definition. One of the leading cases was *Hyam v DPP* (1975), in which the House of Lords held that a person intends a result which he foresees as a (highly) probable result of his actions. This decision was, however, rarely followed as it was felt to blur the distinction between intention and recklessness.[6]

In the 1980s, a series of cases adopted a different approach to the question of intention. In the first, *Moloney* (1985), the House of Lords held that, ordinarily, the judge need not define the word 'intention', except to explain that it is not the same thing as either 'desire' or 'foresight'.[7] In 'rare' and 'exceptional' cases, however – those in which the primary purpose of the defendant was not to cause the defined harmful consequence – the judge may instruct the jury that, if the defendant foresaw the consequence as a natural consequence of his act, then they may infer that he intended it.

It is likely that Lord Bridge used 'natural consequence' believing that it conveyed the concept of a very high probability, but the guidelines did not make that clear.[8] The problems caused by the guidance were raised in 1986 in the case of *Hancock and Shankland*. Two miners on strike had pushed a concrete block from a bridge onto a three lane highway on which a miner was being taken to work by taxi. The concrete block hit the taxi and killed the driver. The defendants were charged with murder. They said that they merely intended to block the road and to frighten the non-striking miner. Following the *Moloney* guidelines, the judge asked the jury to consider two questions: was death or serious injury a natural consequence of what was done?; and did the defendant foresee that consequence as a natural consequence? The jury convicted the defendants of murder.

The Court of Appeal held that the *Moloney* guidelines were misleading and quashed the conviction. There was an appeal to the House of Lords. In the only speech, Lord Scarman agreed that the *Moloney* guidelines were potentially misleading as they omitted any reference to the probability of death or serious harm occurring. Lord Scarman pointed out that it should be explained to the jury that the greater the probability of a consequence, the more likely it is that the consequence was foreseen and that if the consequence was foreseen, the more likely it is that it was intended.

In the third case, *Nedrick* (1986), the Court of Appeal held that the jury were entitled to draw the inference of intention only where they were sure that the defendant foresaw as a virtual certainty the consequence in question. Indeed, Lord Lane thought that, in those circumstances, the 'inference may be irresistible'.[9]

As a result of these decisions, it appeared that there was no longer a definition of intention. *Hyam* was effectively overruled. Foresight, even of a virtually certain consequence, was merely evidence of intention to be considered along with all other relevant evidence. Intention and foresight were not commensurable.

The decisions were heavily criticised for their failure to provide a definition of intention and for failing to explain how juries were to weigh the evidence of foresight against all the other evidence.[10]

In *Woollin* (1998), the House of Lords reconsidered the earlier decisions. The appellant had lost his temper and thrown his baby son on to a hard surface. His son had sustained a fractured skull and died. The appellant was charged with murder. The Crown did not contend that the appellant desired to cause his son serious injury. The issue was whether the appellant nevertheless intended to cause serious harm. The appellant denied that he had any such intention. The recorder's summing up was largely in accordance with the guidance given in *Nedrick*. However, he instructed the jury that if they were satisfied that the appellant realised that there was a *substantial* risk that he would cause serious injury to his son, then it would be open to them to find that he intended to cause injury to the child.

In the leading judgment, Lord Steyn observed, with the approval of all the Law Lords, that by using the phrase 'a substantial risk', the judge had blurred the line between intention and recklessness. The conviction of murder was quashed and a conviction for manslaughter substituted.

This part of the decision is, in itself, unremarkable, but, in what appears to be a revision of the previous approach, Lord Steyn observed that a consequence foreseen as virtually certain is an intended result. Doing acts with foresight that serious harm is a virtually certain result is a species of intention to cause serious harm.

Lord Steyn believed that this approach to intention was neither too narrow nor likely to confuse a jury. He also noted that it was similar to the definition preferred by the Law Commission in their draft Criminal Code. The Law Commission have proposed that a person acts intentionally with respect to a result if: (a) it was his purpose to cause it; or (b) he is aware that it would occur in the ordinary course of events if he were to succeed in his purpose of causing some other result.[11]

Although the second part of the proposal avoids use of the expression 'knowledge of virtual certainty', it would appear to cover the 'bomb in the plane case', as well as the situation where one event is a condition precedent to another.[12]

The decision in *Woollin* meets the criticisms of the previous approach to the question of intention. It keeps intention within fairly narrow limits. The overlap with 'recklessness' is minimised. And, although it extends intention beyond its ordinary meaning, it is expressed in fairly simple language. Juries should be capable of applying it with little difficulty.[13]

Notes

1   Murder (Abolition of Death Penalty) Act 1965; s 5 of the Offences Against the Person Act 1861.

2   It also corresponds to the meaning of the word in the *Shorter Oxford English Dictionary*.

3   See, for example, the speech of Lord Hailsham in *Hyam v DPP* [1974] 2 All ER 41, pp 51–52.

4   Duff, A, 'Intention, recklessness and probable consequences' [1980] Crim LR 404.

5   See, for example, Ashworth, A, *Principles of Criminal Law*, 1991, p 149.

6   *Belfon* (1976); *Bloomfield* (1978).

7   It is rather strange that the House of Lords in *Moloney* should express approval of the decision of the Court of Criminal Appeal in *Steane* (1947). D had been charged with 'doing acts likely to assist the enemy with intent to assist the enemy' contrary to Defence Regulations of 1939. As a result of threats to himself and his family, he had agreed to take part in propaganda broadcasts for the Nazi Government of Germany during the Second World War. Lord Goddard held that as D's motive was a desire to save his wife and children, he had not intended to assist the enemy.

   The decision is surely wrong and confuses motive with intent. *Steane* intended to assist the enemy as the lesser of two evils. His acquittal should have been based on the basis of duress and not on the absence of intent.

8   In *Walker and Hayles* (1989), the Court of Appeal held that whilst a direction in terms of high probability was not a misdirection, it was preferable to direct the jury in terms of foresight of virtual certainty.

9   Lord Lane, in the debate on the *Report of the House of Lords Select Committee on Murder* (1989), stated that *Nedrick* 'was not as clear as it should have been' and agreed with the definition set out in cl 18(b) of the Draft Code:

   A person acts intentionally with respect to ... a result when he acts either in order to bring it about or being aware that it will occur in the ordinary course of events.

10 Card, R, *Cross and Jones: Criminal Law*, 12th edn, 1992, p 64.

11 Law Commission, *Legislating the Criminal Code: Offences Against the Person and General Principles*, Law Com No 218, 1993.

12 In *Re A (Children) (Conjoined Twins: Medical Treatment) (No 1)* (2000), the Court of Appeal considered whether an operation to separate conjoined twins would be lawful where one of the effects of the operation would be the death of one of the twins. Ward LJ and Brooke LJ acknowledged that the decision in *Woollin* was authoritative on the issue of intention and concluded that a court would inevitably find that the surgeons intended to kill the twin, however little they desired that end, because they knew that her death would be the virtually certain consequence of their acts.

13 In *Matthews and Alleyne* (2003), the Court of Appeal held that the trial judge had gone further than the law permitted when he directed the jury to find the necessary intent in murder proved if they were satisfied that the defendant appreciated that death or grievous bodily harm was virtually certain to result from his actions. Giving the judgment of the court, Rix LJ said that *Woollin* did not lay down a substantive rule of law, but approved the evidential rule in *Nedrick* subject to the substitution of 'find' for 'infer' and thus, where the charge is murder, the jury should be directed that they are not entitled to find the necessary intention unless they feel sure that death or serious bodily harm was a virtual certainty as a result of the defendant's actions and that the defendant appreciated that such was the case. According to this view, the House of Lords in *Woollin* did not provide a definition of intention in terms of foresight of virtual certainty.

It is submitted that the Court of Appeal's interpretation of the decision is wrong. Lord Steyn in *Woollin* attached great importance to a passage in *Moloney* in which Lord Bridge stated that, if a person foresees the probability of a consequence as little short of overwhelming, this will suffice to *establish* the necessary intent (Lord Steyn's emphasis). According to Lord Steyn, a high level of foresight is not merely evidence of intention. It puts the issue beyond dispute.

Question 3

The *Caldwell* test fails to make a distinction which should be made between the person who knowingly takes a risk and the person who gives no thought to whether there is a risk or not. And, on the other hand it makes a distinction which has no moral basis [Smith, JC and Hogan, B, *Criminal Law*, 1992].

Discuss.

Answer plan

The quotation is critical of the *Caldwell* test of recklessness and therefore the discussion should explain the grounds of criticism. It is not sufficient to give an account of the *Caldwell* formula nor is it necessary to mention every case in which the *Caldwell* test has been applied or discussed. The main features of the *Caldwell* test relevant to this question can be demonstrated by reference to a small number of cases.

The first part of the quotation refers to the view of many critics that there is a significant distinction between the advertent and the inadvertent wrongdoer – a distinction which, it is alleged, Lord Diplock in *Caldwell* failed to observe. The implication of the quotation is that the inadvertent wrongdoer should not incur criminal liability or, at least, not to the same extent as the advertent wrongdoer.

The second part of the quotation refers to the apparent arbitrariness of the *Caldwell* 'loophole'.

You should be familiar with:

- the *Caldwell* definition of 'recklessness';
- the justifications for the punishment of the advertently reckless wrongdoer;
- the arguments for and against the punishment of the inadvertently reckless wrongdoer;
- the failure of the *Caldwell* test to recognise differences in the degree of blameworthiness of the advertently and inadvertently reckless wrongdoer;
- the justification for the exemption from liability in cases of the *Caldwell* 'loophole'.

Answer

In *Caldwell* (1982), the House of Lords ruled upon the meaning of the term recklessness in s 1 of the Criminal Damage Act 1971. Lord Diplock stated that a person is reckless with respect to whether any property would be destroyed or damaged:

> ... if (1) he does an act which in fact creates an obvious risk that property would be destroyed or damaged, and (2) when he does the act, he either (a) has not given any thought to the possibility of there being such a risk, or (b) has recognised that there was some risk involved and has nonetheless gone on to do it.

In *Lawrence* (1982), in a judgment concerning reckless driving handed down on the same day as *Caldwell*, Lord Diplock said that the risk must be 'obvious and *serious*'. Dealing with the same offence, the House of Lords in *Reid* (1992) explained that a risk is 'serious' if a reasonable person would consider it not to be negligible. It was also stated that where (2)(b) – the advertent limb – is relied upon, there is no need to prove that the risk was an obvious one; awareness of *some* risk of the particular consequence required will suffice.

Prior to these decisions, it was apparently settled law that the test of recklessness required the prosecution to prove that the accused consciously ran the risk in question. For example, in the case of *Stephenson* (1979), D lit a fire in the hollow of a haystack. The stack caught fire and was destroyed. D claimed that he had not foreseen the damage. Psychiatric evidence was given that D suffered from schizophrenia. This disorder could have deprived Stephenson of the normal capacity to weigh and foresee risks.

The Court of Appeal held that the fact that the risk of damage would have been obvious to any normal person was not sufficient to give rise to criminal liability. The court held that the prosecution were obliged to prove that the defendant himself appreciated the existence of the risk. Recklessness was limited to *advertent* risk taking.

The *Caldwell* formula – (in (2)(a) above) – extends the concept to include inadvertence. Lord Diplock believed that to restrict recklessness to the conscious disregard of a recognised risk would impose an unnaturally narrow meaning on the word. In addition, he felt that, as consciously taking a risk was not necessarily more blameworthy than failing to give any thought to the possibility of risk, to restrict recklessness to advertent risk taking was undesirable as a matter of policy.

However, in a case decided two years later, the harshness of the *Caldwell* test was demonstrated. In *Elliott v C* (1983), the Divisional Court held that, with crimes for which *Caldwell* recklessness will suffice, it is not only unnecessary for the prosecution to prove that the accused was aware of the risk in question, it is also unnecessary to prove that the accused would have or could have been aware of the risk had he stopped to think about it.

The case concerned a 14 year old backward schoolgirl convicted of unlawfully destroying by fire a garden shed and its contents (contrary to s 1(1) of the Criminal Damage Act 1971). She was acquitted by the magistrates who found as a fact that she was unaware that her behaviour carried with it a risk of damage to the shed and contents and would not have appreciated the danger even if she had stopped to think about it. The Divisional Court allowed the prosecutor's appeal, holding that, an 'obvious' risk is one which would have been obvious to an ordinary reasonable person who gave thought to the matter, whether or not it would have been obvious to the accused if he had given thought to the matter (see also *R (Stephen Malcolm)* (1984)).[1]

The quotation from Professors Smith and Hogan above expresses the view shared by a number of critics that the extended definition of recklessness categorises as equivalent levels of fault that are morally quite distinct. They argue that the justifications for imposing criminal liability on the conscious risk taker do not apply to the inadvertently reckless individual. It is to those arguments that we shall now turn.

The traditional justification for imposing criminal liability on the basis of 'advertent' recklessness is that a person who pursues a course of conduct aware of the risks of harm displays that he is willing to take a deliberate chance with the person or property of another. As Professor Hall points out, the subjectively reckless individual has *deliberately* chosen to increase the risk of a defined harm occurring.[2]

And, although a person who takes a risk in causing harm is regarded, in general, as less blameworthy than the person who sets out *intentionally* to cause harm, there is unanimity among commentators that the individual who willingly and consciously takes a risk with respect to another's protected interests *deserves* to be punished.

The commentators are divided, however, with respect to whether criminal liability should be *restricted* to the advertent wrongdoer. Those who maintain that advertence ought to be a *necessary* condition of liability argue that the standard justifications and objectives of punishment are implicitly based on a concept of 'subjective' fault.

They argue that the retributive theory, for example, is based on the notion that punishment should be administered if, but only if, the accused deserves it, and that an accused deserves punishment *only* where he has chosen to gain an unfair advantage by breaking the primary rules of social life.

The deterrent theory, it is said, also presupposes the existence of a 'guilty mind'. Punishment is threatened to discourage the potential wrongdoer from deliberately causing harm or taking risks with respect to the person or property of another. According to this theory, the interests recognised by the criminal law are protected by discouraging potential offenders from deliberately acting in a way that will violate those interests. Similarly, where an individual has deliberately chosen to risk causing harm, the theory of individual deterrence justifies punishing him to discourage him from taking similar risks in the future.[3]

Is there any justification for imposing criminal liability on the basis of 'inadvertent' recklessness?

Opponents of objective tests of liability contend that a person who has failed to perceive a risk has not deliberately chosen to break the law and hence does not deserve to be punished. Further, it is argued, there is no room for the deterrence justification as one cannot be discouraged from taking risks of which one is unaware.

Duff, however, has argued that the person of full capacity who fails to consider an obvious risk may be as culpable as the person who consciously runs a risk. He suggests that the person who is unaware of an obvious risk may manifest not merely stupidity but an attitude and values which reflect a lack of concern for the interests of others.[4] Similarly, Fletcher argues that, if the inadvertent wrongdoer could have done otherwise, if he failed to utilise his faculties to estimate and avoid risks inherent in his proposed conduct, his actions are correctly described as voluntary.[5] And Professor Hart argues that, if the capacities of the defendant are taken into account, there is no injustice in punishing the 'objectively reckless' wrongdoer.[6]

From a utilitarian standpoint, the threat of punishment for inadvertence is said to promote adherence to a particular standard of care by encouraging reflection. A potential actor is encouraged to consider the possible consequences of his conduct. And, if a person causes harm, having failed to consider an obvious risk, then punishment may serve the purpose of encouraging him to reflect on the potential consequences of his actions in the future.

Of course, these arguments do not justify the punishment of an individual like the defendant in the *Elliott* case.[7] Nor do they justify treating the inadvertently reckless as morally equivalent to the conscious risk taker, as the *Caldwell* test does. Criminal law recognises *degrees* of blameworthiness. Thus, even if we accept that the inadvertent wrongdoer is culpable and that there is some utility in punishing him, ought he not to be distinguished in terms of formal liability from the conscious risk taker?

Professor Kenny argues that the advertent risk taker is not only more wicked than the inadvertent wrongdoer, he is also, in general, more dangerous and that, from a utilitarian standpoint, the threat of a more severe punishment is necessary to discourage a person from pursuing a course of conduct which he knows carries a risk of harm than is necessary for the less dangerous inadvertent actor.[8]

Brady agrees that there is a significant *moral* distinction between the person who consciously runs a risk and the individual who fails to consider a risk. The former is *more* culpable because he has 'manifest[ed] a trait' which demonstrates a *greater* degree of indifference to the interests of others. For this reason, we are justified in punishing him more severely.[9]

The decision in *Caldwell* fails to recognise this distinction at the substantive level. It may be the case, of course, that differences in blameworthiness will be recognised at the *sentencing* stage. In many cases, however, this will not be possible. The morally relevant information may be lacking, for example, if the defendant pleads guilty. Greater precision in the substantive law results in more specific categorisation of the guilty prior to sentencing.[10]

For these reasons, it is submitted that if criminal liability is to be imposed on the inadvertently reckless, a specific offence should be targeted at them and should reflect the lower degree of blameworthiness with an appropriately lower maximum penalty.

The second part of the quotation refers to the fact that if the defendant considered a risk but, for whatever reason, concluded there was none, he is not reckless. This so called loophole or lacuna in the *Caldwell* test was acknowledged, *obiter*, by the Court of Appeal in *Reid* (1990).

Professors Smith and Hogan argue that the distinction between somebody who considers a risk but negligently dismisses it and the person who negligently fails to think about a risk is unsound.[11]

Those in favour of the test argue, however, that the individual who has thought about the risk but dismissed it has not displayed that same degree of indifference or disregard as either the conscious risk taker or the inadvertently reckless individual, and as the purpose of the test is to discourage conscious risk taking and to encourage reflection, the loophole exemption is a valid one.[12]

In conclusion, it has been argued by a number of commentators that the extended meaning given to recklessness by Lord Diplock in *Caldwell* fails to acknowledge an important distinction in terms of the degree of fault of the advertently and inadvertently reckless actor. It not only results in the attribution of responsibility to a defendant like the young girl in *Elliott's* case, but treats her and the conscious risk taker as equally blameworthy.[13]

Notes

1   In *R v Gemmell; R v Richards* (2003), the defendants, aged 11 and 12, were charged with and convicted of arson. They had set fire to some newspapers in a bin behind a store. The fire spread and the store caught fire. They stated that they had expected the newspapers to burn themselves out and that it had not occurred to them that there was a risk that the fire might spread. The judge directed the jury in accordance with *Caldwell* and stated that the question of whether or not there was an obvious risk of property being damaged had to be assessed by reference to the reasonable man, not a person endowed with the characteristics of the defendants.

The defendants appealed on the ground that the jury should have been instructed to take into account their age when considering whether the risk was obvious. The test as expressed by the judge was incompatible with Art 6 of the European Convention on Human Rights because it effectively rendered reckless arson an offence of strict liability, since a child was incapable of advancing a defence based on his or her immaturity and lack of understanding.

The Court of Appeal dismissed the appeal, holding that it was bound by *Caldwell* to apply an objective test. The characteristics or qualities of the particular defendant were irrelevant. Furthermore, the objective test was not incompatible with the right to a fair trial under Art 6 of the Convention, because Art 6 was not concerned with the fairness of provisions of substantive law. It was a matter for the contracting state to choose how to define the substantive elements of a particular offence.

2   Hall, J, 'Negligent behaviour should be excluded from penal liability' [1963] Colum L Rev 1.

3   See Fine, RP and Cohen, GM, 'Is criminal negligence a defensible basis for penal liability?' (1967) 16 Buffalo L Rev 749.

4   Duff, A, 'Recklessness' [1980] Crim LR 282.

5   Fletcher, GP, 'The theory of criminal negligence: a comparative analysis' (1971) U Pa L Rev 401.

6   See extract from Hart, HLA, 'Punishment and responsibility', 1968, in Clarkson, CMV and Keating, HM, *Criminal Law: Text and Materials*, 4th edn, 1998, p 187.

7   Although the decision of the Divisional Court in *Elliott v C* was not referred to in *Reid*, three of their Lordships made reference to the situation where a failure to advert to a risk is a consequence of a lack of capacity.

Lord Keith said that a driver may be regarded as not having driven recklessly where his capacity to appreciate risks was adversely affected by some condition not involving fault on his part. It is not at all clear that when he made this statement, Lord Keith had circumstances like those in *Elliott v C* in mind ([1992] 3 All ER 673, p 675c–d).

Lord Goff made a similar statement in his speech, but he restricted himself to cases where the lack of capacity is caused by the sudden onset of an illness or shock which impairs D's capacity to consider the possibility of risk (p 690j).

Lord Ackner rejected, as far as reckless driving was concerned, the appellant's submission that recklessness would be lacking if ignorance of the relevant risk was attributable to incapacity due, for example, to age or mental deficiency of the defendant. It would appear that his Lordship might have been prepared to accept the submission if the case had concerned an offence under the Criminal Damage Act 1971 (p 683e–h). In Cole (1994), however, the Court of Appeal gave their approval to the approach taken by the Divisional Court in *Elliott v C*.

8   Kenny, A, *Freewill and Responsibility*, 1978.

9   Brady, JB, 'Recklessness, negligence, indifference and awareness' (1980) 43 MLR 381.

10 In *Hoof* (1980), the Court of Appeal stated that where D is charged under s 1(2) and (3) of the Criminal Damage Act 1971 there should be two counts:

(a)   arson with *intent* to endanger life; and

(b)   arson being *reckless* as to whether life would be endangered.

This is to ensure that, for the purposes of sentencing, the court is aware of the jury's verdict with respect to the degree of D's blameworthiness. However, as the law currently stands, no distinction can be drawn within category (b) between those who are inadvertently reckless and those who are subjectively reckless. They are treated as legal equivalents although they are not moral equivalents: see also *Hardie* (1984).

11 Smith, JC and Hogan, B, *Criminal Law*, 9th edn, 1999.

12 In *Reid*, Lord Browne-Wilkinson appeared to suggest that the loophole applies
    in situations where 'despite D being aware of the risk and deciding to take it, he
    does so because of a reasonable misunderstanding' [1992] 3 All ER 673, p 696f.
    There are two objections to this:

    (a)   if D takes a risk of which he is aware, he is reckless. As explained above,
    the lacuna in *Caldwell* applies where D has considered whether there is a
    risk and concluded there is *none*;

    (b)   there is no justification for narrowing the lacuna to the situation where D
    reasonably concludes there is no risk. As Lord Goff pointed out, both limbs
    of the *Caldwell* test of recklessness are tests of *mens rea* and a *bona fide*
    mistaken belief that there was no risk will excuse. The reasonableness of
    the mistake is merely evidence of whether it was genuinely held (at
    p 690f–h). In *Merrick* (1996), the Court of Appeal held that taking steps to
    remedy a risk which has been created will not absolve a defendant of
    recklessness, even if the remedial steps were planned before the risk was
    created. See Cowley, D, 'Criminal damage: the nature of the lacuna in
    Caldwell recklessness' (1996) 160(25) JP 407.

The *Caldwell* definition of recklessness is limited to offences of criminal damage
and a limited number of regulatory offences. See, for example, *Information
Commissioner v Islington Borough Council* (2002).

13 The Draft Criminal Code Bill, if enacted, would restrict recklessness to where D
    is aware of a risk that a circumstance exists or will exist, or that a result will
    occur and it is, in the circumstances known to D, unreasonable to take the risk.

Question 4

[T]here has for centuries been a presumption that Parliament did not intend
to make criminals of persons who were in no way blameworthy in what they
did. That means that whenever a section is silent as to *mens rea* there is a
presumption that, in order to give effect to the will of Parliament, we must
read in words appropriate to require *mens rea*.

In the absence of a clear indication in the Act that an offence is intended to be
an [offence of strict liability], it is necessary to go outside the Act and
examine all relevant circumstances in order to establish that this must have
been the intention of Parliament [*per* Lord Reid in *Sweet v Parsley* (1970)].

Discuss.

Answer plan

A fairly straightforward question. It requires a discussion of the approach of
the courts to the task of interpreting statutory offences where it is not clear

whether Parliament intended the offence to be one requiring proof of *mens rea*.

The following points need to be discussed:

* the presumption of *mens rea*;
* the meaning of strict liability;
* intrinsic/extrinsic aids to interpretation.

Answer

A crime of strict liability is one where there is no requirement of *mens rea* or negligence in respect of one or more of the elements of the *actus reus*. For example, in *Woodrow* (1846), the accused was convicted of the offence of 'having in his possession adulterated tobacco', despite his lack of knowledge that the tobacco was adulterated.

As the quotation indicates, most such offences are statutory and it is a question of interpretation whether a particular offence requires *mens rea* or not. Certain words or expressions (for example, 'knowingly', 'intentionally', 'recklessly', etc) clearly indicate that proof of a particular form of *mens rea* is necessary. However, the absence of a *mens rea* term is not conclusive that the offence is one of strict liability. The presumption referred to by Lord Reid means that, if a section is silent as to *mens rea*, the courts should imply *mens rea* unless Parliament has indicated a contrary intention either expressly or by implication. This is a corollary of the principle that, where a penal provision is capable of two interpretations, the interpretation most favourable to the accused must be adopted.

In *B (A Minor) v DPP* (2000), Lord Hutton pointed out that the test is not whether it is a reasonable implication that the statute rules out *mens rea* as a constituent part of the crime – the test is whether it is a *necessary* implication. Lord Nicholls explained that 'necessary implication' connotes an implication which is compellingly clear.

In one of the earliest cases to deal with the issue, *Sherras v de Rutzen* (1895), Wright J stated that, to give effect to the intention of Parliament, it is important, first of all, to consider the actual words used in the statute and, secondly, to consider the subject matter of the provision. This accords with the normal principle of interpretation that the court should look only to extrinsic factors when the intention of Parliament is not clear from the words of the statute.

The words of the statute

The court may look to the wording of the provision in its overall context. Words and terms used in other provisions of the same statute may provide a clue as to the intention of Parliament. For example, in *Pharmaceutical Society of Great Britain v Storkwain* (1986), the House of Lords decided that s 58(2)(a) of the Medicines Act 1968 was one of strict liability. They were influenced by the fact that, whereas s 58(2)(a) was silent with respect to fault, there were express requirements of *mens rea* for other provisions of the same statute.

In *Cheshire County Council Trading Standards Dept ex p Alan Helliwell & Sons (Bolton) Ltd* (1991), D was charged with an offence contrary to the Transit of Animals (Road and Rail) Order 1975 of permitting unfit animals to be carried so as to be likely to cause them unnecessary suffering (Art 11(1)). The court held that the offence was one of strict liability. It was partly influenced by the fact that another provision of the Order, concerning the transportation of pregnant animals, expressly imposed a requirement of knowledge.

On the other hand, in *Sweet v Parsley*, Lord Reid stated that the fact that other sections of the statute expressly required *mens rea* is not itself sufficient to justify a decision that a section which was silent as to *mens rea* created an absolute offence. And, in *Sherras v de Rutzen* (1895), the Divisional Court held that a provision of the Licensing Act 1872 should be interpreted to impose a requirement of *mens rea* even though it contained no *mens rea* term and despite the fact that another sub-section used the word 'knowingly' (cf *Cundy v Le Cocq* (1881)).

In *B (A Minor) v DPP* (2000), the defendant was charged with inciting a girl under the age of 14 to commit an act of gross indecency with him contrary to s 1(1) of the Indecency with Children Act 1960. The issue for the House of Lords was whether it was necessary for the prosecution to prove the absence of a genuine belief on the part of the defendant that the child was over the specified age of 14. The section was silent in respect of the issue. The Crown argued that the 1960 Act together with the Sexual Offences Act 1956 formed a code of sexual offences and that where Parliament intended belief as age to be a defence, it had expressly so provided.

The House rejected the argument. Whilst accepting that the statutes formed a code, there was no clear or consistent pattern within the 1956 Act that provided compelling guidance in respect of the question whether an age related defence applied to the offence under s 1.

In *R v K* (2001), the House considered a similar issue in respect of the offence of indecent assault contrary to s 14 of the 1956 Act. The offence requires proof that the defendant touched a woman indecently without her consent. Section 14(2) provides that a girl under the age of 16 cannot in law give consent. The question for the House was whether a man who indecently touches a girl under the age of 16 but believes her to be over 16 and believes her to have consented to the contact is entitled to be acquitted. Again, the section was silent on this issue.

The Crown pointed out that sub-ss (3) and (4) defined circumstances in which a defendant's belief, knowledge or suspicion exonerate a defendant from liability for what would otherwise be an indecent assault and contended that if it had been intended to excuse a defendant who believed a complainant to be 16 or over, this ground of exoneration would have been expressed in sub-s (2).

The House rejected the argument. Section 14 was not part of a single coherent legislative scheme; its provisions were derived from a variety of sources and thus no significance could be attached to the inclusion of grounds of exoneration in sub-ss (3) and (4) and the omission of such a ground from sub-s (2). The 1956 Act was a consolidating statute and had perpetuated the anomalies of the previous legislation. Neither in s 14 nor elsewhere in the 1956 Act was there any express exclusion of the need to prove an absence of genuine belief on the part of a defendant as to the age of an underage victim. Had it been intended to exclude that element of *mens rea*, it would have been very easy to do so by an appropriately worded provision in or following sub-s (2).

Nor was there anything in the language of the statute which justified, as a matter of necessary implication, the conclusion that Parliament must have intended to exclude this ingredient of *mens rea* from the offence of indecent assault. As far as the age related offences of the statute were concerned, a compellingly clear implication displacing the presumption could only be established if the supplementation of the text by reading in words appropriate to require *mens rea* resulted in an internal inconsistency of the text. Section 14(2) could have provided that a genuine belief by the accused that the girl was over 16 was no defence but, equally, it could have provided that a genuine belief that the girl was under 16 was a defence; such a provision would not have been conceptually inconsistent with any part of s 14. Thus, there was nothing in s 14(1) which clearly indicated the displacement of the presumption.

The subject matter of the offence

It is often stated that, if the subject matter of the provision relates to 'acts which are not criminal in any real sense', the presumption against no fault liability may be displaced (Wright J in *Sherras v de Rutzen*). The same principle was expressed in a positive form in *Gammon v Attorney General of Hong Kong* (1985), where Lord Scarman stated that the presumption in favour of the implication of a fault requirement is particularly strong where the offence is 'truly criminal' in character.

In *Sweet v Parsley*, the House of Lords implied a requirement of *mens rea* into the offence of 'being concerned in the management of premises used for the purpose of smoking cannabis' contrary to s 5(1)(b) of the Dangerous Drugs Act 1965. The House was influenced by the fact that the offence was regarded as serious, attracting 'social obloquy' (see also *Alphacell v Woodward* (1972)). And in *B v DPP*, the House was influenced by the fact that gross indecency is a serious offence carrying a maximum penalty of 10 years' imprisonment and to which the notification requirements under Pt I of the Sex Offenders Act 1997 applied. It was also felt that the presumption was reinforced by the fact that the offence was broad and would cover conduct ranging from predatory advances by an adult paedophile to consensual sexual contact, in private, between young teenagers. Lord Steyn observed that as the *actus reus* extends to incitement to an act of gross indecency, the sub-section applies to verbal sexual overtures between teenagers if one of them is under 14. For the law to criminalise such conduct of teenagers by *offences of strict liability* would be far reaching and controversial.

By contrast, in *Gammon v Attorney General of Hong Kong*, the Privy Council were prepared to impose strict liability in the case of an offence punishable with a fine of $250,000 and imprisonment for three years. And in *Hussain* (1981), the Court of Appeal held that s 1 of the Firearms Act 1968, which prohibits the unlawful possession of a firearm, should be interpreted strictly even though it carried a maximum penalty of three years' imprisonment.[1]

A factor that may influence the court in favour of imposing strict liability is where the provision is concerned with an issue of public safety and, particularly, where the dangerous activity is performed predominantly by corporate undertakings (see, for example, *Gammon Ltd v Attorney General of Hong Kong*).

Indeed, most offences of strict liability are contained in legislation concerned with the sale of food and drugs, the operation of licensed premises, industrial activity (for example, pollution) and other hazardous activities which individuals may voluntarily engage in like driving a car.

The courts often express a willingness to impose strict liability out of a protectionist concern for the welfare of 'ordinary' citizens exposed to the hazardous activities of others. In *Alphacell v Woodward*, for example, it was said that the imposition of strict liability might encourage businesses to comply with important social welfare regulations. In *Sweet v Parsley*, Lord Diplock stated that, where the subject matter of a statute is the regulation of an activity involving potential danger to public health or safety, the court may impose liability on a strict basis to enforce the obligation to take whatever measures may be necessary and without reference to considerations of cost or business practicability.

In response to the argument that it is 'unfair' to use the weight of the criminal law in this way and that principles of justice prohibit the imposition of criminal liability where the defendant has not chosen to break the law, the proponents of strict liability point out that those principles are not appropriate when we are dealing with questions of corporate liability. A corporate enterprise, when deciding whether to engage in the activities in question, is in a position to consider and weigh the potential costs of any unintentional infringement of the law.

In any event, the presumption of *mens rea* remains unless it can be shown that the objects of the legislation will be better promoted by strict liability (see *Gammon*, above, and also *Lim Chin Aik v R* (1963)). Thus, for example, one of the factors influencing the Divisional Court in the *Cheshire County Council* case was the difficulty of proving *mens rea* of one of the controlling officers of the respondent company. By dispensing with a requirement of *mens rea*, liability could be imposed on the company, thereby encouraging the officers to take positive steps to prevent an offence being committed in the future.[2]

Conclusion

There is no single test that the courts will apply in deciding whether the presumption is displaced in respect of a particular offence. The courts are influenced by a number of intrinsic and extrinsic factors.[3] Although there is a great deal of inconsistency, the modern cases concerning strict liability have tended to look principally to the subject matter of the offence when in doubt as to Parliament's intentions. And, although there have been a number of cases where the presumption of no liability without fault has been re-affirmed, it would appear that it is most likely to be rebutted where the subject matter of the offence relates to a serious social danger or a matter of social concern and adherence to the law is perceived to be more likely to be achieved by the imposition of strict liability.

Notes

1   In *Howells* (1977), which concerned s 58 of the same Act, the Court of Appeal stated that the danger to the community resulting from the possession of lethal firearms is so obviously great that an absolute prohibition against their possession must have been the intention of Parliament. This implies that the more serious the offence, the stronger the argument that Parliament intended strict liability.

2   [1991] Crim LR 221.

3   In *R v Muhamad* (2002), the Court of Appeal rejected the submission that, in order to be compatible with Art 7 of the European Convention on Human Rights, a provision had to be read so as to import a requirement of *mens rea*. States are free to enact offences of strict liability. The case concerned an offence contrary to s 362(1)(a) of the Insolvency Act 1986. The court held that the offence was one of strict liability. The statute created 'a clear and coherent regime'. The majority of the offences included an express requirement of a mental element. The fact that s 362 was one of the few provisions which did not specify a mental element was 'a clear pointer to Parliament's intention'. Further support was found from the fact that offences for which no mental element was specified attracted considerably lower sentences and, furthermore, the legislation dealt with an issue of social concern. See also *R (Grundy & Co Excavations Ltd and Parry) v Halton Division Magistrates' Court* (2003).

Question 5

Part (a)

In what circumstances does the criminal law impose a duty to assist other individuals?

Part (b)

Gorge was employed as a lifeguard at a beach. He had just returned from lunch when he noticed that one of the swimmers, Flop, appeared to be distressed and was screaming and shouting. Gorge was about to take steps to rescue her when Flop stopped screaming. She had become too tired. Gorge thought she had stopped screaming as she was no longer in danger. He returned to the life station. Flop drowned.

Discuss Gorge's criminal liability.

Would your answer differ if Gorge had returned from lunch in a state of drunkenness and concluded that Flop was screaming with enjoyment?

Answer plan

You should discuss:

- liability for omissions;
- duty to act;
- duty of care in negligence;
- manslaughter – basic intent and drunkenness.

Principal authorities: *Miller* (1983); *Stone and Dobinson* (1977); *Adomako* (1994); *DPP v Majewski* (1977).

Answer

Part (a)

Criminal law is in general concerned with prohibiting certain forms of behaviour. Offences are normally defined in active terms and not in terms of a failure to do something. Liability for a failure to act will only arise in those rare situations where a legal duty to act is recognised.

The law in this area has developed considerably in recent years, but there are still some uncertainties. First, the House of Lords in *Miller* (1983) held that a person who accidentally creates a potentially harmful situation is under a duty, upon becoming aware of the risk of harm, to take steps to minimise the effects of his act. Lord Diplock said that if a defendant failed to take measures to counteract a danger that he himself has created, then his failure can be regarded as amounting to the commission of the *actus reus* of an appropriate offence. One is under a duty (Lord Diplock preferred the word 'responsibility') to take steps that lie within one's power to rectify the danger created. A person who neglects to discharge the duty is guilty of an offence, provided the failure to act was accompanied by the appropriate *mens rea*.

The case concerned criminal damage but it is clear that Lord Diplock intended the principle to apply to all result crimes and in *Lawford* (1994), the Supreme Court of South Australia held that if a defendant was responsible for a person being rendered unconscious and, as a consequence, placed in a dangerous situation, a duty to take positive steps to render assistance would arise and the defendant would be guilty of murder by omission if the *mens rea* elements of the offence were proved.[1]

Secondly, duties may be imposed on individuals as a result of their relationship with the victim. The Children and Young Persons Act 1933, for example, imposes duties on parents. By virtue of s 1, it is an offence for a parent to wilfully neglect a child in a manner likely to cause unnecessary suffering or injury to health. This offence carries a maximum sentence of 10 years' imprisonment (s 45 of the Criminal Justice Act 1988).

In addition to this statutory duty, the common law recognises a parental duty to act which may give rise to liability for an offence against the person. Thus, for example, although there is no general duty to take steps to save the life of another, a parent would be under a duty to take reasonable steps to save the life of his or her child. A failure to discharge such a duty may result in liability for either murder or manslaughter, depending on the defendant's *mens rea*. *Gibbons and Proctor* (1918) provides a rare case of murder by omission. The defendants killed the child of the father by withholding food. As the parties failure to look after the child was accompanied by 'malice aforethought', they were guilty of murder. Most commonly, in cases of 'neglect' of this sort, it will be difficult to prove an intent adequate for murder and the person will normally be guilty of manslaughter 'by gross negligence'.[2]

It is not clear to what other familial relationships the common law duty extends. It is not clear, for example, whether a duty is owed by one spouse to another or whether an adult child owes a duty to his or her parent. There are a couple of 19th century decisions which denied the existence of a duty towards adult sons and daughters (*Smith* (1826); *Shepherd* (1862)) suggesting that the parental duty is terminated when the child becomes 'independent'.

In addition to familial relationships, it has been held that a duty may be imposed on one who has voluntarily undertaken the care of another. In *Stone and Dobinson* (1977), Stone's sister, Fanny, whilst living with the defendants, had become unable to care for herself. She became extremely ill and died. It was held, as a matter of fact, that the defendants had undertaken to care for her. Such an undertaking gave rise to a legal duty to care for her. As they had committed a 'reckless' breach of that duty – by failing to get medical assistance – they were both guilty of manslaughter.[3]

In *Pittwood* (1902), it was held that a duty may arise from contract. In that case, a railway gatekeeper failed to comply with his contractual duty to close a gate at a level crossing. As a consequence, a person crossing the tracks was killed. Wright J held that the defendant could not rely on the doctrine of privity of contract to deny the existence of a duty to users of the crossing. The obligation arose from the fact that others were dependent on the proper performance of the contract. Likewise, a duty may arise by virtue of the 'office' that a person holds (see *Curtis* (1885); and *West London Coroner ex p Gray* (1987)).

It is not clear what other situations or relationships might give rise to a legally recognised duty to provide assistance.[4] In *Adomako* (1994), an anaesthetist failed to respond appropriately to obvious signs that his patient had ceased to breathe as a tube supplying him with oxygen had become disconnected. The appellant was convicted of manslaughter by gross negligence. His appeal to the House of Lords was unsuccessful. However, although Lord Mackay, in a speech with which the other Lords agreed, regarded Adomako's liability as stemming from a series of omissions, his Lordship made no reference to the legal basis of the duty to act.[5]

In *Khan* (1998), the Court of Appeal held that whether a duty to act exists is a matter of law and the judge should make a ruling as to whether the facts were capable of giving rise to a duty to act. The appellant had sold heroin to a 15 year old girl (V). V was a first time user. She snorted an amount of heroin that was twice the quantity an experienced user might take. V went into a coma whilst still at the appellant's flat. He left the flat and returned the following day to discover her dead. The appeal against conviction for manslaughter was allowed as the trial judge had failed to direct the jury as to whether the facts were capable of giving rise to a duty to summon assistance.[6]

Part (b)

Provided that Flop's life could have been saved had Gorge taken reasonable steps to rescue her, then her death may be attributed to Gorge's failure to act. As explained above, a duty to act may arise from a contractual obligation (*Pittwood*).

Whether he is guilty of an offence of unlawful homicide depends on his *mens rea* at the relevant time.

There is no suggestion that he had the *mens rea* for murder but he may be guilty of manslaughter. In *Adomako* (1994), the House of Lords held that, in cases of manslaughter by gross negligence involving a breach of duty, the ordinary principles of the law of negligence apply. Where the death of the victim is attributable to a breach of duty to take care, it is for the jury to determine whether the breach was such serious departure from the proper standard of care as to amount to gross negligence and, therefore, to give rise to criminal liability. Thus, in this case, the central question for the jury is whether, having regard to the risk of death from his failure to go to Flop's aid, Gorge's conduct was, in all the circumstances, so bad as to amount in their judgment to a criminal omission.

Alternative facts

Provided Gorge's failure to act was the imputable cause of Flop's death, he is guilty of manslaughter. A person charged with an offence of *basic intent*, like manslaughter, cannot rely on voluntary intoxication as a defence if his act was causative of the death of the victim (*DPP v Majewski* (1977); *Lipman* (1970); *Caldwell* (1982)).

Notes

1   In *DPP v K* (1990), the defendant, a schoolboy, had created a dangerous situation by concealing acid in a face dryer. As he had failed, recklessly, to take steps to rectify that situation, he was guilty of assault occasioning actual bodily harm when a fellow pupil was scarred after turning on the drier.

2   In *Russell and Russell* (1987), the Court of Appeal held that both parents have a duty to intervene to prevent the ill treatment of their child.

3   Stone was the deceased's brother, but it is not clear from the judgment whether the family relationship alone would have given rise to a duty to act. In *Sogunro*

(1997), the defendant was convicted of manslaughter by gross neglect (*sic*) for failing to provide for his fiancée. She died of starvation after he kept her without food and drink.

4   The recognition of a duty to act for the helpless and infirm arose from the Poor Law obligations and was initially based exclusively on status. The courts imposed a legal duty on those who occupied certain defined positions. Responsibility was based on the dependent relationship (economic or physical) between the parties.

5   The decision in *Adomako* is primarily concerned with the nature of gross negligence and the *duty of care*. This is a separate issue from the question of whether there is a legal *duty to act*. In criminal law terms, the issue whether there is a duty to act relates to the *actus reus* of the offence in question, whereas a duty of care is a component of the *fault* requirement of manslaughter by gross negligence.

Presumably, the duty to act arose out of the fact that the victim was dependent upon Adomako performing his contractual obligations to the health authority.

6   The Court of Appeal acknowledged that to impose a duty to summon medical assistance on a supplier of heroin to a user suffering an overdose would have the effect of enlarging the class of persons to whom a duty could be owed, but they expressed no opinion on the merits of so doing.

Question 6

Part (a)

Julian and Dick decided to have a picnic in Farmer Giles' field. Julian decided to build a fire next to a haystack. When Dick asked him whether it would be safe, Julian explained that the wind was blowing from a direction that would keep the flames away from the haystack. Julian made the fire and began to prepare the food. After a few minutes, the wind changed direction, blowing the flames towards the haystack. Part of the haystack started to smoulder. Dick suggested that they should pour the contents of their bottle of wine to douse the fire. Julian disagreed and told Dick to help him quickly pick up their belongings and move to a neighbouring field. This they did. The haystack was destroyed.

Part (b)

Anne was taking a walk by a lake. She noticed a young boy in the lake. He was having difficulty swimming and called for help. Anne swam out to him and dragged him back to the edge of the lake. His breathing had stopped. Anne did not give mouth to mouth resuscitation as she was afraid of catching disease. She ran to a nearby public telephone and called an ambulance. When the ambulance arrived, the boy was already dead.

Discuss the criminal liability of the parties.

Answer plan

A relatively straightforward question in which both parts relate to the question of liability for omissions. The first part raises the issue in the context of criminal damage where D fails to take steps to counteract a dangerous situation for which he was 'responsible'. The problem can be seen as one relating to the issue of coincidence of *actus reus* and *mens rea*. The second part concerns liability for omissions in the context of unlawful homicide.

The principal issues are:

- the rule in *Miller* (1983);
- the meaning and application of 'recklessness' for the purposes of the offence of criminal damage;
- the voluntary assumption of a duty to act for the benefit of another.

Answer

Part (a)

Julian may be liable for the offence of criminal damage contrary to s 1(1) of the Criminal Damage Act 1971. This provides that a person who without lawful excuse destroys or damages any property belonging to another, intending to destroy or damage any such property or being reckless as to whether any such property would be destroyed or damaged shall be guilty of an offence. By virtue of s 1(3), where, as in this case, the unlawful destruction or damage of property is by fire, the offence is charged as arson. By s 4, arson is punishable with a term of imprisonment for life.

Julian was probably not guilty of the offence when the haystack first caught fire. Although he committed the *actus reus* of criminal damage, he was not reckless at that stage of the proceedings.

A person is reckless in this context if his conduct: (1) created a (serious) risk of causing damage to the property of another; and (2) he either: (a) gave no thought to possibility of there being any such risk where the risk was in fact obvious; or (b) he recognised that there was some risk of damage, but nevertheless went on to take it (*Caldwell* (1982)).

A risk is serious if a reasonable person would not have treated it as negligible (*Reid* (1992)). The obviousness of a risk relates to whether the reasonable prudent person would have been aware of the risk irrespective of whether D was or could have been aware of the risk (see *Elliott v C* (1983); *Stephen Malcolm R* (1984)).

Julian thought the construction of the fire near the haystack was safe. He did not consider there to be a risk of damage. Nor had he failed to give any thought to the question of whether there was a risk. He had considered the possibility of there being a risk and discounted it. His state of mind falls within what is known as the *Caldwell* loophole.

However, he may be guilty of arson for his later failure to take steps to extinguish the fire that he had caused.

In *Miller* (1983), the House of Lords pointed out that the *actus reus* of criminal damage may continue over some considerable period of time. If D does an act which he believes initially to be harmless, but he later becomes aware that that act has set in train events that present an obvious risk that property belonging to another will be damaged, then he is under a duty to try to prevent or reduce the damage by taking such steps as are reasonable and without danger or difficulty to himself.

The defendant's state of mind throughout the entire period from immediately before the property caught fire to the completion of the damage is relevant to the issue of liability.

Julian could have used the wine to extinguish the fire and, therefore, as he failed to take what, it is submitted, would amount to reasonable action to prevent further damage, he is guilty of arson.

Dick has committed no offence. He is clearly not liable as a principal offender nor can he be regarded as an accomplice to the offence perpetrated by Julian. Although he assisted Julian to remove their belongings and to get away from the scene, Dick neither assisted nor encouraged Julian to commit criminal damage.

Part (b)

Anne's liability for unlawful homicide will depend first upon showing that her failure to provide resuscitation was a factual cause or *sine qua non* of the boy's death. If medical evidence reveals that he was already dead when she pulled him on to the bank or if, for some other reason, attempted resuscitation would have been pointless, then the death will not be attributable to Anne's inaction (see, for example, *White* (1910)).

If her failure was a *sine qua non* of the boy's death, it must also be shown that it was a *legal* cause of his death.

In English law, there is generally no liability for omissions. Thus, it is often said that D incurs no criminal liability if he stands and watches a stranger drown even where he could have acted to save the stranger without risk to himself. The death of the stranger in these circumstances is not regarded in law as a consequence of D's inaction. A failure to act which, as a matter of fact, causes the death of another will give rise to liability only where the defendant was under a duty to act.

In *Stone and Dobinson* (1977), the Court of Appeal held that where one undertakes a duty to care for another incapable of looking after themselves, then a failure to discharge this duty may result in criminal liability. The Court of Appeal agreed with the trial judge that the proper approach is to leave the question of whether there has been a voluntary assumption of a duty to the jury.

The evidence in that case showed that the deceased, Fanny, had lodged with Stone and Dobinson for three years, that the defendants had looked after her for many weeks and had been aware of her deteriorating condition for a similar period, during which they had taken ineffectual steps to help her.

In Anne's case, although the period of involvement was much shorter, it is submitted that there is sufficient evidence of an assumption of duty to warrant consideration by the jury. The boy's welfare was dependent on the continued provision of care by Anne.

Even the duty to act is, however, not an absolute duty. A conviction for manslaughter will not follow unless the prosecution prove that her failure to discharge the duty was 'grossly negligent'.

In *Adomako* (1994), the House of Lords held that whether or not the defendant's conduct was grossly negligent is a question to be decided by the jury. Lord Mackay explained that where the death of the victim resulted from a breach of duty by the defendant, the jury should consider whether, having regard to the risk of death involved, the conduct of the defendant was so bad in all the circumstances as to amount in their judgment to a criminal act or omission.

Consequently, whether or not Anne's conduct and, in particular, her decision to call the ambulance service negatives 'gross negligence' is a question of fact for the jury.[1]

Thus, the crucial questions in this problem are whether Anne was under a duty to provide assistance and, if so, whether she failed to discharge that duty in a manner which was grossly negligent. Provided the jury reach affirmative conclusions with respect to both of these issues, Anne may be convicted of manslaughter – an offence which, by virtue of s 5 of the Offences Against the Person Act 1861, carries a maximum penalty of life imprisonment.

Note

1   In *Stone and Dobinson*, it was said that the appellants could have discharged their duty by summoning outside help.

Question 7

All punishment in itself is evil. It ought only to be admitted in so far as it promises to exclude some greater evil [Bentham, J, 'An introduction to the principles and morals and legislation', in Bentham and Mill, *The Utilitarians*, 1961].

It is only as deserved or undeserved that a sentence can be just or unjust [Lewis, CS, 'The humanitarian theory of punishment' (1953) VI Res Judicatae 224].

Assess critically both of the above statements. With which of the above statements do you agree?

Answer plan

Occasionally, examiners in criminal law include a question concerning the aims, objectives and justifications of punishment. The question above requires a critical assessment of the utilitarian thesis (Bentham) and the retributive thesis (Lewis). You are also asked to express a preference for one.

Answer

The first quotation expresses the reductive or utilitarian view that punishment is justified to the extent that it is administered with the objective of reducing the overall level of 'evil' or 'harm' in society. The argument runs that punishment normally takes the form of penalties, for example, deprivation of liberty, financial penalties, etc, which would in themselves constitute 'evils' were they not justified by reference to the objective of an overall reduction in the balance of social 'evil'.

Thus, reductive theories are primarily concerned with the preventive consequences of punishment. Legitimacy of punishment stems from the attempt to reduce further crime.

The objective may be to deter the *individual* wrongdoer from repeating the offence. (Most sentencers probably have this objective in mind – at least partly – when they impose punishment on convicted criminals.) In addition, the sentencer might attempt to influence the behaviour of potential wrongdoers. This is known as the general deterrence objective. The imposition of punishment is justified according to the utilitarian hypothesis if the reduction in criminal behaviour is greater than the pain inflicted on the individual offender.

Deterrence theories are based on the idea that we are rational creatures motivated by self-interest and that we weigh up the consequences of our actions before acting. It is hoped that when faced with the choice of breaking or observing the law, the threat of punishment will persuade us to choose the latter course.

Empirical research based on reconviction rates is often pessimistic regarding the effectiveness of punishment as an individual deterrent. It is more difficult to measure the effectiveness of punishment as a general deterrent. How can one know the number of occasions when potential wrongdoers decided against breaking the law because they feared detection and punishment?

It is often argued that deterrent effects of punishment are likely to be greater for planned crimes rather than for impulsive or opportunist crimes. In addition, where detection rates are low the potential criminal might feel that his interests are best served by breaking the law.[1]

Reductivists contend that punishment also serves an educative purpose. It is suggested that members of any society learn to avoid behaviour that they know attracts penalties. Punishment, it is said, expresses general disapproval of the behaviour, reinforces certain standards and (as human beings are presumed to be motivated to avoid pain and to gain social approval) results in learned inhibitions against violating those standards.

It is sometimes argued that the educative effects of punishment are of even greater value than deterrent effects because obedience resulting from the absorption of values will not be adversely affected by the perception that the chances of detection are low.[2]

There are enormous difficulties, however, in assessing empirically the educative effects of punishment. How could one reliably determine whether law abiding behaviour was a result of having internalised a particular set of social values, rather than, say, a conscious fear of detection and punishment? For many people, the consequences of conviction may be so unpleasant that even a relatively low risk of detection would discourage them from breaking the law. Indeed, the inverse relationship between the likelihood of detection on the one hand and willingness to break the law on the other implies that, for many members of the community at least, educative effects are weak.

Rehabilitation, as an objective of punishment, is also reductive. It is based upon the premise that criminal behaviour is maladjusted. The development of the behavioural sciences such as psychology and sociology in the 19th century challenged the view that criminality would respond positively to deprivation. Indeed, as the causes of human behaviour were examined, anti-social behaviour was perceived as a response to privations and adopted only where the drive to behave in a pro-social way had been inhibited for some reason or another. The individual may have chosen his criminal career because there were, or there appeared to be, no other opportunities available. The criminal may simply not realise that his interests would be better served by adopting a law abiding course of conduct. He may require retraining so that he can satisfy his economic and social needs in socially approved ways. It may be necessary for him to learn the effect of his criminal acts on his victims.

The rehabilitative ideal stimulated reform of punishment and, in particular, reform of the prisons. Research concerning the effectiveness of rehabilitation, however, has not been encouraging.[3]

In addition to criticisms regarding the effectiveness of deterrent and rehabilitative sentencing, there are a number of 'principled' objections to reductive justifications.

The major objection is that the reductive approach would justify the imposition of a disproportionately severe sentence in certain cases. An individual offender might receive a greater punishment than he 'deserves' because, for example, there is a perceived epidemic of the type of crime he has committed. Similarly, the rehabilitative ideal might justify the imposition of a severe penalty even for a trivial infraction if that was felt necessary to 'cure' him of his criminal attitudes.

This 'retributivist' objection, expressed in the second of the quotations, above, is based, partly, on the Kantian view that respect for individual autonomy requires that a person should never be treated solely as a means whereby certain social ends are achieved. Thus, we ought to punish a criminal because *he* or *she* deserves it and the punishment should be proportionate to the seriousness of the offence. Advocates of this approach point out that it ensures uniformity in sentencing practice and does not result in the criminal being used unfairly to achieve some further social purpose.

But, what does it mean to say that an offender 'deserves' to be punished?

Desert theory is often based upon the notion that the offender has gained an 'unfair advantage' by breaking the law. The equilibrium with other law abiding members of society must be restored by punishment. Alternatively, it is argued that the offender has broken the 'social contract' which binds him and his fellow citizens to observing the law.

Critics of this approach ask: 'in what sense can a theory of real obligations be based upon the fiction of a social contract?' In addition, the concept of 'desert' is said to be too vague a basis for sentencing.[4]

Professor Hart, among others, has argued that, although 'just desert' should be the guiding principle when determining whether a given individual should be punished and calculating the appropriate level of punishment that an individual should suffer, it cannot provide the justification for the institution of punishment as a whole. The 'general justifying aim' of punishment is to reduce or at least contain the level of criminality in society. According to this 'hybrid' theory, 'desert' is a necessary but not a sufficient condition of punishment in any individual case; the principle of 'just desert' operates as a limitation on the utilitarian objectives discussed above. It means, for example, that no punishment may be imposed on a person, even for laudable utilitarian purposes, unless he has voluntarily committed a clear breach of the criminal law. Thus, for example, even though the punishment of a friend or relative of an offender might result in greater obedience by deterring potential offenders, it cannot be justified as neither the friend nor the relative has broken the law. There is, it is argued, no positive obligation to punish on the basis of 'desert' but, on the other hand, there is an obligation not to punish if punishment is not deserved.

Hyman Gross points out that there is no inherent incompatibility between punishment administered with the objective of reducing the level of crime in society yet limited, out of respect for individual autonomy, to those deserving it. Indeed, individual autonomy – which includes the freedom to plan one's life according to one's own preferences – can only flourish in a legally ordered society and, thus, respect for the moral distinctness of persons informs both the general justifying aim and the principles governing the distribution of punishment.[5]

On the other hand, it has been argued that there is no need to turn to abstract notions of 'desert' to explain why victimisation is unacceptable: limiting rules on the application of punishment to those who have broken the law are a feature of reductivism. The deterrent effect of the law depends partly at least on the legal institutions being respected. Victimisation of an innocent person would be counter-productive as it would weaken that respect. In addition, by punishing only those who are guilty, the general population are reminded what conduct amounts to an offence and should, therefore, be avoided. Furthermore, if it were known that an innocent person might be punished instead of the guilty person, the deterrent effect of the law would be weakened.

The point has been made, however, that it is conceivable that unjust victimisation could be an effective deterrent if, for example, the general public were fooled into believing that the convicted person was guilty and, therefore, it follows that reductivist objectives cannot be a sufficient justification of punishment.

In conclusion, the dominant theory of punishment reflects both of the views expressed in the quotations above. Punishment is justified if two conditions are satisfied – it is deserved and it is aimed at reducing criminal conduct in the future.

Notes

1   See, for example, Ashworth, A, *Sentencing and Criminal Justice*, 3rd edn, 2000, p 60.

2   See Clarkson, CMV and Keating, HM, *Criminal Law: Text and Materials*, 4th edn, 1998, pp 42–47.

3   See Ashworth, A, *Sentencing and Criminal Justice*, 2000, p 63.

4   See extract from Lacey, N, 'State punishment: political principles and community values', pp 24–26, in Clarkson, CMV and Keating, HM, *Criminal Law: Text and Materials*, 4th edn, 1998, p 33.

5   See extract from Gross, H, 'A theory of criminal justice', 1979, pp 382–85, in Clarkson, CMV and Keating, HM, *Criminal Law: Text and Materials*, 4th edn, 1998, p 63.

CHAPTER 2

FATAL AND NON-FATAL OFFENCES AGAINST THE PERSON

Introduction

The questions in this chapter concern offences against the person, ranging from common assault at one end of the spectrum to murder at the other. Offences of this type are graded partly in terms of the harm caused but also by reference to the *mens rea* of the accused. The harm caused will define the range of offences that ought to be considered, that is, if D kills V, then liability for murder, manslaughter and/or causing death by dangerous driving, if appropriate, should be considered.

Similarly, if serious bodily harm is the result of D's actions, then liability for the offences under ss 18, 20 and 23 of the Offences Against the Person Act 1861 should be examined. Normally, therefore, it is wise, when attempting to resolve a problem involving the offences against the person, to analyse issues relating to the *actus reus* prior to considering issues relating to the *mens rea*.

It should be noted that most examiners set questions where the facts are 'open' with respect to D's *mens rea*. That is, the *mens rea* is normally not disclosed in the facts of the problem. This provides you with the opportunity to display your knowledge of the ingredients of liability for a number of offences. For example, if the facts of a question revealed that 'D killed V, intending to cause grievous bodily harm', then it is clear that, in the absence of a defence, *there is only one conclusion* – D is guilty of murder. If, on the other hand, the facts report, in effect, that 'D killed V', without specifying his *mens rea*, the answer involves an explanation of the possible *alternative* conclusions (which, of course, will depend upon D's *mens rea*). The second question provides an opportunity to explain the *mens rea* requirements of murder *and* manslaughter. Where there are 'gaps' in the facts, it is not your responsibility to fill them – answers should be expressed in the alternative.

Similarly, if – as is commonly the case – the facts are 'open' with respect to the severity of the bodily harm caused or whether a particular defence is available, provide alternative answers.

Checklist

The questions in this chapter concern, principally, the following offences:

- homicide:
  - murder;

- o   manslaughter;
- o   causing death by dangerous driving, contrary to s 1 of the Road Traffic Act 1988 as substituted by s 1 of the Road Traffic Act 1992;
- non-fatal offences against the person:
  - o   common assault;
  - o   battery;
  - o   aggravated assaults under the Offences Against the Person Act 1861, that is, wounding with intent contrary to s 18; malicious wounding contrary to s 20; assault occasioning actual bodily harm contrary to s 47;
  - o   offences of poisoning contrary to ss 23 and 24 of the 1861 Act;
  - o   sexual offences – rape contrary to s 1(1) of the Sexual Offences Act 1956; procuring sexual intercourse by false pretences, contrary to s 3(1); indecent assault contrary to ss 14 and 15.

In addition, the following defences are dealt with in this chapter:

- provocation;
- diminished responsibility;
- consent.

It is important that you have mastered some of the issues dealt with in detail in the previous chapter – in particular, the definitions of 'intention' and 'recklessness'.

As 'mixed problems' are popular with some examiners, a couple of questions also raise issues of liability for property offences.

Question 8

Colin disliked Matthew, a player for a local football team. He threw a stone at Matthew's car as he was being driven past. The stone hit the windscreen and smashed it. George, the driver, lost control of the car. The car mounted the pavement and crashed into a bus queue, seriously injuring three children. Sandra, their mother, saw the car collide with her children and suffered a heart attack from which she died. George was slightly bruised as a result of the collision and Matthew suffered shock.

Consider Colin's criminal liability.

Answer plan

This problem requires discussion and application of a range of offences from common assault and battery to murder.

Principal issues:

* the ingredients of assault and battery;
* the ingredients of the aggravated assaults – ss 47, 20 and 18 of the Offences Against the Person Act 1861;
* the doctrine of transferred malice;
* the principle that 'one must take one's victim as one finds them';
* the *mens rea* requirements of murder and manslaughter;
* liability for criminal damage.

Principal authorities: *Ireland; Burstow* (1998); *Savage; Parmenter* (1991); *Adomako* (1994).

Answer

Non-fatal offences against the person

Assault and battery

Assault and battery are two distinct offences (*DPP v Little* (1991)).[1] The *actus reus* of assault consists of causing another to apprehend the application of immediate and unlawful force (*Venna* (1976)). Thus, the prosecution must prove that Colin caused either Matthew or George or both to anticipate that they would be struck.

The *mens rea* requirement for assault is that the accused intended to cause the victim to apprehend the application of immediate and unlawful force or was reckless with respect to that (*Venna*).

The 'recklessness' required in this context is known as '*Cunningham*-type' recklessness. That is, the prosecution must prove that Colin, if he did not intend to cause apprehension of force, was at least aware of the risk that his actions might cause Matthew or George to apprehend force (*Spratt* (1991), overruling *DPP v K* (1990)).

A battery, or 'assault by beating', comprises the intentional or reckless infliction of unlawful personal violence by the accused upon another person. Again, *Cunningham*-type recklessness is required (*Spratt*).

Section 39 of the Criminal Justice Act 1988 provides that common assault and battery are summary offences whose maximum penalty is a term of imprisonment not exceeding six months.

Aggravated assaults

More importantly, Colin may be guilty of one of the aggravated assaults in respect of the injuries sustained by George, Matthew and the children. For these offences, it is necessary to prove that the injuries were caused by the actions of the defendant. It is for the judge to direct the jury with reference to the relevant principles of law relating to causation, and then to leave it to the jury to decide, in the light of those principles, whether or not the necessary causal link has been established (*Pagett* (1983)).

In the present case, the jury would be directed to consider whether George's 'instinctive' reaction was reasonably foreseeable, that is, within the range of responses that one might reasonably expect from a person in George's situation, in which case the resulting injuries would be attributed to Colin (*Williams and Davis* (1992)).

(It shall be assumed for the purposes of further analysis that George's reaction was reasonably foreseeable.)

With respect to George and Matthew, Colin may have committed the offence of 'assault occasioning actual bodily harm' contrary to s 47 of the Offences Against the Person Act 1861. Bruising is clearly capable of amounting to actual bodily harm.[2] However, as far as the shock experienced by Matthew is concerned, the position is less clear. In *Ireland; Burstow* (1997), the House of Lords endorsed the approach adopted by the Court of Appeal in *Chan Fook* (1994). It was held that an identifiable psychiatric condition is capable of amounting to 'bodily harm' if supported by medical evidence. Mere emotional reactions such as fear, distress, panic or difficulties with coping are not, in themselves, however, instances of bodily harm (see also *Morris* (1998)).[3]

For liability under s 47, the prosecution are required to prove that the defendant committed an intentional or reckless assault or battery (as above) and that the assault or battery caused actual bodily harm: *Burstow* (1997). It is unnecessary to prove any *mens rea* with respect to the harm caused (*Savage; Parmenter* (1991), confirming *Roberts* (1971) and overruling *Spratt* on this point).

As the children have suffered 'serious' injuries, it is proposed to consider Colin's liability for maliciously inflicting grievous bodily harm under s 20 of the Offences Against the Person Act 1861 and causing grievous bodily harm with intent contrary to s 18 of the same Act.[4]

In *Ireland; Burstow* (1997), the House of Lords held that there is no radical difference in meaning between 'causing gbh' in s 18 and 'inflicting gbh' in s 20 – and that it is unnecessary in either case to prove a direct or indirect application of force (see also *Mandair* (1995)).[5]

The *mens rea* requirement for s 20 is (subjective) recklessness with respect to some harm, albeit not serious harm. Thus, if Colin was aware that throwing the stone at the car carried the risk that some person might suffer harm, he is guilty of the offence under s 20 (*Savage; Parmenter*).

The maximum penalty for an offence under s 20 is a term of imprisonment not exceeding five years.

If Colin intended to cause grievous bodily harm, then he may be convicted of the more serious offence of causing grievous bodily harm with intent, contrary to s 18 of the 1861 Act.

By virtue of the doctrine of transferred malice, Colin may be convicted of the offence under s 18 with respect to the injuries sustained by the three children if he intended to cause serious injuries to George or Matthew (see *Latimer* (1886)).[6] And the jury are entitled to find that grievous bodily harm was intended, even if it was not Colin's purpose, if he knew that grievous bodily harm was a virtually certain consequence of his actions (*Bryson* (1985); *Woollin* (1998)).

Homicide

Can Colin be convicted of the manslaughter of Sandra? The assault committed against George or Matthew would amount to an unlawful and dangerous act for the purposes of constructive manslaughter (see, for example, *Larkin* (1943)) and, by virtue of the doctrine of transferred malice, it may provide the basis of liability for Sandra's death.[7]

(The requirement of dangerousness is satisfied by proving that all sober and reasonable people would inevitably recognise that D's act subjected another person to the risk of harm, albeit not serious harm. It is not necessary to prove that D was aware of the risk of harm (*Church* (1966); *Goodfellow* (1986); *Newbury* (1977).)

Professor Williams, however, argued that the doctrine of transferred malice should not be applied where an injury intended for V1 causes fright and consequent injury to V2:

> ... the law of constructive manslaughter and transferred intention should not be pushed so far as to say that if D assaults V1 he becomes guilty of the

manslaughter of V2, a mere spectator who, remarkably, dies of fright or shock in witnessing what happens to V1.

He may, however, be guilty of manslaughter by gross negligence. Colin owed a duty of care towards Sandra (*Hambrook v Stokes Bros* (1925); *Alcock v Chief Constable of South Yorkshire Police* (1992)). The question for the jury is whether the breach of duty was so bad in all the circumstances as to amount to the crime of manslaughter (*Adomako* (1994)).[8]

The maximum punishment for manslaughter is a term of imprisonment for life (s 5 of the Offences Against the Person Act 1861).

Criminal damage

Colin may be convicted of the offence of criminal damage, contrary to s 1(1) of the Criminal Damage Act 1971, for smashing the windscreen. The maximum penalty for this offence is a term of imprisonment not exceeding 10 years.[9] The prosecution must prove either that he intended to damage property belonging to another or was reckless with respect to property being damaged (the meaning of intention is discussed above).

A person is reckless as to whether any property is damaged if his conduct creates a serious risk of damage and he either fails to give any thought to the risk where it is obvious to a reasonable person or he is aware that there is some risk and nonetheless goes on to take it (*Caldwell* (1982)).

By virtue of s 1(2) of the Act, a person who intentionally or recklessly destroys or damages property belonging to another 'intending by the destruction or damage to endanger the life of another or being reckless whether the life of another would be thereby endangered' is guilty of the more serious offence of 'aggravated' or 'dangerous' damage. The maximum penalty for this offence is life imprisonment.

In *Steer* (1988), it was held that it is not sufficient to prove that D was reckless with respect to damaging property and that he was reckless with respect to endangering life. It must be shown that D was reckless as to whether life would be endangered *by the destruction or damage* of the property (see also *Walker* (1995)).[10]

Notes

1   In *DPP v Little*, the Divisional Court held that assault and battery are statutory offences. The better view is that they are common law offences whose penalties are prescribed by statute (s 39 of the Criminal Justice Act 1988). This approach was taken by Lawi LJ in *Haystead v Chief Constable of Derbyshire* (2000).

2   Note, however, that as a result of prosecuting policy, it would be most unlikely that D would be charged with the offence under s 47 if the only injuries suffered

by V were minor bruises. The Code for Crown Prosecutors, *Offences Against the Person*, June 1994, offers the following guidance:

> ... although any injury can be classified as actual bodily harm, the appropriate charge will be contrary to s 39 where injuries amount to no more than the following: grazes, scratches, abrasions, minor bruising, swellings, reddening of the skin, superficial cuts, a 'black eye' [para 2.4].

> When the injuries amount to no more than those described above, any decision to charge an offence contrary to s 47 would only be justified in the most exceptional circumstances or where the maximum available sentence in the magistrates' court would be inadequate [para 2.5].

3   In *T v DPP* (2003), it was held that, although there was no discernible physical injury, a momentary loss of consciousness, resulting from being kicked, amounted to bodily harm.

4   If the psychological injuries suffered by Matthew are serious, then Colin may be guilty of an offence under s 20 or s 18 in respect of them too, depending on his *mens rea* (*Ireland; Burstow*).

5   It is not clear whether this part of the decision in *Ireland; Burstow* is restricted to cases involving the infliction of psychiatric harm but, in any case, even if it were to be so limited, grievous bodily harm was inflicted indirectly by force on the children. Lord Ackner in *Savage* stated that there would be an infliction of grievous bodily harm where D frightens V who suffers serious injury as a result of taking evasive action, or where D interferes with the brakes of a car causing the driver to suffer serious harm in an accident.

6   The doctrine of transferred malice states that if D aims to strike V1 but 'accidentally' misses with the result that V2 is struck, then D will be guilty for the injuries sustained by V2 *to the same extent* as he would have been had those same injuries been sustained by V1 (see *Attorney General's Reference (No 3 of 1994)* (1997)).

7   There is one possible further requirement – that the act was 'directed at another' (*Dalby* (1982); and see *Ball* (1990)). It is not clear whether this raises issues independent of the requirement that D's act caused the death (*Goodfellow* (1986)). However, even if there is such a requirement, it was held in *Mitchell* (1983) that it is not necessary to prove that the act was directed at the person who was actually killed. This approach was endorsed by the House of Lords in *Attorney General's Reference (No 3 of 1994)* (1997).

8   The 'egg shell skull' principle applies in these circumstances and Colin's liability would be unaffected by the medical evidence revealing that Sandra had a weak heart (*Brice v Brown* (1984); *Martin* (1832)).

9   If the value of the property damaged is less than £5,000, the offence is triable summarily and the maximum penalty is six months' imprisonment and/or a fine (s 22(1) and (2) of the Magistrates' Courts Act 1980). See *Alden* (2002).

10 In *Walker* (1995), Lord Taylor CJ stated at p 497:

> [I]f a defendant throws a brick at the windscreen of a moving vehicle, given that he causes *some* damage to the vehicle, whether he is guilty under s 1(2) does not depend on whether the brick hits or misses the windscreen, but whether he intended to hit it and intended that the damage *therefrom* should endanger life or whether he was reckless as to that outcome.

Question 9

Jack had been burgled and his wife viciously attacked. As he was nervous of a further attack, he kept a baseball bat by the side of his bed. One night, he woke up as he heard footsteps from a neighbouring room. He picked up the baseball bat and went to confront the apparent intruder. He saw a young man about to enter his daughter's bedroom.

In fact, the young man was Carruthers, the new boyfriend of Jack's daughter, Cynthia. Cynthia had invited Carruthers to spend the night with her. Jack had met Carruthers only once and in the dark of the hallway he did not recognise him.

Jack struck Carruthers over the head with the baseball bat. Carruthers slumped, unconscious, to the floor.

Jack made a cursory examination of the body. He recognised the youth. Jack was horrified at what he had done. Believing that Carruthers was dead, Jack decided to dispose of the body. He weighted the body and threw it in a nearby lake.

Medical evidence has revealed that Carruthers died from drowning and thus was still alive when thrown in the lake.

Discuss Jack's criminal liability.

Answer plan

This question raises a number of quite separate issues in the context of unlawful homicide.

In particular, the answer involves analysis and application of the following:

- the *Thabo Meli* principle;
- 'private' and 'public' defence and the treatment of mistaken beliefs in this context;
- manslaughter by gross negligence;
- the *Caldwell* 'loophole'.

Principal authorities: *Thabo Meli* (1954); *Le Brun* (1992); *Williams* (1987); *Owino* (1996).

Answer

Homicide

The *mens rea* for murder or 'malice aforethought' is satisfied on proof of an intention to kill or cause grievous bodily harm (*Moloney* (1985)). 'Grievous bodily harm' means 'serious bodily harm' (*DPP v Smith* (1961); *Saunders* (1985)).

The facts of the problem state that Jack intended to cause Carruthers serious harm and therefore we may conclude that, at the moment he delivered the blow, he acted with the 'malice aforethought' for murder.

However, although accompanied by 'malice aforethought', the blow struck by Jack did not result in death and the concealment of the body, although the immediate cause of death, was not accompanied by 'malice aforethought'. As he believed Carruthers was dead, Jack clearly had no intention to kill or cause grievous bodily harm when he disposed of the body. There is a well established principle of English law that the *actus reus* and *mens rea* of an offence must coincide temporally. The relevant *mens rea* must be present at the time of the act constituting the *actus reus* (*Fowler v Padget* (1798)).

It has been held, however, that if the immediate cause of death is part of what might be regarded as one 'series of acts' or one 'transaction', then liability for murder may be imposed if the defendant acted with malice aforethought at some point during that 'series' or 'transaction' (*Thabo Meli* (1954); *Church* (1966)).

In *Le Brun* (1992), the Court of Appeal held that if a person unlawfully assaults another and, believing he has delivered a fatal blow, attempts to conceal or otherwise dispose of the body, then he will be guilty of murder if the blow was struck with malice aforethought, even if the immediate cause of death stems from the concealment. Thus, in this case, Jack may be charged with murder.[1]

He may, however, be able to take advantage of the defences of public or private defence. These defences are complete defences and apply to all crimes. In *Cousins* (1982), the Court of Appeal held that a person may in appropriate circumstances take advantage of both defences; the principles applicable are the same. By virtue of s 3(1) of the Criminal Law Act 1967, a person may use such force as is reasonable in the circumstances in the prevention of crime. And, at common law, a person may use such force as is reasonable in the defence of his own person or another's. A person who uses force in these circumstances is acting lawfully (*Abraham* (1973)).

Although, as far as these defences are concerned, the prosecution has the burden of proving that the force was used unlawfully, the defendant has the burden of adducing sufficient evidence that he acted in defence (*Abraham*; *Anderson* (1995)).

In *Attorney General for Northern Ireland's Reference (No 1 of 1975)* (1977), Lord Diplock, expressing the opinion of the House of Lords, pointed out that the question whether the force used was reasonable is a question of fact for the jury and never a point of law for the judge. The jury should reject the defence only if they are satisfied that no reasonable man in the circumstances would have considered exposing the victim to the risk of harm that was foreseeable. All the circumstances should be taken into account, including the serious nature of the harm which the force was intended to prevent and whether it could have been prevented without the use of force (*Allen v MPC* (1980)).

The courts have recognised on a number of occasions that detached reflection cannot be expected from the defendant in circumstances of defence. In *Palmer* (1971), for example, Lord Morris stated that if, in the opinion of the jury, the defendant responded to an attack in a way that he honestly and instinctively thought was necessary, then that is 'potent evidence' that he took reasonable defensive action. And, in *Attorney General for Northern Ireland's Reference (No 1 of 1975)*, Lord Diplock said that the jury should consider the time available for reflection.

In addition, a pre-emptive strike may be justified. It may be the case, however, that what constitutes reasonable force in the case of a pre-emptive strike is somewhat less than would be justified against an actual attack (*Beckford v R* (1987)).

It is in the light of the above principles that the jury should consider whether Jack used reasonable force when he attacked Carruthers.

The judge should explain to the jury that the question whether the force is reasonable should be answered by reference to the facts as Jack believed them to be. In *Williams* (1987), D attacked V believing that V was unlawfully attacking a youth. In fact V was acting lawfully. D was charged with assault occasioning actual bodily harm. The Court of Appeal held that, as the *mens rea* for assault is an intent to apply *unlawful* force, a person who applies force which would be reasonable were the circumstances as he believed them to be lacks the necessary intent. This principle was applied by the Privy Council in *Beckford v R* (1988).

In *Owino* (1996), the Court of Appeal stressed that the question whether the force used was reasonable, in the circumstances believed to exist, is a question of fact exclusively for the jury.

And so if, in the opinion of the jury, the blow struck by Jack was or may have been necessary and reasonable in the circumstances as he perceived them, then he is not guilty of murder. If, on the other hand, the force would have been excessive in those circumstances, then he is guilty of murder. The English courts have not adopted the principle (which at one time applied in Australia) that, if a person used excessive force in circumstances where lesser force in defence would have justified the homicide, the person was acquitted of murder and convicted of manslaughter (*Howe* (1987); *Clegg* (1995)).[2]

Even if Jack's attack on Carruthers is excused on the grounds of necessary defence, it is arguable that he committed manslaughter when he threw the body into the lake. Clearly, at that time he was not acting in self-defence. The test to be applied in cases such as this involves assessing whether the defendant's conduct was grossly negligent (*Adomako* (1994)). In other words, the jury should be directed to consider whether, having regard to the objective risk of death, Jack's conduct in disposing of the body was so bad in all the circumstances as to amount in their judgment to the offence of manslaughter.

Notes

1   In *Attorney General's Reference (No 3 of 1994)* (1997), the House of Lords explained the rule in these cases in terms of the ordinary principles of causation. Lord Mustill said:

> The existence of an interval of time between the doing of an act by the defendant with the necessary wrongful intent and its impact on the victim in a manner which leads to death does not in itself prevent the intent, the act and the death from together amounting to murder, so long as there is an unbroken causal connection between the act and the death.

2   In *R v Martin (Anthony Edward)* (2001), Lord Woolf CJ stated at para 9:

> What has been the subject of debate is whether a defendant to a murder charge should be convicted of murder if he was acting in self-defence but used excessive force in self-defence. It is suggested that such a defendant should be regarded as being guilty of manslaughter and not murder. He would not then have to be sentenced to life imprisonment but usually instead to a determinate sentence the length of which would be decided upon by the judge, having regard to the circumstances of the offence. If it is thought that this should not be the law then the change would have to be made by Parliament. It was not even suggested on this appeal that it would be open to this court by judicial decision to bring about such a change. However, even in the case of a life sentence for murder the circumstances of the offence are taken into account. The Home Secretary, having considered the recommendations of the trial judge and the Lord Chief Justice of the day, fixes the tariff period, that is, the period which has to elapse before a defendant can be recommended for parole by the Parole Board.

Question 10

What is meant by an 'unlawful act', for the purposes of constructive manslaughter?

Answer plan

The principal issues are:

- the definition of an unlawful act;
- the question of whether the prosecution are required to prove that D acted with the *mens rea* for the unlawful act;
- the meaning of 'dangerousness'.

Answer

The essence of constructive crime is that liability for one offence is based upon the commission of another less serious offence. It was once the law that a person was guilty constructively of murder if he killed in the course of a felony, and guilty of manslaughter if he killed in the course of a misdemeanour. Although the felony murder rule was abolished by the Homicide Act 1957 and the distinction between felonies and misdemeanours was abolished by the Criminal Law Act 1967, this species of manslaughter remains. Liability for the death of the victim is constructed upon an 'unlawful act' for which the defendant would have been liable even if death had not resulted.

It is not every unlawful act, however, that will suffice for constructive manslaughter. A tort is insufficient (*Franklin* (1883)). Furthermore, it was settled by the House of Lords in *Andrews* (1937) that an offence whose basis is negligence is not an unlawful act for the purposes of constructive manslaughter. *A fortiori*, an offence of strict liability ought not to suffice. In *Lowe* (1973), the Court of Appeal held that the commission of the offence under s 1(1) of the Children and Young Persons Act 1933 – of wilful neglect of a child – did not make the parent liable for constructive manslaughter. Lord Phillimore stated that a criminal omission would not generally give rise to liability for constructive manslaughter.[1]

Most commonly, the unlawful act will be an assault or some other offence against the person (see, for example, *Larkin* (1943)), but it need not be. An offence of criminal damage may, in appropriate circumstances, suffice (*Goodfellow* (1986)) and, in *Watson* (1989), the Court of Appeal held that liability might be constructed upon a burglary contrary to s 9(1)(a) of the Theft Act 1968.

Whether or not it is necessary for the prosecution to prove that D had the *mens rea* for the unlawful act is, surprisingly, a moot point. In other words, it is unclear whether the prosecution are required to prove that, even if death had not occurred, D could have been convicted of some offence, limited by reference to the above criteria. In *Lamb* (1967), the defendant pointed a revolver at his friend. He neither intended to injure nor alarm his friend, nor was the friend alarmed. Lamb and his friend thought it was safe to pull the trigger. They did not realise that the gun was primed. Lamb pulled the trigger and the friend was shot dead. The trial judge took the view that the pointing of the revolver and the pulling of the trigger was something which could, in itself, be unlawful, even if there was no attempt to alarm or intent to injure. This was rejected by the Court of Appeal. The defendant lacked the *mens rea* for a criminal assault or battery and consequently had not committed an unlawful act 'in the *criminal* sense of the word' (*per* Sachs LJ). Constructive manslaughter could not be established without proving that element of intent without which there could be no assault.

Similarly, in *Jennings* (1990), the Court of Appeal held that possession of a knife in a public place was not an unlawful act unless the prosecution could prove that the defendant possessed it with intent to cause injury – that is, the intent necessary for the offence of possession of an offensive weapon contrary to s 1(1) of the Prevention of Crime Act 1953.

These cases support the principle that there can be no 'unlawful act' unless the defendant has committed the *actus reus* of an identified offence with the requisite *mens rea* for that offence. However, the decision of the House of Lords in *Newbury* (1977) casts doubt on this principle. Two 15 year old boys pushed part of a paving stone from the parapet of a railway bridge on to the path of an oncoming train. The stone went through the glass window of the driving cab and struck and killed the guard. The boys were convicted.

On appeal, the House of Lords upheld the conviction.[2] Lord Salmon, with whose speech the other Law Lords concurred, stated that, as manslaughter was a crime of 'basic intent', the only *mens rea* that needed to be proved was 'an intention to do the acts which constitute the crime'. Lord Edmund-Davies said that, for manslaughter, it is sufficient to prove the 'intentional' commission of the unlawful act. And, in the later case of *Goodfellow* (1986), the Court of Appeal held that, for constructive manslaughter, the act must be intentional and unlawful.

These statements are ambiguous. They could mean (and the general tenor of the speeches in *Newbury* supports this interpretation) that all that is required for constructive manslaughter is that the accused's actions are performed deliberately, that is, voluntarily. Although Lamb lacked the *mens rea* for an assault, his actions were performed *deliberately*, in the sense that he pulled the trigger of the gun consciously. The gun did not go off 'by accident'. He was not an automaton. This, perhaps, is the reason that Lord Salmon in *Newbury* thought that Lamb was 'lucky' to have his conviction quashed on appeal.

The other possible (but less natural) interpretation of the opinion of the House in *Newbury* is that the statement that the unlawful act must be performed intentionally was not meant to be understood as a complete account of the mental element of manslaughter and that, since an act is unlawful for the purposes of the criminal law only if performed with the appropriate *mens rea*, manslaughter is not committed constructively unless D acted with that *mens rea*.

Lord Salmon stated that there was no basis upon which counsel for the defendant could dispute that his act was unlawful. Without specifying the unlawful act, it is difficult to assess this statement.

Another difficult decision is that of the Court of Appeal in *Cato* (1976). D caused the death of his friend, V, having injected him with heroin. V had consented to the administration of heroin. The Court of Appeal stated that the offence under s 23 of the Offences Against the Person Act 1861 would suffice as an unlawful act. The court added, however, that, even if it had not been possible to rely on the s 23 offence, there would have been the unlawful act of 'injecting the friend with heroin which the accused had unlawfully taken into his possession'. This is puzzling. There is neither a statutory nor a common law offence of 'injecting heroin'. *Cato* suggests that the unlawful act need not be an offence!

In *Kennedy* (1999), D supplied V with a syringe containing heroin. V injected himself and died from the effects of the drug. The Court of Appeal dismissed D's appeal against conviction for manslaughter. The self-injection of heroin by V was unlawful and as D had assisted and wilfully encouraged V, he too was acting unlawfully. Furthermore, the court held that D had committed an offence contrary to s 23 of the Offences Against the Person Act 1861.

This ruling attracted widespread criticism and in *Dias* (2001), a case involving similar facts, the Court of Appeal cast doubt on the decision. Self-injection was not an unlawful act and thus, even though he had assisted and encouraged V to take the heroin, D could not be guilty as a secondary party to the manslaughter of V, as there was no offence of self-manslaughter to which D was an accessory.

The court added that there may be situations where a jury could find manslaughter in cases such as these so long as they were satisfied that the chain of causation between the supply of the drug and V's death was not broken. That, however, was not the case in *Dias*, because the issue was not left to the jury and the self-injection was clearly capable of breaking the chain. Furthermore, assistance and encouragement by D should not be equated automatically with causation. The judge, after identifying the unlawful act on the part of the defendant, must direct the jury to ask whether that act was at least a substantive cause of the victim's death.[3]

The approach of the House of Lords in *Newbury* and that of the Court of Appeal in *Cato* and *Kennedy* is harsh. The decisions imply that a person may be convicted of the serious offence of manslaughter without proof of a recognised unlawful act. It is submitted that the approach of the Court of Appeal in *Jennings* is preferable.[4]

Finally, the unlawful act must be 'dangerous'. In *Church* (1966), Lord Edmund-Davies, delivering the judgment of the Court of Appeal, explained the meaning of 'dangerous'. He said that an unlawful act is dangerous if *all sober and reasonable people* would inevitably recognise that the unlawful act subjected the victim to the risk of some harm, albeit not serious harm.[5] This was endorsed by the House of Lords in *Newbury* (above). In addition, the House approved the decision of the Court of Appeal in *Lipman* (1970), to the effect that the test for 'dangerousness' is framed in objective terms. For constructive manslaughter, it is quite unnecessary for the prosecution to prove that *the defendant* knew that his conduct carried the risk of harm.

But, as the earlier discussion reveals, it would seem that the House did not appreciate that the requirement that the act be dangerous is additional to, and not a replacement for, the requirement that the unlawful act is performed with full *mens rea*.

Notes

1 The facts may, however, justify a verdict of manslaughter by gross negligence.

2 The unlawful act may have been an offence of criminal damage, but the House of Lords was not clear on this issue.

3 See also *Richards* (2002). In *Rogers* (2003), D held a tourniquet to V's arm while V injected himself with heroin. V died. The Court of Appeal, whilst agreeing that self-injection was not an unlawful act, held that as D had actively participated in the mechanics of injection, he had committed the offence contrary to s 23 and thus was guilty of manslaughter by an unlawful act.

In *Andrews* (2002), D, with his consent, injected V, an alcoholic, with some insulin which he had obtained from a diabetic. V died and D's conviction for manslaughter was upheld. The administration of the insulin was an offence contrary to s 58(2)(b) of the Medicines Act 1968 and V's consent did not negative guilt.

4   The decision of the Court of Appeal in *O'Driscoll* (1977) supports the view that there is no unlawful act without proof of the *mens rea* for the offence in question. The court held that, if the unlawful act is an offence of specific intent, there can be no conviction in the absence of that intent and evidence of intoxication is admissible to support a contention that D lacked the requisite intent.

5   In *Dawson* (1985), the Court of Appeal held that the 'harm' referred to in the test means 'physical harm'. Emotional disturbance *per se* is insufficient. Further, it was decided that the objective test should be applied in the context of the circumstances known to the accused. If the accused is unaware of a peculiar vulnerability of the victim, then the 'sober and reasonable man' is also taken to lack this knowledge in assessing whether the conduct was objectively dangerous.

Question 11

Jason decided to go out for the evening and drove to a local public house. At the pub, he met Julie. As there were not many people there, Jason suggested that they go to a club in a neighbouring town. Whilst driving to the club, Jason made advances towards Julie. When Julie rejected those advances, Jason told her that he had beaten up girls who had refused him in the past. Julie jumped out of the moving car and suffered serious injuries. She was taken to hospital where she was informed that she needed a blood transfusion. As she feared contracting AIDS, she refused the transfusion and died.

Discuss Jason's criminal liability.

Answer plan

This problem is a standard question concerning murder and manslaughter. It raises issues of causation and is 'open' with respect to the *mens rea* of Jason. In these circumstances, as murder and manslaughter share a common *actus reus* and differ according to their *mens rea* requirements, it is sensible to consider the issues of causation before dealing with those concerning the *mens rea*.

The principal issues to be discussed include:

• principles of causation in cases where the victim of an assault takes evasive action and where the victim refuses medical treatment;

• the *mens rea* requirements for murder and manslaughter.

Answer

Unlawful homicide

The first issue to consider in answering this question is whether Julie's death is attributable to Jason's actions – that is, whether he has caused the death of Julie.

It is convenient to deal with the issue of causation in two stages: first, to examine whether Jason's actions were the cause of Julie's injuries; and, secondly, assuming that they were, to establish whether the injuries were the cause of Julie's death. If Jason's actions were the legal cause of Julie's injuries and the injuries were the legal cause of death, then, logically, we may attribute Julie's death to Jason.

(Note that it is for the judge to direct the jury with reference to the relevant principles of law relating to causation, and then to leave it to the jury to decide, in the light of those principles, whether or not the necessary causal link has been established (*Pagett* (1983).)

In *Williams and Davis* (1992), the Court of Appeal held that where, as in the present case, a person leaps from a moving car to avoid some threatened attack, the jury should be directed to consider whether that evasive action was within the 'range of responses' that might reasonably be·expected from a person in that situation. If the response of the deceased was disproportionate to the threat, then it should be regarded as a voluntary act, breaking the 'chain of causation'.

It was said that, in applying this test, the jury should consider appropriate characteristics of the victim.[1] Presumably, these characteristics include the age and sex of the victim. In addition, the jury should bear in mind that the victim might, in the agony of the moment, act without proper reflection.[2]

To allow further analysis of the problem, it shall be assumed that Julie's evasive reaction was reasonably foreseeable and proportionate to the threat and, therefore, that Jason's intimidatory behaviour caused the injuries sustained.

Were the injuries the cause of death? In *Blaue* (1975), a Jehovah's witness, having been stabbed by D, refused a blood transfusion on religious grounds. The Court of Appeal held that the cause of death was the original stab wound. Lawton LJ, extending the principle that 'one must take one's victim as one finds them' (that is, that a defendant may not point to a particular vulnerability or peculiarity of the victim as the cause of death), stated that, if D attacks another, he may not argue that the religious beliefs of the victim, which prevented treatment, were in the circumstances unreasonable; the refusal to have treatment does not break the chain of causation.

In *Blaue*, it was the victim's religious convictions which prevented her from having a blood transfusion. It is not clear whether the principle is of wider application and, in particular, whether it covers a situation like that of the present problem, where the victim refuses treatment because of an (irrational) fear of contracting a disease.

If the principle in *Blaue* does apply to the present problem, then the injuries are the cause of death and, assuming, as we have above, that those injuries are attributable to Jason, he has committed the *actus reus* of unlawful homicide.

(If the court were to distinguish *Blaue* and to hold that responsibility for the death of Julie was attributable to Jason only if the refusal of the blood transfusion was reasonably foreseeable (and the jury were to conclude that it was not reasonably foreseeable), then Jason could not be convicted of an offence of homicide. His liability would extend only to the initial injuries sustained as a result of Julie's evasive action in jumping from the car. For an analysis of his liability in those circumstances, see the discussion of 'aggravated assaults' (below).)

The next issue to consider is Jason's *mens rea*, for it is his intent at the time of the intimidatory behaviour which will determine whether he is to be convicted of murder or manslaughter.

The *mens rea* for murder is satisfied on proof that he either intended to kill or cause grievous bodily harm (*Moloney* (1985)).

If his aim or purpose was to cause death or grievous bodily harm, then he intended death or grievous bodily harm. If it was not his aim or purpose, but the jury are satisfied that he was aware that either death or grievous bodily harm was virtually certain to result from intimidating Julie, then the jury are entitled to find that he intended death or grievous bodily harm (*Hancock and Shankland* (1986); *Nedrick* (1986); *Woollin* (1998); *Matthews v Alleyne* (2003)).

If, however, as the facts imply, he did not intend to kill or cause grievous bodily harm, his liability for manslaughter should be considered.

For constructive manslaughter, the prosecution must prove that the defendant intentionally committed an unlawful and dangerous act that resulted in death (*Goodfellow* (1986)).

In this case, it would appear that, when he intimidated Julie, Jason committed an unlawful act, that is, an assault. An assault is any act by which the defendant intentionally or recklessly causes the victim to apprehend immediate and unlawful personal violence (*Venna* (1976)). Although recklessness will suffice, the facts of the problem indicate that Jason *intentionally* assaulted Julie.[3]

An unlawful act is 'dangerous' if all sober and reasonable people would inevitably recognise that some harm, albeit not serious harm, was likely to result from the unlawful act (*Church* (1966)). Thus, if the jury are satisfied that it was reasonably foreseeable that Julie might jump from the car and sustain some injury then the requirement of 'dangerousness' is satisfied. It is unnecessary to prove that the defendant was aware that his unlawful act was dangerous (see, for example, *Lipman* (1970); *Williams and Davis*; *Newbury* (1977)).

The issue of causation was discussed in detail above.

As we have seen, Jason's liability is dependent upon a number of questions of fact for the jury. Thus, it is not possible to provide a conclusive answer to this problem. The facts do, however, imply liability for manslaughter, in which case Jason would face a maximum sentence of imprisonment for life (s 5 of the Offences Against the Person Act 1861).

Aggravated assaults

If the court were to conclude that, although the injuries sustained by Julie were attributable to Jason, her death was not (see the discussion of *Blaue*, above), then Jason's liability would be limited to one of the non-fatal offences against the person according to the gravity of those injuries and his *mens rea*.

As the question states that Julie suffered 'serious injuries', it is proposed to consider, first, those offences involving grievous bodily harm, that is, causing grievous bodily harm with intent contrary to s 18 of the Offences Against the Person Act 1861 and maliciously inflicting grievous bodily harm contrary to s 20 of the same Act (see *Saunders*, above).

To establish liability under s 18, the more serious offence, the prosecution would have to prove that Jason intended to cause serious harm. Recklessness will not suffice (*Belfon* (1976)). Intention probably bears the same meaning for this offence as it does for murder (*Bryson* (1985); *Purcell* (1986); *Woollin* (1998)).[4]

If intention cannot be proved, then liability under s 20 should be considered. As far as the *actus reus* of this offence is concerned, there were a number of decisions which implied that 'inflicts' was a narrower concept than 'causes'. The effect of the House of Lords decision in *Wilson* (1984) was understood to restrict s 20 to cases where force was applied directly or indirectly to the body of the victim. In *Ireland; Burstow* (1997), however, the House of Lords held that there is no significant difference in meaning between 'causing grievous bodily harm' in s 18 and 'inflicting grievous bodily harm' in s 20. It is unnecessary in either case to prove a direct or indirect application of force (see also *Mandair* (1995)). It is not clear whether this part of the decision in *Ireland; Burstow* is restricted to cases involving the infliction of psychiatric harm, although this seems unlikely. In any case, even if it were to be so limited, serious injury was inflicted indirectly by force in the instant problem. Lord Ackner in *Savage; Parmenter* (1991) stated that grievous bodily harm is inflicted where D frightens V into taking reasonably foreseeable evasive action and V suffers injury as a result (and see *Lewis* (1970)).

The *mens rea* requirement for s 20 is (subjective) recklessness with respect to some harm. This imposes on the prosecution the burden of proving that Jason was aware that intimidating Julie might result in her suffering some harm, albeit not serious harm (*Savage; Parmenter; Rushworth* (1992)).

The maximum punishment for the offence under s 20 is five years' imprisonment and, under s 18, life imprisonment.

If it is not possible to prove that Jason had the *mens rea* for either of these offences, his liability for the offence under s 47 – assault occasioning actual bodily harm – ought to be considered. For this offence, it is sufficient to prove that D assaulted V as a result of which V suffered some harm. It is not necessary to prove that D intended or was reckless as to the occasioning of harm (see *Savage*, above).[5]

Notes

1   In *Marjoram* (2000), the Court of Appeal rejected the appellant's submission that the question whether the evasive action of V was reasonably foreseeable should be determined by reference to the foresight of a reasonable person of the same age and sex as the *defendant*. The test was objective and thus the personal characteristics of the assailant were irrelevant.

2   In *Corbett* (1996), the victim was a mentally handicapped man who was extremely drunk at the time he was attacked by D. He ran away and was fatally struck by a passing car. The Court of Appeal approved the trial judge's direction that the jury had to consider whether what the victim had done was something that might reasonably be expected as a reaction of somebody in that state.

3   'Recklessness' in this context bears a 'subjective' meaning. It would be sufficient for the prosecution to prove that Jason was aware that there was a risk that his actions would cause Julie to apprehend immediate and unlawful personal violence (see *Savage; Parmenter* (1991)).

4   In *Dakou* (2002), Sachs J cited with approval a passage from the judgment of Diplock LJ in *Mowatt* (1967) which appears to suggest that an intention to cause serious harm or an intention to wound will suffice for an offence under s 18. This is not correct. Only an intention to cause serious injury will suffice.

5   The ingredients of assault and the relevant principles of causation are discussed above.

Question 12

Part (a)

Who, for the purposes of the defence of provocation, is the 'reasonable man'?

Part (b)

Fernando was told by his wife, Isabel, that she was having an affair with Carlos, the waiter. Fernando, seething with rage, went into the kitchen and, intending serious injury, hit Carlos with his chopper. Carlos slumped to the floor and died immediately.

Discuss Fernando's criminal liability.

How would your answer differ if the facts were amended as follows: Fernando, having attacked Carlos, sat down and smoked a cigarette. He then examined Carlos and noticed that he was still breathing. Fernando decided to leave Carlos to die. Carlos died 30 minutes later.

Answer plan

The first part of the question requires analysis of a number of key decisions concerning the characteristics of the defendant that may be attributed to the reasonable man in provocation. The second part involves application of the defence and consideration of the *Miller* (1983) principle.

Principal authorities include:

- *DPP v Camplin* (1978);
- *Morhall* (1996);
- *Luc Thiet Thuan* (1996);
- *Smith* (2000).

Answer

Part (a)

The defence of provocation is a partial defence, applicable only to murder. If successfully pleaded, liability is reduced to manslaughter. There are two limbs to the defence: first, the question whether provocation had temporarily deprived the person provoked of the power of self-control as a result of which he committed the unlawful act which caused death; and, secondly, whether the provocation would have made a reasonable man lose his self-control and do as the defendant did.[1]

The defence is of common law origin but was significantly modified by s 3 of the Homicide Act 1957. Whereas at common law verbal insults alone could not constitute provocation, s 3 provides that 'anything done or *said*' or a combination of things done and things said may give grounds for the defence (and see *Acott* (1997)). In addition, the section provides that if there was evidence that the accused was provoked to lose his self-control, then the question whether the reasonable man would have reacted as the defendant did is to be left to the jury. The judge is not entitled, as he could at common law, to withdraw the issue from the jury if, in his opinion, there is no evidence upon which a jury could reasonably consider that the reasonable man might have done as the defendant did.[2] As a corollary of this, the section prevents the judge from instructing the jury how the reasonable man would have reacted in the circumstances.

The question which came before the House of Lords in *DPP v Camplin* (1978) was whether, in addition to the two express changes in the law, the section had, by implication, abolished the rule in *Bedder v DPP* (1954) which provided that the 'reasonable person' was not to be endowed with the defendant's characteristics.

Bedder v DPP (1954)

In *Bedder*, an impotent youth visited a prostitute and attempted unsuccessfully to have sexual intercourse with her. She taunted him and, in the course of a struggle to break free from his grasp, slapped, kicked and punched him, whereupon he took a knife out of his pocket and killed her. The House of Lords approved the judge's direction to the effect that the jury should ignore the fact that the youth was impotent when considering whether the deceased's conduct amounted to such provocation as would cause a reasonable or ordinary person to do as the defendant did. In effect, the jury were instructed to allow the defence only if, in their opinion, the ordinary potent man would have responded in the same way as the accused.

DPP v Camplin (1978)

In *Camplin*, the appellant, a boy aged 15, lost his self-control and killed a man who had buggered him and then laughed at him. At his trial for murder, the judge directed the jury that the proper test was the effect of the provocation, not on a reasonable 15 year old boy, but on a reasonable man. The House of Lords disagreed and held that the age of the accused was to be taken into account in determining the degree of self-control to be expected of an ordinary person. Furthermore, the House decided that the principle expressed in *Bedder* no longer represented the law. Since provocation by words was frequently directed at some characteristic of the accused, such as a disability or race, the change in the law which now allowed words to constitute provocation would be ineffectual if the accused had to be assumed to lack such a characteristic.

However, as the function of the test is to set a standard of self-control, characteristics which reduced the defendant's powers of self-control, such as exceptional excitability or pugnacity, were not attributable to the reasonable person. And thus, according to Lord Diplock in *Camplin*, the judge should explain to the jury that the reasonable man is a person with the powers of self-control that might fairly be expected of someone of the age and sex of the accused who shares those characteristics of the accused, whether normal or abnormal, that might affect the gravity of the provocation upon him. In addition to characteristics of the defendant, the defendant's history or personal circumstances might also be relevant in assessing the gravity of the provocation and should be considered by the jury when dealing with the second limb of the defence.

Morhall (1996)

This approach was followed in *Morhall*. The appellant, who had been sniffing glue, was taunted about his addiction by V. A fight ensued, in the course of which the appellant stabbed V, who subsequently died. The appellant was charged with murder. At his trial, he put forward a defence of provocation. The judge in his summing up made no reference to any special characteristics of the appellant which the jury might think would affect the gravity of the provocation to him. The appellant was convicted. He appealed to the Court of Appeal, contending that his addiction to glue sniffing was a characteristic which should have been taken into account as affecting the gravity of the provocation. The Court of Appeal dismissed his appeal on the grounds that a self-induced addiction to glue sniffing was 'repugnant' to the concept of the 'reasonable man' referred to in s 3 of the 1957 Act. It was not a characteristic of the accused which the jury could take into account as affecting the gravity of the provocation. The appellant appealed to the House of Lords.

The House of Lords reversed the decision. The mere fact that a characteristic of the defendant was discreditable did not exclude it from consideration. The appellant's addiction to glue sniffing should have been taken into account as affecting the gravity of the provocation, since it was this characteristic which was the subject of the words of the deceased which were said to constitute provocation.[3] The judge should have directed the jury to take into account the fact of the appellant's addiction to glue sniffing when considering whether a person with the *ordinary person's power of self-control* would have reacted to the provocation as the appellant did. A distinction was to be drawn between the situation where the characteristic affected the gravity of the provocation, as with taunts directed at the characteristic, and which would be attributable to the reasonable person and one where the characteristic impaired the defendant's powers of self-control, where it would not.

Luc Thiet Thuan (1996)

In *Luc Thiet Thuan* (1996), the Privy Council held (Lord Steyn dissenting) that brain damage reducing the powers of self-control of the defendant was not to be attributed to the reasonable man.

The test of provocation was an objective test, namely whether the provocation was enough to make a reasonable man do as the defendant did, and individual peculiarities of the defendant affecting his powers of self-control should not, as such, be taken into account for the purposes of that test. In his advice, Lord Goff pointed out that to do so would undermine the objective test, something which, he noted, appeared to have occurred in a series of decisions of the Court of Appeal.

In the first of those decisions, *Ahluwalia* (1992), the court suggested, *obiter*, that 'post-traumatic stress disorder' and 'battered woman syndrome' were 'mental characteristics' which may be attributed to the reasonable person. In *Dryden* (1995), it was held that the defendant's obsessive personality and clinical depression ought to have been left to the jury for their consideration and, in *Humphreys* (1995), the relevant 'characteristics' to be attributed included 'abnormal immaturity' and 'attention seeking' by wrist slashing (see also *Thornton (No 2)* (1996); *Raven* (1982)).[4]

It is by no means clear from these decisions whether the Court of Appeal took the view that the abnormal characteristics of the defendant were relevant to the issue of self-control, or whether they should be taken into account solely when considering the gravity of the provocation. Nonetheless, Lord Steyn, dissenting in *Luc Thiet Thuan*, understood the Court of Appeal to have decided that psychological characteristics which impaired self-control ought to be attributed to the reasonable person. Lord Steyn believed that to restrict consideration of these characteristics to the subjective question would puzzle the jury and lead to injustice.

In *R v Campbell* (1997), the Court of Appeal considered the majority opinion in *Luc Thiet Thuan* (1996) and held that it would continue to follow the earlier decisions of the Court of Appeal and the minority opinion of Lord Steyn. And in *Parker* (1997), the Court of Appeal held that psychiatric evidence that the defendant, a chronic alcoholic, had suffered brain damage which might have rendered him more susceptible to provocation was admissible.

Smith (2000)

The issue arose for the consideration of the House of Lords in the case of *Smith* (2000). During the course of an argument at his flat, the defendant stabbed his friend, McCullagh, several times with a kitchen knife, fatally wounding him. He was charged with murder. Smith put forward a number of defences including diminished responsibility and provocation. He claimed that he was provoked to lose his self-control as a result of McCullagh's refusal to admit that he had stolen the appellant's carpentry tools.

The defence put forward psychiatric evidence that Smith was suffering from a severe form of depression which made him more volatile.

In his summing up, the trial judge told the jury that the fact that the depressive illness might have disinhibited the respondent from behaving violently was not relevant, as far as provocation was concerned, when deciding whether a reasonable person would have done as the defendant did. The jury were required to consider whether a person with *ordinary* powers of self-control would have done as the defendant did.

The jury rejected Smith's defences and, by a majority of 10 to 2, convicted him of murder. The defendant appealed, contending that the judge ought to have directed the jury that the evidence of the two psychiatrists as to his mental state and its impact on his response to the provocation was relevant to the question whether a reasonable person would have done as he did in response to the provocation.

The Court of Appeal allowed the defendant's appeal and substituted a verdict of manslaughter. The jury should have been directed to consider whether the hypothetical reasonable man possessing the appellant's characteristics including his depressive illness might have reacted to the provocative conduct in the way that the appellant had. The court recognised, however, that a thorough review of the authorities was necessary, gave leave to appeal and certified the following point of law of general public importance for the House of Lords' consideration:

> Are characteristics other than age and sex attributable to a reasonable man, for the purpose of s 3 of the Homicide Act 1957, relevant not only to the gravity of the provocation to him but also to the standard of control to be expected?

The House of Lords, Lords Hobhouse and Millet dissenting, answered the certified question affirmatively and dismissed the appeal. The judge should not have directed the jury as a matter of law that the effect of Smith's depression on his powers of self-control was 'neither here nor there'. It was a matter for the jury whether to take it into account when deciding whether the behaviour of the accused had measured up to the standard of self-control which ought reasonably to be expected of him.[5] Lord Hoffmann took the view that s 3 of the Homicide Act 1957 made the jury sovereign in respect of the objective element. It was for them to determine not only whether the behaviour of the accused complied with a standard of self-control, but what the appropriate standard in the particular case should be. It followed, in Lord Hoffmann's opinion, that it would be inconsistent with the section for the judge to tell the jury as a matter of law that they should ignore a characteristic of the accused when deciding whether the objective element of provocation had been satisfied.

The House held that no distinction should be drawn, when attributing characteristics for the purposes of the objective part of the test imposed by s 3 of the Homicide Act, between their relevance to the gravity of the provocation to a reasonable man and his reaction to it. Account may be taken of a relevant characteristic in relation to the accused's power of self-control, whether or not the characteristic is the object of the provocation. In Lord Hoffmann's view, there was no justice in applying a standard of self-control that the defendant was incapable of attaining. In *Camplin*, although the provocation was not directed at D's age, the defendant's youthfulness was to be taken into account by the jury because the principle of human compassion to human infirmity required one to do so and, the majority concluded, there was nothing in the judgment to say that the same principle of compassion was not applicable to other characteristics which a jury might on similar grounds think should be taken into account.

Comment

The decision in *Smith* has enlarged the scope of the defence of provocation and, it is submitted, is inconsistent with *Camplin*, *Morhall* and s 3. The function of the reasonable man test is to set an objective standard by reference to 'the degree of self-control to be expected of the ordinary person with whom the accused's conduct is to be compared' (Lord Diplock in *Camplin*, p 717). Whilst agreeing that those who are incapable of exercising ordinary self-control may have a partial excuse for their actions, the minority pointed out that the defence of provocation is not the appropriate defence. Where an individual is provoked by a trivial insult and, because of mental abnormality cannot exercise ordinary self-control, his loss of self-control should be ascribed to his psychological make-up rather than to the provocation he received and, if the offence is to be mitigated, it ought to be on the basis that his mental abnormality has diminished his responsibility.

Section 2 of the 1957 Act specifically creates the defence of diminished responsibility, which provides an excuse for those whose mental responsibility is impaired as a result of an abnormality of mind. By allowing abnormal psychiatric conditions as such to be attributed, an element of diminished responsibility is indirectly incorporated into the law of provocation and whereas the burden of proving diminished responsibility falls on the defendant in the case of provocation, the burden is with the prosecution. The majority approach in *Smith* allows a defendant to escape the burden of proof imposed by s 2 by raising the defence of provocation, either alone or in conjunction with diminished responsibility, and introducing medical evidence of an abnormal condition impairing the defendant's powers of self-control.

In conclusion, it is submitted that the approach of the majority in *Smith* means that the accused is to be judged by his own impaired powers of self-control and, in effect, eliminates the objective element of the defence. By introducing a variable standard of self-control, the foundation of the defence is undermined.[6]

Part (b)

Fernando may be charged with murder. He committed unlawful homicide intending to cause grievous bodily harm (*Saunders* (1985); *Moloney* (1985)). He may, however, be able to take advantage of the defence of provocation to reduce his liability to manslaughter. As explained above, provocation may take a purely verbal form and the fact that it originates from some source other than the deceased does not preclude the defence.

The loss of self-control must be 'sudden and temporary' and the fact that Fernando reacted spontaneously to his wife's revelations is good evidence of that (*Ahluwalia* (1992)).[7]

If the jury believe that Fernando may have lost his self-control when he attacked Carlos, they must allow the defence unless they are sure that a reasonable man would not have done as he did (s 3 of the 1957 Act). This entails considering whether the defendant exercised the powers of self-control that might reasonably be expected of him. The jury should take all matters into account, including the characteristics of the defendant as well as the circumstances in which the death occurred. The judge should not tell the jury that they should, as a matter of law, ignore any matter (*Smith*; *Weller* (2003); *Lowe* (2003)).

Alternative facts

The defence of provocation applies only where the defendant lacked self-control *at the time he killed the deceased*. Provided, therefore, that the jury are sure that Fernando did not lack self-control after smoking the cigarette or if he did lack self-control that the reasonable man would not have left Carlos to die, they should return a conviction for murder.

In *Miller* (1983), Lord Diplock said that a person is under a duty to take measures that lie within his power to counteract a danger that he himself has created. If he fails to take those steps, then his failure can be regarded as causative of any particular result that ensues and he may be convicted of an appropriate offence provided the failure to act was accompanied by the relevant *mens rea*.[8]

Carlos' vulnerable state was brought about by the act of Fernando. Fernando was under a duty to attempt to remedy the situation. As he failed to discharge that duty, his inaction may be regarded as causative of Carlos' death. As the facts indicate that at that time he intended to let Carlos die, he is guilty of murder.

Notes

1   These two requirements are commonly called the subjective and objective elements of the defence respectively.

2   The judge may withdraw the defence from the jury only if there is no evidence of a sudden and temporary loss of self-control. See *Acott* (1997); *Kromer* (2002). If there is evidence that D was provoked to lose his self-control, the defence must be left to the jury. The probative burden is on the prosecution to satisfy the jury beyond reasonable doubt that either D was not provoked to lose his self-control at the relevant time or that the reasonable man would have not done as D did (*McPherson* (1957)). In *Pearson* (1992), where two sons, William and Malcolm, killed their violent father, the Court of Appeal held that in deciding whether William had lost his self-control, the jury were entitled to take into account those words and conduct of the father directed against Malcolm which had come to the notice of William. Provocation was not limited to his own personal experience of his father's conduct (see also *Peter Davies* (1975)).

3   In *Newell* (1980), the provocation was not directed at the appellant's alcoholism and thus could not be imputed. Lord Lane, however, left open the possibility of chronic alcoholism being regarded as a characteristic attributable to the reasonable man in an appropriate case.

4   In *Raven*, the accused was 22 years old but had a mental age of nine. The Recorder of London ruled that the jury should be directed to consider the effect of the provocation upon 'a reasonable man who has lived the same type of life as the defendant for 22 years but who has the mental age of the defendant'.

5   In *Camplin*, Lord Diplock stated that the question whether the reasonable man would have done as the defendant did is to be decided by the jury 'drawing on their experiences of how ordinary human beings behave in real life' and 'that since [the] question is one for the opinion of the jury, the evidence of witnesses as to how they think a reasonable man would react to the provocation is not admissible' (*Camplin* (1978), p 711). It would seem therefore that expert psychiatric evidence as to the effects of mental abnormalities is, strictly

speaking, inadmissible. This was the view taken by Lord Clyde in *Smith*. Medical evidence concerning the effect the characteristic might have on self-control was not admissible. The jury are somehow expected to take account of the defendant's mental impairment without hearing evidence regarding its effects on behaviour!

6   *Smith* was applied in the case of *Roberts* (2002), where it was held that D's depressive condition was attributable to the reasonable man.

7   It is not necessary that the defendant suffered a complete loss of control such that he was not aware of what he was doing; it is sufficient that he could not restrain himself (*Richens* (1994)).

Whilst there must be a sudden and temporary loss of self-control, the jury should consider any history of potentially provocative behaviour by the deceased (*Smith (Josephine)* (2002)).

8   Lord Diplock articulated the rule in the context of criminal damage, but it is clear that the principle was intended to apply to all result crimes. In *Lawford* (1994), the Supreme Court of Australia applied the rule to a case involving murder. *Miller* involved a situation where D, having becoming aware of the fact that he had accidentally created a dangerous situation, failed to take steps to rectify it. Presumably, the rule applies also to a situation like the present one, where a defence which may have been available to D at the time he created the dangerous situation is not available when he fails to take remedial steps. D is responsible for the victim being in a vulnerable state.

Question 13

Iago lied to Othello, telling him that Othello's wife, Desdemona, was having a passionate affair with Othello's friend, Cassio, and that he had just seen them both going into Othello and Desdemona's apartment. Othello was an extremely jealous individual and what Iago had told him made him furious. He told Iago that he was going to kill Cassio and asked Iago to lend him a knife. Iago gave him the knife and Othello rushed off to find Cassio. A few minutes later, he arrived at their apartment to find his wife alone and asleep. Intending to kill her, he fatally wounded Desdemona.

Discuss the criminal liability of Iago and Othello.

How would Othello's liability differ if Desdemona had suffered serious injuries but survived his attack?

Answer plan

This question requires consideration of the defences of provocation and diminished responsibility. Both are defences to murder and, if successfully pleaded, reduce liability to manslaughter. In addition, issues concerning accessorial liability and incitement are raised.

The principal issues are:

- application of the defence of provocation;
- application of the defence of diminished responsibility;
- liability of accomplices where the principal has a defence;
- application of the law relating to attempts.

The principal authorities are: s 3 of the Homicide Act 1957; s 2 of the Homicide Act 1957; s 1 of the Criminal Attempts Act 1981.

Answer

Othello

As Othello intentionally killed Desdemona, he may be charged with murder (*Moloney* (1985)). He may contend, however, that he was acting under provocation. This is a common law defence, modified by s 3 of the Homicide Act 1957, which, if successfully pleaded, reduces liability from murder to manslaughter. There are two elements to the defence. The first is whether, at the relevant time the accused had, as a result of provocation, lost his self-control. The second involves assessing whether the reasonable man would, in the circumstances, have done as the accused did. Although the accused bears an evidential burden in support of his plea, the burden of disproving provocation lies with the Crown and thus the defence will succeed if the jury believe the accused may have lost his self-control and a reasonable man might also have lost his self-control and done as the accused did (*Woolmington v DPP* (1935); *McPherson* (1957)).

With respect to the first element, Devlin J in *Duffy* (1949) held that there must be a 'sudden and temporary loss of self-control'. (This was endorsed in *Thornton* (1992) and *Ahluwalia* (1992).) The facts of the problem indicate that Othello reacted fairly spontaneously to Iago's lies and this is good evidence that he suddenly lost his self-control (*Ahluwalia*).

The fact that Othello was provoked by Iago's lies and not by an act of Desdemona does not preclude the defence. First, s 3 of the Homicide Act 1957 provides that provocation may be verbal; and, secondly, the Court of Appeal in *Davies* (1975) held that the defence is not to be denied merely because the provocative words are spoken by someone other than the victim.[1]

The second element – whether the reasonable man would have done as the accused did – is exclusively a matter for the jury. In *Smith* (2000), the

House of Lords held that, ordinarily, the judge should not direct the jury to ignore a characteristic of the accused in deciding whether the reasonable man would have done as the defendant did. However, concerned that the objective element of the defence might otherwise be eroded, Lord Hoffmann expressed the view that certain characteristics including obsessive jealousy were not an acceptable reason for loss of self-control and suggested that the judge should explain to the jury that they should be ignored in relation to the objective element.[2] In *Weller* (2003), the Court of Appeal noted that Lord Hoffmann's comments concerning obsessive jealousy were simply a 'suggestion' and his Lordship was not 'commending an approach'. Delivering the judgment of the court, Mantell LJ stated that the overall tenor of the majority speeches in *Smith* indicated that, when considering the objective element of the defence, the jury should take all matters into account, including characteristics of the defendant and the circumstances in which the death occurred and held that the trial judge had quite properly allowed the jury to take into account the defendant's obsessive jealousy.

Furthermore, the House had made it clear that the judge is not required to express the test by reference to a reasonable man provided the principles underlying the defence are explained to the jury. And so, in the instant case, the jury may be directed to consider whether the circumstances were such as to make Othello's loss of self-control sufficiently excusable to reduce the gravity of the offence from murder to manslaughter.[3]

As an alternative to the defence of provocation, Othello may be able to take advantage of the defence of diminished responsibility, introduced into English law by s 2 of the Homicide Act 1957. In common with provocation, it is a partial defence which, if successfully pleaded, reduces liability from murder to manslaughter (s 2(3) of the Homicide Act 1957).

For a successful plea, Othello bears the burden of proving, on the balance of probabilities (s 2(2); *Dunbar* (1958)), that:

(a) he was suffering from an 'abnormality of mind',

(b) resulting from a condition of arrested or retarded development of mind or any inherent causes or induced by disease or injury,

(c) that substantially impaired his responsibility for the killing.[4]

In *Dix* (1981), the Court of Appeal held that the defence must not be left to the jury unless there is medical evidence in support of these three elements. The elements (a) and (b) are issues for the jury, who should take into account all the evidence, but, if the medical evidence is unanimous, and there is nothing in the facts or circumstances which could lead to a contrary conclusion, they are bound to accept it (*Byrne* (1960); *Matheson* (1958); *Kiszko* (1978)). The second element concerns the aetiology or cause of the abnormality. This issue is to be resolved solely by reference to the medical evidence (*Byrne*).

Although killings motivated by simple hatred or jealousy fall outside the scope of the defence of diminished responsibility, it has been held to apply where the defendant's abnormality involves morbid or pathological jealousy substantially impairing his ability to control himself (*Vinagre* (1979); *Miller* (1972); *Nicholls*, (1974); *Asher* (1981); *Sangha* (1997)).[5] Thus, the question whether Othello is able to take advantage of the defence will depend upon the jury's assessment of all the evidence and, in particular, the testimony of the medical experts.

If Othello successfully pleads diminished responsibility or provocation, he will be convicted of manslaughter and the court will have a discretion as to sentence, ranging from absolute discharge to life imprisonment[6] or, if appropriate, a hospital order may be made under s 37(1) of the Mental Health Act 1983.[7]

Iago

It is proposed to consider first Iago's liability as an accomplice to Desdemona's murder. Section 8 of the Accessories and Abettors Act 1861, as amended by s 12 of the Criminal Law Act 1977, provides that a person who aids, abets, counsels or procures the commission of an offence is liable to be tried and punished for that offence as a principal offender.

To 'aid' means to provide help or assistance to the perpetrator, and it is immaterial whether or not the accomplice is present at the time the offence is committed. In *NCB v Gamble* (1959), Devlin J stated that supplying a knife to commit a murder is clearly capable of amounting to assistance. It should also be noted that Iago may be convicted of murder even if Othello is convicted only of manslaughter as a result of successfully pleading provocation (*Howe* (1987)) and/or diminished responsibility (s 2(4) of the Homicide Act 1957).

However, although Iago intended to assist Othello to commit murder, his intention was to assist Othello in the murder of Cassio, not Desdemona, and it is generally accepted that, in such circumstances, the alleged accomplice attracts no liability.[8] It is submitted, however, that, if Iago contemplated or foresaw as a real or serious risk that Othello might intentionally kill Desdemona, then he may be convicted of her murder (see *Rook* (1993)).

Iago's liability for the common law offence of incitement ought to be considered. For a conviction on indictment, the penalty is a fine and/or imprisonment at the discretion of the court. An offence is committed whether or not the person incited does what he is urged to do. There must, however, be some element of persuasion (*Fitzmaurice* (1983)). In this case, although Iago knew that Othello intended to kill Cassio and supplied the weapon, it does not appear that Iago actually encouraged Othello to commit murder and, thus, it would seem that he is not guilty of the offence.

Alternative facts

Othello may be convicted of attempted murder contrary to s 1(1) of the Criminal Attempts Act 1981. The facts of the problem indicate that he had the necessary intention to kill (*Whybrow* (1951); *Cunningham* (1982)) and, clearly, his acts were 'more than merely preparatory' to the commission of the full offence.

In addition, he may be convicted of the offence of wounding with intent contrary to s 18 of the Offences Against the Person Act 1861. Again, it is clear that he committed the *actus reus* with the necessary *mens rea* – an intention to do really serious bodily harm (*Belfon* (1976)).

The maximum penalties for each of the above offences is a term of imprisonment for life (s 4(1)(a) of the Criminal Attempts Act 1981; s 18 of the Offences Against the Person Act 1861).

The fact that Othello was provoked by Iago's lies into attacking Desdemona is no defence to either of these offences, although it may amount to substantial mitigation (*Kingston* (1994)).

Notes

1　See also *Pearson* (1992).

2　See [2000] 4 All ER 289 at p 309.

3　In *Jenkins and Others*, it was held that no 'particular formula' is required but, in most cases, a summing up is not defective if the expression 'reasonable man' is used. The term is used in s 3 and its use is not proscribed in *Smith*. In *Lowe* (2003), the Court of Appeal held that the judge need not expressly refer to characteristics which are not directly relevant, and in *Paria v The State of Trinidad and Tobago* (2003), the Privy Council held that as there was no evidence that D's depression was pathological, it did not constitute a 'characteristic' which the jury were required to take into account in applying the objective test. As there was no evidence that the condition had affected the way that D had reacted when he killed V, it would have been 'sheer speculation on their part if the jury had taken account of this factor in relation to either the subjective or the objective test'.

4　In *Ali; Jordan* (2001), the Court of Appeal held that the requirement in s 2(2) that the defendant bears the burden of proof in respect of diminished responsibility does not contravene Art 6 of the European Convention for the Protection of Human Rights and Fundamental Freedoms 1950, which provides that 'in the determination of any criminal charge against him, everyone is entitled to a fair and public hearing' and that 'everyone charged with a criminal offence shall be presumed innocent until proved guilty according to law'. The defence provided by s 2 is not an ingredient of the offence of murder. It is of benefit to defendants who are in a position to take advantage of it; if the defendant does not seek to rely on it, he is not required to prove anything.

5　Note the following remark made in the *Report of the Committee on Mentally Abnormal Offenders* (the Butler Committee), 1975, Cmnd 6244, para 19.7:

Sometimes, depression and jealousy can properly be diagnosed as mental disorders; but the distinction between conditions which can be so diagnosed and normal depression or normal jealousy may be one of degree only, and the effect of the present law is to put strong pressure on the psychiatrist to conform his medical opinion to the exigency of avoiding a very severe sentence, fixed by law, for a person for whom everyone has the greatest sympathy.

It would appear, from the decisions of the Court of Appeal in *Campbell* (1997); *Parker* (1997); and *Smith* (1998), that Othello's pathological jealousy may be attributed to the reasonable man for the purposes of the defence of provocation.

6   Section 5 of the Offences Against the Person Act 1861.

7   Hospital orders are not normally made in respect of defendants whose abnormality involves morbid jealousy; they are generally given short custodial sentences, probation orders or conditional discharges. See the Criminal Law Revision Committee, 14th Report, Cmnd 7844, 1980, para 92.

8   See Williams, G, *Textbook of Criminal Law*, 2nd edn, 1983, p 357.

Question 14

Part (a)

Molar visited his dentist, Spitoon, for a dental examination. Spitoon discovered that one of Molar's teeth needed filling. Molar, who did not realise that Spitoon had been suspended from practice by the General Dental Council (GDC), agreed to the surgery and it was performed there and then. Later that afternoon, Kite, a newcomer to the area, visited the surgery needing an emergency extraction. John, the receptionist, had always wanted to be a dentist. He had watched Spitoon at work, had read the best dentistry books and was confident of his ability. So he pretended to be Spitoon and performed the treatment. (Spitoon was drunk and asleep in one of the treatment rooms.)

In both cases, the treatment was perfect.

Discuss the criminal liability of Spitoon and John.

Part (b)

Mark and Jodie were engaged to be married when Jodie decided she no longer wished to see Mark. He was extremely angry and, over the course of the next few months, he made a number of telephone calls to her during which he did not speak. As a result of these calls, Jodie suffered a psychological breakdown.

Discuss Mark's criminal liability.

Answer plan

Both parts of this question raise issues concerning a number of the non-fatal offences against the person.

In addition, the first part involves the defence of consent. The second part deals with liability where psychiatric harm, without physical harm, results from the defendant's unlawful conduct. Note that it is not possible to provide a definitive answer to the second part, as a number of relevant facts are not disclosed.

The principal authorities are: *Ireland; Burstow* (1997); *Clarence* (1888); *Richardson* (1998); *Chan Fook* (1994); *Savage; Parmenter* (1991).

Answer

Part (a)

It is proposed to consider liability of both parties for the offence of assault occasioning actual bodily harm under s 47 of the Offences Against the Person Act 1861. The basic ingredients of liability for this offence are that the defendant intentionally or recklessly performed an assault or a battery which resulted in some injury (*Ireland; Burstow* (1997)).

There are a number of circumstances where consent may operate to prevent conduct which would otherwise be classified as an assault from being so treated. One of those is where the victim gives his consent to surgery. In these circumstances, the infliction of harm is regarded as being in the public interest (*Attorney General's Reference (No 6 of 1980)* (1981)).

The issue in this problem concerns the effect on the validity of consent where a fraud is practised.

In *Clarence* (1888), it was held that fraud does not necessarily negative consent. Only where the fraud goes to the nature of the act performed or the identity of the person performing it is any apparent consent vitiated.[1] This principle was considered in *Richardson* (1998). The Court of Appeal here had to decide whether the consent given to the defendant, a dentist, to perform treatment had been nullified by the defendant's implied and false representation that he was qualified. The dentist had been suspended from practice by the GDC. The Court of Appeal held that the consent had not been negatived. The complainants were fully aware of the appellant's identity. They knew who he was. The Crown's submission that 'the identity of the person should be extended to cover the qualifications or attributes of the dentist on the basis that the patients consented to treatment by a qualified dentist and not a suspended one' was rejected.[2]

In *Tabassum* (2000), the appellant had examined three women's breasts, having led the women to believe that he was medically qualified and was carrying out research into breast cancer. Each of the three women said that they had only consented because they thought the appellant had either medical qualifications or relevant training.

At his trial on charges of indecent assault, he submitted that the case should be stayed on the basis that the prosecution could not prove the absence of consent and therefore no assaults had taken place. The judge ruled against that submission; the nature and quality of the act performed was different from that consented to. His appeal against conviction was dismissed. As the appellant had no medical qualifications, he could not have been touching the complainants' breasts for a proper medical purpose. The complainants had consented to a medical act and not a sexual act and thus although there was consent as to the nature of the act, there was no consent as to its quality.

The Court of Appeal distinguished *Richardson* as that case proceeded solely by reference to the issue of identity. The Crown had not argued that the act performed by Richardson differed in nature and quality from the act consented to. It is submitted that it is unlikely that such an argument would have been successful. The appellant had consented to dental treatment and that is what Richardson performed. As in the current problem, there was consent as to the nature and quality of the act.[3]

John, on the other hand, did practice a fraud as to his identity. He represented, by his conduct, that he was the dentist in practice and, as a result of this fraud, Kite was induced to give consent to the treatment. John is guilty of the offence under s 47.

Part (b)

Can psychiatric illness amount to bodily harm?

In *Ireland; Burstow* (1997), the House of Lords, approving the decision of the Court of Appeal in *Chan Fook* (1994), decided that a recognisable psychiatric illness, whether of a neurotic, psychoneurotic or psychotic nature, may amount to bodily harm.[4]

Whether or not psychiatric illness amounts to 'actual' or 'grievous' bodily harm depends, of course, upon the seriousness of the illness in question and is ultimately a question for the jury.

As the extent of Jodie's psychological illness is not disclosed, it is proposed to consider liability for a number of offences including 'unlawfully causing grievous bodily harm with intent', 'maliciously inflicting grievous bodily harm', and 'assault occasioning actual bodily harm' contrary to s 18, s 20 and s 47 of the Offences Against the Person Act 1861, respectively.

Liability under s 47 – was there an assault occasioning actual bodily harm?

An assault is committed where D intentionally or recklessly causes V to apprehend an imminent application of violence (*Savage; Parmenter* (1991)). Might there be an apprehension of immediate and unlawful violence in a case such as the present, where there was a lack of physical proximity between the defendant and the victim and when the act complained of consisted of telephone calls?

The House of Lords in *Ireland*, overruling *Meade and Belt* (1823), decided that an assault can be committed by words alone or indeed silence and that silent telephone calls may amount to an assault provided the victim is caused to fear immediate personal violence or the possibility thereof (see also *Constanza* (1997), decided before *Ireland*).[5]

As far as the *mens rea* of the offence under s 47 is concerned, the prosecution must prove that the accused either intended the victim to apprehend violence or foresaw the risk that the victim might apprehend violence (*Savage; Parmenter*).

The maximum penalty for this offence is five years' imprisonment.

Liability under s 20 – was there an infliction of grievous bodily harm?

Counsel for Burstow argued that the House of Lords in *Wilson* (1984) decided that a direct or indirect application of force was necessary for the s 20 offence. Lord Steyn agreed that there were passages which supported the appellants' argument, but he believed overall that the judgments on this point were 'neutral'. In addition, Lord Steyn and Lord Hope considered the 'troublesome authority' of *Clarence* (1888). This decision appeared to hold that a battery – a direct application of violence – was a necessary element of the s 20 offence. Both of their Lordships considered the decision to be of little weight as it was decided before the concept of psychiatric injury had been recognised. The decision was dated. As a matter of current usage, 'inflict' could embrace the idea of one person causing psychiatric injury to another without any need for an assault or other application of force (see also *Mandair* (1995)).

As far as the *mens rea* for this offence is concerned, it is sufficient to prove that the defendant intended or foresaw the risk of some harm, not necessarily serious harm (*Mowatt* (1967), referred to with approval in *Savage; Parmenter*).

The maximum penalty for maliciously inflicting grievous bodily harm is a term of imprisonment not exceeding five years.

Liability under s 18

Provided the psychiatric injury sustained was serious, the only practical difficulty in prosecuting under this section will be proving that the defendant intended to cause grievous bodily harm. Nothing less will suffice (*Belfon* (1976)). If the approach to intention adopted by the House of Lords in *Woollin* (1998), in respect of murder, applies also to this offence, then the prosecution must prove either that it was Mark's desire to cause serious harm or that he foresaw that serious harm was *virtually certain* to result.

Other offences

Section 43(1) of the Telecommunications Act 1984 makes it an offence persistently to make use of a public telecommunications system for the purpose of causing annoyance, inconvenience or needless anxiety to another. The maximum penalty is six months' imprisonment.

Sections 1 and 2 of the Protection from Harassment Act 1997 make it an offence to pursue a course of conduct which amounts to harassment of another and which the accused knows or ought to know amounts to harassment.[6]

A person guilty of this offence is liable, on summary conviction, to a term of imprisonment not exceeding six months or a fine not exceeding level 5 on the standard scale (s 2(2)).

Section 4(1) of the same statute creates a more serious offence, where a person, D, whose course of conduct causes another to fear, on at least two occasions, that violence will be used against him and where D knows or ought to know that his course of conduct will cause the other so to fear on each of the occasions. The maximum penalty for this offence is a term of imprisonment not exceeding five years (s 4(4))[7] – a penalty which Lord Steyn in *Ireland* thought was inadequate to deal with the persistent offender who causes serious injury to his victim.

Notes

1 Compare Law Commission, *Consent and Offences Against the Person*, Consultation Paper No 134, 1994, paras 26.2, 27.2 with *Consent in the Criminal Law*, Consultation Paper No 139, 1995, para 6.27.

2 Similarly, in *Papadimitropoulos* (1957), a mistake as to the defendant's 'qualifications' – in this case, concerning his marital status – was regarded as having no effect on the complainant's consent.

3   It is an offence contrary to s 38 of the Dentist Act 1984 to practise or hold oneself out to practise dentistry when not qualified. The maximum penalty on summary conviction is a fine not exceeding level 5 on the standard scale.

4   Simple states of fear or 'problems in coping with everyday life' are not, however, included.

5   The House acknowledged that immediacy of the violence was not an issue in *Ireland*, as he had pleaded guilty, but that it was likely to prove problematic in cases involving silent callers. Lord Steyn did accept that:

> ... the concept of an assault involving immediate personal violence as an ingredient of the s 47 offence is a considerable complicating factor in bringing prosecutions under it in respect of silent telephone callers and stalkers. That the least serious of the ladder of offences is difficult to apply in such cases is unfortunate.

See also *Cox* (1998).

6   In *Kelly v DPP* (2002), the Divisional Court held that three threatening and abusive calls in five minutes constituted a 'course of conduct'.

7   Lord Steyn believed that it may be difficult to secure a conviction for this offence in respect of a silent caller as the offence requires that the victim fears that violence will be used against him.

Question 15

Fred, an alcoholic, was drinking heavily in his local pub. He thought he heard Albert, the barman, make insulting comments about Fred's girlfriend to another customer, John. In fact, Albert had been talking about his own wife.

Fred, intending serious injury, picked up a heavy ashtray and threw it at Albert. The ashtray missed Albert and hit John on the head. John had an abnormally thin skull and died from the blow.

Discuss Fred's criminal liability.

Answer plan

This question raises the defences of provocation and diminished responsibility. Although the facts state that Fred had been drinking heavily, there is no need to refer to the *Majewski* principle as the facts also state that Fred intended serious injury – that is, he acted with malice aforethought.

The particular issues are:

- the 'egg shell skull' principle;
- the doctrine of transferred malice;
- the defence of provocation;
- the defence of 'diminished responsibility'.

The principal authorities include: *Camplin* (1978); *Newell* (1980); *Luc Thiet Thuan* (1996); *Morhall* (1996); *Smith* (2000); *Byrne* (1960); *Tandy* (1989).

Answer

Murder

Fred may be charged with the murder of John. His actions were the legal cause of John's death. Any argument by Fred to the effect that John's condition, that is, his thin skull, was the cause of death will be rejected by the court. There is a principle of English law that 'one must take one's victim as one finds him'. This means that one cannot point to a peculiar vulnerability of the victim as the legal cause of death (see *Hayward* (1908)). The fact that John had a thin skull, rendering him more vulnerable to fatal injury, does not affect the attribution of the death to Fred.

Furthermore, the facts indicate that Fred had the *mens rea* for murder. It was finally settled by the House of Lords in *Cunningham* (1981) that an intention to cause grievous bodily harm to another amounts to 'malice aforethought' and grievous bodily harm means 'serious bodily harm' (*Saunders* (1985)). The fact that Fred intended serious injury to Albert but missed him and hit John is of no legal consequence. The doctrine of transferred malice, as explained in the old case of *Latimer* (1886), provides that if D aims a blow at 'V1' (Albert), misses and accidentally hits 'V2' (John), D is responsible for the injuries sustained by 'V2' to the same extent as he would have been had those injuries been sustained by 'V1'.[1]

Fred may be able, however, to take advantage of the defence of provocation or, alternatively, the defence of diminished responsibility, both of which reduce liability to manslaughter.[2]

Provocation – manslaughter

Provocation is a common law defence, modified by s 3 of the Homicide Act 1957.

The elements of the defence are first, that at the relevant time, the defendant had lost his self-control as a result of provocation (*the subjective condition*) and, secondly, that the reasonable man in those circumstances would have done as the accused did (*the objective condition*).

Although the accused bears an evidential burden in support of his plea that he was provoked to lose his self-control, the burden of disproving provocation lies with the Crown (*Woolmington v DPP* (1935); *Macpherson* (1957); *Acott* (1997)) and thus where evidence of provocation is raised, the jury should allow the defence unless they are sure that one or both of the elements were not present.[3]

The fact that Fred mistakenly believed that his girlfriend was being insulted is, it is submitted, no bar to the defence. First, the Homicide Act 1957 provides that provocation may take the form of spoken insults and, secondly, in *Letenock* (1917), it was held that even if the accused acts under a mistaken belief induced by drunkenness that he was being provoked, he should be judged in accordance with the facts as he mistakenly believed them to be (see also *Safi* (2003)).

The defence of provocation is only available if the defendant suffered a 'sudden and temporary loss of self-control' (*Duffy* (1949); *Thornton* (1992)). The facts of the problem disclose that Fred reacted spontaneously to the perceived insults. This is good evidence that he suddenly lost his self-control (*Ahluwalia* (1992)).

The jury must be satisfied, however, that the reasonable man would have done as Fred did in the circumstances which Fred supposed to exist. Who is the reasonable man in this context?

According to the House of Lords in *Camplin* (1978), the reasonable man is a person having the power of self-control to be expected of a person of the same age and sex as the accused and sharing such characteristics of the accused as they think would affect the gravity of the provocation to him. As the function of the objective test is to set a standard of self-control, characteristics which do not affect the gravity of the provocation but impair the defendant's powers of self-control ought not to be attributed.

It is clear that Fred's drunkenness may not be attributed to the reasonable person (*Newell* (1980); *Morhall* (1996); *Pearce* (2001)), but might his alcoholism? In *Newell* (1980), the Court of Appeal held that chronic alcoholism could not be attributed to the reasonable man as there was no connection between it and the deceased's taunts about the accused's former girlfriend. Had the insults been directed at his condition, it would have been attributable to the reasonable person as it would have affected the gravity of the taunts (see *Morhall* (1996)).

In *Luc Thiet Thuan* (1996), the Privy Council, following the logic of *Camplin*, held that the response of the victim should be assessed by reference to the powers of self-control of an ordinary person and not a person sharing the defendant's mental impairment.

However, in *Ahluwalia*, Lord Taylor observed that a psychological condition of 'learned helplessness' or 'battered woman syndrome', if supported by medical evidence, would be relevant to the objective test. This *dictum* was followed in *Dryden* (1995), where the Court of Appeal held that obsessive personality disorder and depression were characteristics imputable to the reasonable person (see also *Thornton (No 2)* (1996); *Humphreys* (1995)). In none of these cases was the provocation directed at the relevant characteristic. Nonetheless, in *Campbell* (1997), Lord Bingham regarded these decisions of the Court of Appeal as authoritative and, in *Parker* (1997), it was held that the trial judge had erred in refusing to admit evidence that D was a chronic alcoholic with brain damage which rendered him more susceptible to provocation. The court did not regard itself bound by the decision of the Privy Council in *Luc Thiet Thuan*.

This approach was endorsed by the House of Lords in *Smith* (2000). The defendant was suffering from a severe depressive illness which reduced his powers of self-control. The defence raised the defences of provocation and diminished responsibility and put forward psychiatric evidence that Smith was suffering from severe depression which reduced his 'threshold for erupting with violence'. The trial judge instructed the jury that the fact that the depressive illness might have disinhibited the respondent from behaving violently was not relevant, as far as provocation was concerned, when deciding whether a reasonable person would have done as the defendant did. The jury were required to consider whether a person with ordinary powers of self-control would have done as the defendant did.

The jury rejected Smith's defence and convicted him of murder. The defendant appealed, contending that the judge ought to have directed the jury that the psychiatric evidence was relevant to the objective question in provocation.

The Court of Appeal allowed the defendant's appeal and substituted a verdict of manslaughter. The Crown appealed to the House of Lords.

The House, by a majority of three to two, held that s 3 of the Homicide Act 1957 made the jury sovereign in respect of the objective element. It was for them to determine not only whether the behaviour of the accused complied with a standard of self-control, but what the appropriate standard in the particular case should be. It followed, in Lord Hoffmann's opinion, that it would be inconsistent with the section for the judge to tell the jury as a matter of law that they should ignore a characteristic of the accused when deciding whether the objective element of provocation had been satisfied. The judge should simply tell the jury that the question whether the defendant's behaviour fell below the standard which should reasonably have been expected of him was entirely a matter for them. Thus, if the jury believe that Fred's alcoholism affected the degree of control that could reasonably be expected of him, they are entitled to take it into account when considering the objective question.[4]

Diminished responsibility – manslaughter

The defence was introduced into English law by s 2 of the Homicide Act 1957. Like provocation, it is a partial defence which reduces liability from murder to manslaughter (s 2(3)). For a successful plea, Albert bears the burden of proving (s 2(2))[5] on the balance of probabilities (*Dunbar* (1958)) that at the time he committed the *actus reus*:

(a) he was suffering from an 'abnormality of mind',

(b) resulting from a condition of arrested or retarded development of mind or any inherent causes or be induced by disease or injury,

(c) that substantially impaired his responsibility for the killing.

In *Dix* (1982), the Court of Appeal held that the defence must not be left to the jury unless there is medical evidence in support of these three elements.[6]

Fred's alcoholism may have caused him to suffer an abnormality of mind. In *Byrne* (1960), it was held that the expression means a state of mind so different from that of ordinary human beings that the reasonable man would term it abnormal and includes not only abnormalities of perception or cognition, but also an abnormality affecting the ability to exercise will power. And in *Tandy* (1989), the Court of Appeal held that an abnormality due to alcoholism might diminish responsibility if it were of such a degree that either the brain had been injured resulting in impaired judgment or increased volatility or, even where the brain had not been so damaged, the accused was unable to resist taking a first drink (see also *Inseal* (1992)).

As far as the third element is concerned, the jury would have to be satisfied that the difficulty Fred experienced in controlling himself was substantially greater than that which would be experienced in like circumstances by an ordinary person (*Lloyd* (1967)).

In *Dietschmann* (2003), the House of Lords held that where the defendant suffers from an abnormality of mind of the type defined in s 2(1) and has also taken alcohol before the killing, the jury should find him not guilty of murder but guilty of manslaughter if they are satisfied that, notwithstanding the alcohol he had consumed and its effect on him, his abnormality of mind substantially impaired his mental responsibility for the fatal acts. The subsection does not require the abnormality of mind to be the sole cause of the defendant's acts; even if the defendant would not have killed if he had not consumed alcohol, the causative effect of the alcohol does not prevent an abnormality of mind suffered by the defendant from substantially impairing his mental responsibility for the fatal acts (see *Fenton (Martin Charles)* (1975) and *Gittens (Charlesworth Alexander)* (1984) approved and *Atkinson (John)* (1985) and *Egan (Shaun Daniel)* (1992) disapproved).

If Fred successfully pleads diminished responsibility or provocation, he will be convicted of manslaughter and the court will have a discretion as to sentence ranging from absolute discharge to life imprisonment[7] or, if appropriate, a hospital order may be made under s 37(1) of the Mental Health Act 1983. If, on the other hand, neither plea is successful, he will be convicted of the murder of John and by virtue of the Murder (Abolition of the Death Penalty) Act 1965 sentenced to life imprisonment.

Notes

1   In *Gross* (1913), the principle was applied in a case involving provocation.

2   He may plead both together as alternatives for the jury's consideration.

3   Lord Steyn, delivering the opinion of the House of Lords in *Acott*, stressed the requirement that there had to be specific evidence of provocative conduct before the defence could be put to the jury but declined the invitation to state what would amount to sufficient evidence. But in that case, there was no evidence at all of provocative conduct perceived or otherwise. And in *Luc Thiet Thuan* (1996), Lord Goff, delivering the majority opinion of the Privy Council, assumed that an innocent remark by the deceased which was misunderstood by the defendant may amount to provocation.

4   In *Pearce* (2001), D stabbed his brother to death. There was evidence that he was a persistent heavy drinker and was drunk at the time of the killing. The trial judge told the jury to disregard the alcohol when considering the defence of provocation. On appeal, the defence contended that, in the light of the decision of the House of Lords in *Smith*, alcoholism was a characteristic of D which should have been taken into account by the jury both when considering the effect of the conduct of the deceased on the appellant and when considering the acceptability in law of the appellant's level of response. The Court of Appeal dismissed his appeal. A 'drink problem' is not a characteristic that the jury are required to take that into account when considering the defence of provocation. D's consumption of alcohol was voluntary. Kennedy LJ agreed with the Crown submission, para 22, that:

> The evidence ... went no further than to show that the appellant frequently drank to excess, and was pugnacious when drunk, so the jury was rightly told not to have regard to the effects of alcohol upon him.

5   In *Ali; Jordan* (2001), the Court of Appeal held that the requirement that the defendant bears the burden of proof in respect of diminished responsibility does not contravene Art 6 of the European Convention for the Protection of Human Rights and Fundamental Freedoms 1950.

6   The first and third elements are issues for the jury, who should take into account all the evidence, but if the medical evidence is unanimous and there is

nothing in the facts or circumstances which could lead to a contrary conclusion, they are bound to accept it (*Byrne* (1960); *Matheson* (1958)). The second element concerns the aetiology or cause of the abnormality. This issue should be resolved solely by reference to the medical evidence (*Byrne*).

7   Section 5 of the Offences Against the Person Act 1861.

Question 16

Late one night, Spit went to Tara's house and, for 'a prank', climbed a ladder to the open window of her bedroom, intending to scare her. When he looked through the window, she appeared to be asleep. He changed his mind about frightening her and decided to make his way home. However, just as he was about to climb down the ladder she said: 'Is that you Tom? Come in.' She made it very clear that she wished to have sexual intercourse.

(Tom, as Spit knew, was Tara's new boyfriend. They were very similar in appearance and had been mistaken for each other in the past.)

Without saying anything, Spit entered Tara's bedroom.

Tara and Spit had sexual intercourse. When Spit asked her if she had enjoyed it, Tara realised that the person with her was not Tom. She was extremely angry and told him to leave.

Assuming that Spit, Tara and Tom are all 16 years of age, advise Spit and Tara with respect to their criminal liability.

Would your answer differ if Spit was 13 years old?

Answer plan

This question raises issues concerning the offences of rape, procuring sexual intercourse by false pretences, indecent assault and burglary.

The principal issues concern the effect on Spit's liability of the various different mistakes made by Tara:

- the effect on liability for rape of a mistake of the victim as to the identity of the man;
- indecent assault and mistake as to identity;
- the issue of trespassory entry in burglary and mistake as to identity;
- the issue of trespassory entry in burglary and ulterior intent;
- indecent assault, consent and the age of the victim.

Answer

Spit

Rape

A man commits rape if he has unlawful sexual intercourse with a person (whether vaginal or anal) who, at the time of the intercourse, does not consent to it and he knows that the person does not consent to the intercourse or is reckless as to whether that person consents (s 1 of the Sexual Offences Act (SOA) 1956, as substituted by s 142 of the Criminal Justice and Public Order Act 1994). The maximum punishment is life imprisonment (Sched 2 and s 37 of the SOA 1956).

The absence of consent on the part of the woman and knowledge or recklessness with respect to that fact are essential ingredients of the offence (s 1(2) of the SOA 1956). Thus, one of the principal issues, as far as this question is concerned, is whether the 'consent' which Tara gave was vitiated by the mistake she made in respect of Spit's identity.

Until recently, the law was not settled. Section 1(3) of the SOA 1956 incorporated s 4 of the Criminal Law Amendment Act 1885, which provided that a man who induces a married woman to have sexual intercourse with him by impersonating her *husband* commits rape. It was not clear whether an equivalent common law rule applied where the man impersonated someone other than the husband of the woman. The issue was resolved in *Elbekkay* (1995). The Court of Appeal held that the vital issue in rape is the lack of real consent and that no valid distinction could be drawn between the situation where a woman mistakenly believes that the man she is having sexual intercourse with is her husband and the situation where she mistakenly believes it is some other man. In addition, by stressing that the fundamental issue concerns the presence or absence of consent, mistake as to the identity of the man vitiates the consent, whether or not there was fraud.[1]

Thus, it would appear that Spit committed the *actus reus* of rape. And, as it would seem from the facts of the problem that he knew that Tara was mistaken as to his identity and that her apparent consent was not real, he performed the *actus reus* with the appropriate *mens rea*.

Procuring sexual intercourse by false pretences

Section 3(1) of the 1956 Act provides that it is an offence for a person to procure a woman by false pretences or false representations to have unlawful sexual intercourse. The maximum penalty is two years' imprisonment (Sched 2 to the Sexual Offences Act 1956).

Spit, however, did not induce the false belief in the mind of Tara. Except in a number of fairly stereotyped situations where a false representation can be implied, silence does not generally amount to a deception or a false pretence in English law. Nor is a person under a duty to correct the self-deception of another (*MPC v Charles* (1977); *Smith v Hughes* (1871)). In addition, procurement implies a positive and purposive act on behalf of the defendant which was not present in Spit's case (see *Attorney General's Reference (No 1 of 1975)* (1975); *Christian* (1913)).

Indecent assault

By s 14 of the 1956 Act, as amended by s 4(3) of the Sexual Offences Act 1985, indecent assault is an offence punishable with 10 years' imprisonment.

Consent negatives an assault but, as a mistake as to identity vitiates consent (see discussion above and *Clarence* (1888)), Spit has committed an indecent assault on Tara. There is no need to prove that the contact was either hostile or aggressive (*Faulkner v Talbot* (1981)).

Burglary

By virtue of s 9(1)(a) of the Theft Act 1968, a person commits burglary if he enters a building as a trespasser intending, among other things, to commit rape therein. The maximum punishment is a term of imprisonment not exceeding 14 years (s 9(4)).

Trespass is a civil law concept involving presence on property without the consent of the occupier. In *Collins* (1973), the application of this concept in the context of burglary was discussed. A girl, mistaken as to the identity of the defendant, invited him into her parent's house to have sexual intercourse with her. The Court of Appeal made a number of points.

First, it was held that, for the purposes of burglary, a person does not enter as a trespasser unless he knows or at least is reckless with respect to the facts or circumstances that would make his entry trespassory. Further, it was stated, *obiter*, that, although the son or daughter of the owner is not, in law, the occupier of the premises for the purposes of the criminal law, he or she has a general implied permission to invite guests into the house.

The effect of a mistake as to identity on consent and trespass was not, however, discussed by the Court of Appeal. As Collins did not know of the mistake (nor was reckless in respect of it), it was unnecessary to decide the point. Smith argues that a mistake as to identity generally vitiates consent and that, provided the defendant is aware of the mistake, his entry should be regarded as trespassory.[2] It is not necessary to resolve the issue in answer to the instant question because, in *Jones and Smith* (1976), it was held that if a person is given a general permission to enter premises but enters with an ulterior intent, the entry is trespassory. Therefore, as Spit entered Tara's room intending to commit rape (see the discussion above), he was guilty of burglary under s 9(1)(a).

Alternative facts

Spit's liability

The rebuttable presumption at common law that a child over the age of 10 years and under the age of 14 was *doli incapax*, that is, incapable of crime, was abolished by s 34 of the Crime and Disorder Act 1998 and the presumption that a boy under the age of 14 was incapable of sexual intercourse was abolished by ss 1, 2(2) and (3) of the Sexual Offences Act 1993. Consequently, Spit's liability would be unaffected were he 13 years old.

Tara's liability

Section 15 of the 1956 Act provides that it is an offence for a person to make an indecent assault on a man (including a boy).

Although there can be no assault if the 'victim' consents, a boy under the age of 16 cannot give a valid consent (s 15(2)). However, in *K* (2001), the House of Lords held that a genuine belief that the girl was over that age of 16 was a defence to indecent assault on a woman contrary to s 14 of the Act, an offence paralleling that under s 15. In cases of indecent assault where the sexual activity was consensual but the girl or boy was under the age of 16, the prosecution are required to prove that the defendant did not mistakenly believe that she was over that age. Thus, as Tara believed that the boy was her 16 year old boyfriend, she committed no offence.

Notes

1   See also the decision of the High Court of Australia in *Papadimitropoulos* (1957).
2   Smith, JC, *Law of Theft*, 8th edn, 1997, p 193.

CHAPTER 3

GENERAL DEFENCES

Introduction

There are a number of defences of general application in criminal law. Most of them are dealt with in this chapter. Defences which apply only to particular crimes – for example, provocation – appear in the chapter concerning the appropriate offence.

Questions concerning the general defences are necessarily set in the context of a particular crime. You should deal with the positive ingredients of liability before discussing the availability of appropriate defences.

Although 'automatism' and 'mistake' are not truly defences, but rather a lack of the positive requirements of 'voluntariness' on the one hand and *mens rea* on the other, they have been dealt with in this chapter because of their relationship to other defences.

Note that the point made regarding 'open' questions in the introduction to the previous chapter applies with equal force to problem-type questions under this heading. The facts of the problem do not always disclose the state of mind of the defendant. In addition, in the case of many of the defences discussed, a successful plea depends upon the action or response of D being 'reasonable' (for example, in self-defence, the force used must be reasonable). The question is generally one for the jury. Thus, it may not be possible to come to a conclusive answer in respect of the availability of a defence.

Checklist

The following issues are covered in this chapter:

- automatism: the distinction between 'sane' and 'insane' automatism; the *M'Naghten Rules*; the meaning of a 'disease of the mind';
- mistake: the various types of mistakes and their effect upon liability, including mistakes induced by drunkenness and mistakes of law;
- compulsion: necessity and duress; the ingredients of the recognised defences; the limitations on the availability of defences of compulsion; duress and murder;
- the effect of drunken mistakes upon liability: the distinction between crimes of 'specific' and 'basic' intent;

- the *Dadson* principle: the availability of defences where D is unaware of the justifying or excusing conditions;
- the distinction between justifications and excuses.

Question 17

No act is punishable if it is done involuntarily and an involuntary act in this context – some people nowadays prefer to speak of it as 'automatism' – means an act which is done by the muscles without any control by the mind [*per* Lord Denning in *Bratty v Attorney General for Northern Ireland* (1963)].

Discuss.

Answer plan

This question requires a discussion of the legal treatment of involuntary conduct.

The principal issues are:

- the general principle regarding automatism;
- automatism caused by a 'disease of the mind';
- automatism caused by the voluntary consumption of alcohol or 'dangerous' drugs;
- other cases of self-induced automatism.

Principal authorities: *Brady* (1963); *Quick* (1973); *Majewski* (1977); *Bailey* (1983); *Sullivan* (1984); *Hennessy* (1989); *Burgess* (1991).

Answer

Automatism is recognised as a defence to all crimes. It refers to the situation where the accused's actions are involuntary in the sense that they are beyond his control. Typical examples are sleep-walking, acts done in a hypnotic trance, reflex actions and convulsions.[1]

There are a number of authorities which imply that automatism does not involve a total loss of control. An effective loss of control inconsistent with responsibility for one's actions will suffice (*Charlson* (1955); *Kemp* (1957); *Burgess* (1991)). However, in *Attorney General's Reference (No 2 of 1992)* (1993), the Court of Appeal held that automatism is only available where there was a complete destruction of voluntary control. This is rather surprising and it is submitted that, whilst in the context of driving related offences, such a principle may have some merit, it would be unjustifiably restrictive if applied generally.[2]

The rationale for the defence of automatism is quite clear. The defendant in such a situation is not responsible for the consequences of his 'actions'. The act is, in a sense, not his own. He does not deserve to be punished, nor would punishment serve any rational purpose. Although automatism has been referred to as a 'defence', the legally accurate analysis is that, since voluntariness is a basic ingredient of criminal liability and the onus is on the prosecution to prove beyond reasonable doubt that the conduct of the accused was willed, they will not be able to do so where the defendant's acts were involuntary. However, the prosecution are obliged to prove that the acts of the accused were voluntary only if the accused has adduced evidence (generally of a medical type) that he was an automaton at the relevant time (*Hill v Baxter* (1958); *Bratty* (1963); *Stripp* (1978); *Pullen* (1991); *Roach* (2001)[3]).

Automatism caused by a 'disease of the mind'

It is not always the case, however, that automatism will result in a simple verdict of not guilty. If the automatism results from a 'disease of the mind', the condition amounts to what, in law, is known as insanity. In such circumstances, the defendant is entitled only to a qualified acquittal, that is, not guilty by reason of insanity.[4] Where a defendant is found not guilty by reason of insanity, the judge must make one of a number of various orders, which include a hospital order with or without restrictions on discharge (s 5 of the Criminal Procedure (Insanity) Act 1964, as substituted by Sched 1 of the Criminal Procedure (Insanity and Unfitness to Plead) Act 1991).[5]

Insanity is, of course, a defence. However, in *Bratty*, it was held, following *Kemp* (1957), that, if the defendant adduces evidence of automatism, the prosecution are permitted to adduce evidence that the condition giving rise to the automatism is a 'disease of the mind' and that the defendant is entitled only to a qualified acquittal. Psychiatric evidence will, of course, be considered as to the nature of the condition, but whether or not the condition is a 'disease of the mind' is a question of law. If the trial judge concludes, on the evidence, that the condition is a disease of the mind, he is entitled to refuse to let the defence of sane automatism go to the jury. In these circumstances, he must instruct the jury that insanity is the only defence available to the defendant (see, for example, *Bratty*; *Sullivan* (1984)).

Any disease which impairs the functioning of the mind may amount to a 'disease'. It matters not whether the cause of the impairment is organic, as in epilepsy, or functional, as in schizophrenia. Nor does it matter whether the impairment is permanent, or transient and intermittent, provided that it was operative at the time of the alleged offence (*Sullivan*).

In *Bratty*, Lord Denning said that any condition which has 'manifested itself in violence and is prone to recur is a disease of the mind'. This reflects what many regard as the central policy underlying the insanity defence: to allow control of those who, although not responsible for the harm caused, are perceived to be suffering from a condition which makes them 'dangerous'.[6]

If, however, the malfunctioning of the mind is caused by an 'external factor', such as a blow to the head, or alcohol or drugs, the condition does not constitute a disease (*Quick* (1973); *Sullivan* (1984)).[7] Thus, whereas *hyper*glycaemia, caused when a diabetic fails to take insulin, is regarded as internally caused (by the diabetes itself) and, therefore, a 'disease of the mind', *hypo*glycaemia, resulting from a failure to take food after taking insulin or taking too much insulin, is regarded as externally caused and amounts to sane automatism (*Hennessy* (1989); *Bingham* (1991)).

Automatism caused by the voluntary consumption of alcohol or drugs

If the automatism is caused by alcohol or drugs then, as these are external factors, the resulting condition is not attributable to a 'disease of the mind' (see *Quick* (1973)). However, automatism caused by alcohol or drugs is not a 'defence' to all crimes.

The rule is that, where the accused lacks the *mens rea* for an offence due to the effects of alcohol or other (non-prescribed) drugs then the absence of *mens rea* is an 'excuse' only for so called crimes of 'specific intent', such as murder, but not for crimes of 'basic intent', such as manslaughter (*DPP v Majewski* (1977); *Lipman* (1970)). Thus, if a defendant kills a person whilst in a state of automatism induced by the voluntary consumption of alcohol or non-prescribed drugs, he will be acquitted of murder and convicted of manslaughter, the prosecution being relieved of the burden of proving the *mens rea* for manslaughter (see, for example, *Lipman*).[8]

The basis for the distinction between crimes of specific intent and basic intent is not at all clear. It seems, however, that the prevailing opinion is that if intention is required with respect to one or more of the elements of the *actus reus*, then it is a crime of specific intent and a crime that may be committed recklessly is a crime of basic intent (see the speech of Lord Elwyn-Jones in *Majewski*).

In addition to murder, the following have been acknowledged as crimes of specific intent: wounding or causing grievous bodily harm with intent contrary to s 18 of the Offences Against the Person Act 1861 (*Pordage* (1975));

theft contrary to s 1 of the Theft Act 1968 (*Ruse v Read* (1949)); handling stolen goods (*Durante* (1972)); and attempts (*Mohan* (1976)).

Offences of basic intent include, in addition to manslaughter: malicious wounding or inflicting grievous bodily harm contrary to s 20 of the Offences Against the Person Act 1861 (*Sullivan* (1981)); assault occasioning actual bodily harm (*Bolton v Crawley* (1972)); rape (*Fotheringham* (1988)).

Other cases of self-induced automatism

In *Bailey* (1983), the Court of Appeal held that self-induced automatism other than that due to intoxication from alcohol or drugs will provide a defence to all crimes except where the defendant was 'reckless' – in a general subjective sense – as to the risk of becoming an automaton.

That is, if the accused knew that by doing or failing to do something (for example, in the case of a diabetic taking too much insulin or not eating after having taken insulin) there was a risk that he might become aggressive, unpredictable or dangerous with the result that he might cause some harm to others, and he persisted in the action or took no remedial action when he knew it was required, then he is regarded as responsible for his condition. In these circumstances, despite the fact that he lacked the *mens rea*, the defendant may be convicted of an appropriate offence of basic intent.

This rule was also applied in *Hardie* (1984), where the defendant took a quantity of valium, a sedative drug. The valium was not prescribed to the defendant and the judge treated the case as an ordinary one of voluntary intoxication, ruling that, as it was self-induced, it was no defence to a crime of basic intent. The Court of Appeal quashed the conviction. The court held, distinguishing *Majewski*, that the rule regarding voluntary intoxication does not apply where the drug is not generally recognised as 'dangerous'. That is, if the drug does not normally cause unpredictable behaviour, automatism resulting from its consumption may provide an excuse to all crimes, even those of basic intent. Only if the defendant was reckless in the *Bailey* sense can he be convicted of an offence (of basic intent).[9]

Conclusion

Although automatism will often afford a 'defence' entitling the defendant to a complete acquittal, the causes of the condition must be examined. If the defendant is 'responsible' for the condition, then he may be convicted, at least as far as basic intent crimes are concerned. If he is not 'responsible' for the automatism, but it is the result of an internal condition that is likely to result in recurrent 'malfunctioning', the defendant will be classified as legally insane and entitled only to a qualified acquittal.

Notes

1   In *Woolley* (1997), the Rochdale magistrates accepted that sneezing could produce a state of automatism. The driver of a lorry was overcome by a sneezing fit lasting a couple of seconds. He lost control of his vehicle and crashed into another, resulting in a serious pile up.

2   Clause 33 of the Draft Criminal Code Bill defines automatism in terms of an *effective* loss of control.

3   In *Roach* (2001), D's appeal against conviction for an offence of wounding with intent was allowed as the judge had not made it clear to the jury that the burden of proof lay upon the prosecution.

4   The defence of insanity is defined in the *M'Naghten Rules* (1843). It must be proved that, at the time he committed the act, the accused was labouring under such a defect of reason, due to a disease of the mind, as either not to know the nature and quality of his act, or, if he did know that, he did not know that what he was doing was wrong.

5   In *DPP v Harper* (1997), the Divisional Court rather surprisingly held that the defence of insanity was not available to strict liability offences. Whatever the merits of this decision, it should, it is submitted, be confined to cases of insanity not involving automatism.

6   In *Burgess* (1991), it was stated that the fact that a condition may not recur does not prevent it being classified as a 'disease of the mind'. Cf cl 34 of the Draft Criminal Code Bill 1989, Law Com No 177.

7   If external factors operate upon an underlying condition which would not otherwise produce a state of automatism, then a defence of non-insane automatism should be left to the jury (*Roach* (2001)).

8   It is submitted that the general tenor of the speeches in *Majewski* supports the notion that the rule is a substantive one – that is, that where a defendant is charged with an offence of basic intent and he raises evidence that, due to drink or drugs, he was not in control of his actions at the relevant time, he can be convicted on proof that he committed the *actus reus*. Liability is, in effect, strict. Cf *Woods* (1982), in which it was held that, as far as rape is concerned, the jury should be instructed to decide whether the defendant had the requisite *mens rea*, but to ignore all evidence of self-induced intoxication! See also *Aitken* (1992) where it was said that for the purposes of s 20 of the Offences Against the Person Act 1861, D acts maliciously if he foresees the risk of injury or *would have foreseen injury but for the drink consumed*.

9   In *Marison* (1996), the defendant, a diabetic, had a hypoglycaemic episode whilst driving. As he was aware that there was a risk he might become an automaton, he was guilty of causing death by dangerous driving before an attack caused him to lose control of the vehicle (see also *Kay v Butterworth* (1947)).

Question 18

Samson is a diabetic. He is required to take insulin regularly to control his condition. On one occasion, he took insulin as prescribed but, not having eaten, he became semi-conscious whilst driving his car. He lost control of the car and it collided with Jeanette, a pedestrian. Jeanette was taken to hospital suffering from multiple fractures. Two weeks later, whilst still in hospital, Jeanette was administered an overdose of a painkilling drug by a nurse. Jeanette died as a result of the overdose.

Discuss Samson's criminal liability.

Would your answer differ if Samson's loss of control had been caused by a failure to take his insulin?

Answer plan

This question involves consideration of liability for a number of offences against the person and the application of the rules concerning involuntary conduct. The same issues of automatism are raised with respect to each of the offences. Repetition may be avoided by reference to principles previously explained.

The principal issues are:

- the question of causation and intervening medical treatment;
- automatism – the loss of control;
- 'reckless' automatism;
- automatism caused by a 'disease of the mind'; the distinction between 'internal' and 'external' causes.

The principal authorities are: *Smith* (1959); *Kemp* (1957); *Cheshire* (1991); *Quick* (1973); *Brady* (1963); *M'Naghten* (1843); *Sullivan* (1984); *Hennessy* (1989).

Answer

Manslaughter

It is proposed initially to consider Samson's liability for manslaughter.

As far as the *actus reus* of this offence is concerned, the only issue requiring consideration is whether Jeanette's death was caused by Samson's actions.

Clearly, his conduct was a *factual* cause of death. That is, *but for* Samson losing control of the car, she would not have suffered the injuries which led to her hospitalisation and subsequent death. The administration of the overdose was also a factual cause of death. The onus is on the prosecution to prove that Samson's actions were a *legal* cause of death.

In *Smith* (1959), D had seriously injured a man who was later subject to improper medical treatment. The man died. The Court of Appeal stated that if the original injuries are still 'operating and substantial' at the time of death then, despite the fact that some other cause of death is also operating, the injuries are a legal cause of death. If, on the other hand, the original injuries are merely the setting in which another cause operates, then the injuries are not a legal cause of death.

The rules were elaborated by the Court of Appeal in *Cheshire* (1991). It was stated that even if negligent treatment of the victim was the immediate cause of the death – the injuries having ceased to be operating and substantial – the responsibility of the defendant will not be excluded if the treatment was itself a direct consequence of the defendant's acts and the contribution of the defendant's acts were still significant at the time of death.

Further, the court stated that a direction in terms of the gross negligence of the doctors would be wrong. The jury should be directed to consider the consequences of the treatment and not the degree of blame attaching to the medical authorities. Only if the medical treatment was a 'potent' cause of death and 'independent' of the defendant's actions would it relieve him of responsibility (and see *Mellor* (1996)).[1]

It is not at all clear from the judgment of the Court of Appeal in *Cheshire* what is meant by either 'independent' or 'potent'. The treatment is always 'dependent' on the acts of the defendant, in the sense that the acts are a *sine qua non* of the treatment. Similarly, if the immediate cause of death was the treatment, it is difficult to see how the jury are to determine whether it was a 'potent' cause of death without reference to the blameworthiness of the medical staff involved.[2]

Assuming, for the purposes of further analysis, that Samson's 'acts' are regarded as a legal cause of death, his criminal liability will be determined by reference to his *mens rea*. It would appear that Samson went into a hypoglycaemic episode – a deficiency of blood sugar resulting in an impairment of consciousness. In these circumstances, he may raise the 'defence' of automatism, which, if successfully pleaded, results in a complete acquittal.

Samson will be required to produce medical evidence to support his claim that, at the relevant time, he was an automaton (*Hill v Baxter* (1958)). Provided he does so, the probative burden lies with the prosecution. In other words, if the prosecution wish to contest his claim, they must satisfy the jury that Samson did not lack conscious control of his actions (*Bratty* (1963)). The facts of the problem state that Samson was *semi*-conscious. It is not clear from the authorities as to whether this amounts to automatism.

There are authorities which support the view that, even where the defendant suffers only a partial loss of consciousness and has some control over his actions, the defence will be available provided he lacks 'effective' control (see *Kemp* (1957); *Charlson* (1955); *Quick* (1973)). On the other hand, in *Attorney General's Reference (No 2 of 1992)* (1993), the Court of Appeal held that a total destruction of voluntary control was required. The appellant, who had been driving with diminished awareness, was not an automaton as he had exhibited some control by managing to steer the vehicle for a distance of about half a mile (see also *Broome v Perkins* (1987)).[3] It is not clear whether Samson's partial loss of consciousness was accompanied by a partial or total loss of control. Control does not always accompany awareness and it is submitted that, if the loss of control suffered by Samson was of such a degree that he could not be said to be responsible for his 'actions', then the defence of automatism should be available to him.

If Samson was in a state of automatism, then, as it was externally caused, it will amount to sane automatism, entitling him to a complete acquittal unless it was 'self-induced' (*Quick* (1973)). That is, Samson is not guilty of an offence unless the prosecution prove that, prior to becoming an automaton, he was aware that by not eating food after taking insulin there was a risk that he might lose conscious control of his actions and deliberately ran that risk. If that is the case, then he will be guilty of an appropriate offence of 'basic intent', in this case, manslaughter (*Bailey* (1983); *Hardie* (1984)).[4]

The maximum punishment for manslaughter is imprisonment for life (s 5 of the Offences Against the Person Act 1861).

Non-fatal offences against the person

If the jury were to conclude that the administration of the drug was an 'independent' and 'potent' cause of death – that is, a *novus actus interveniens* – then, clearly, Samson could not be convicted of manslaughter. In those circumstances, his liability would be limited to the injuries suffered by Jeanette.

Provided the jury conclude that the harm caused was serious and that the automation was 'self-induced', as explained above, then he may be convicted of the offence under s 20 of the Offences Against the Person Act 1861 (see *Brady*).[5]

The maximum punishment for the offence of malicious wounding is a term of imprisonment not exceeding five years.

Dangerous driving and causing death by dangerous driving

Samson may be guilty of the offence of dangerous driving contrary to s 2 of the Road Traffic Act 1988, as substituted by s 1 of the Road Traffic Act 1991; if he is regarded as having caused the death of Jeanette, he may be guilty of causing death by dangerous driving contrary to s 1 of the 1988 Act, as substituted by s 1 of the Road Traffic Act 1991.

Again, even were he an automaton, Samson may be convicted of these offences if the prosecution prove that the automatism was self-induced.

The offence under s 2 carries a maximum punishment of two years' imprisonment and that under s 1 is punishable with up to five years' imprisonment.

Alternative facts – insanity

The ingredients of the defence of insanity were laid down in the *M'Naghten Rules* (1843). These state that insanity consists of a defect of reason due to disease of the mind, such that the defendant either did not know the nature and quality of his act or, alternatively, did not know that what he was doing was wrong.

Consequently, automatism resulting from a condition which, in law, is regarded as a 'disease of the mind' amounts to insanity.

If Samson chose to plead the defence of insanity, then, as there is a presumption of sanity, he would have the burden of proving the defence on a balance of probabilities (*M'Naghten*).

Although insanity is a defence, a successful plea does not result in a complete acquittal. Where a defendant is found not guilty by reason of insanity, the judge must make one of a number of various orders. These include a hospital order, which may be made with or without restrictions on discharge (s 5 of the Criminal Procedure (Insanity) Act 1964, as substituted by Sched 1 to the Criminal Procedure (Insanity and Unfitness to Plead) Act 1991).

Consequently, Samson may choose not to raise the defence of insanity. If, however, he puts his state of mind in issue by raising automatism, the judge may rule that his condition amounts to insanity (*Sullivan* (1984); cf *Thomas (Sharon)* (1995)). And, unfortunately for Samson, it is well established that hyperglycaemia, which may result when diabetes is not controlled by insulin, is a 'disease of the mind'; in contrast to hypoglycaemia, it is perceived as the result of internal factors (*Hennessy* (1989)).

If Samson wishes to avoid an acquittal on the grounds of insanity, he has no alternative but to plead guilty to the offences charged.

Notes

1 In *Mellor*, Lord Schiemann, delivering the judgment of the Court of Appeal, stated:

It is undesirable in most cases for juries to be asked to embark upon the question of whether medical negligence as a significant contributory cause of death has been negatived, because it diverts the jury from the relevant question, namely, has the accused's act contributed significantly to the victim's death?

2 Cf cl 17(2) of the Draft Criminal Code Bill 1989, Law Com No 177:

A person does not cause a result where, after he does [an act which makes a more than negligible contribution to its occurrence] ... an act or event occurs:

(a) which is the immediate and sufficient cause of the result;

(b) which he did not foresee; and

(c) which could not in the circumstances reasonably have been foreseen.

3 The decision in *Broome v Perkins* was criticised by the Law Commission in their commentary on the the Draft Criminal Code which, in cl 33, defines automatism as, among other things, a 'condition depriving a person of *effective* control'.

4 It was decided in *Lipman* (1970) that manslaughter is a crime of basic intent. Murder, on the other hand, is a crime of 'specific intent' (see *Sheehan* (1975)).

5 As a matter of prosecuting policy, the Code for Crown Prosecutors, *Offences Against the Person*, June 1994, paras 2.11 and 2.15, advises that, whereas 'broken or displaced limbs or bones, including fractured skull, compound fractures, broken cheek bone, jaw, ribs, etc' are instances of grievous bodily harm, 'minor fractures' should normally be treated as 'actual bodily harm'.

It was held in *Bratty v Attorney General for Northern Ireland* (1963) that malicious wounding is a crime of 'basic intent' and that the offence under s 18, wounding with intent, is a crime of 'specific intent'.

Question 19

Smart held a party, during which he laced Tippsy's lemonade with a drug. Tippsy began to feel strange and so decided to leave the party. He drove part of the way home but then, as he began to have hallucinations, he parked his car, got out and started to walk the remainder of the journey. As Tippsy approached his house he saw Shifty. Tippsy was convinced that Shifty was about to mug him and so he hit him on the head with his umbrella. In fact, Shifty was waiting for his friend Godot and had no intention of 'mugging' Tippsy.

Shifty had an extremely thin skull and died from the blow.

Tippsy collapsed from the effects of the drug and suffered some damage to his kidneys for which he required hospital treatment.

Advise Smart and Tippsy about their criminal liability.

Answer plan

This question raises issues concerning a number of offences against the person, including poisoning offences, and an offence contrary to the Road Traffic Act 1988. The legal treatment of a (drunken) mistake relevant to an issue of defence is raised with respect to Tippsy's liability. In general, when answering a question which requires analysis of the criminal liability of more than one individual for a number of different offences, it is often sensible to deal with all the issues of liability of relevance to one party before turning to the next. In this case, however, the answer deals with an analysis of Tippsy's liability for Shifty's death followed by an examination of Smart's criminal liability for a number of non-fatal offences against the person and, finally, with an examination of the issues of liability of both parties in respect of a possible driving offence under the Road Traffic Act (RTA) 1988. The RTA issues are dealt with together at the end of the answer as the questions of Smart's liability and Tippsy's liability are interrelated.

The principal issues are:

- the 'egg shell skull' principle;
- self-defence and mistake: the rule in *Williams* (1983) and *Beckford* (1988);
- administration of a 'noxious' thing contrary to ss 23 and 24 of the Offences Against the Person Act 1861;
- the *mens rea* requirement of s 23;
- s 4(1) of the RTA 1988: driving while unfit;
- liability of the 'procurer' of an offence.

Answer

Tippsy – homicide

Tippsy committed the *actus reus* of unlawful homicide, that is, he killed Shifty. The fact that Shifty had a thin skull rendering him more vulnerable to fatal injury does not affect the attribution of the death to Tippsy. There is a principle in English law to the effect that 'one must take one's victim as one finds him'. This means that a defendant whose actions are a cause of death may not point to a peculiar vulnerability of the victim as the legal cause (*Martin* (1832)).

To determine whether Tippsy is guilty of either murder or manslaughter, his *mens rea* at the time of striking the blow must be examined.

For murder, the prosecution must prove that Tippsy either intended unlawfully to kill or to cause grievous bodily harm (*Moloney* (1985)).

A person intends a consequence if it was their aim or objective or they foresaw that it was a virtually certain result of their actions (*Nedrick* (1986), as explained by the House of Lords in *Woollin* (1998)).

For constructive manslaughter, the prosecution must prove that Tippsy intentionally committed an unlawful act which was dangerous and was the legal cause of Shifty's death (*Goodfellow* (1986)).

In this case, the battery committed against Shifty would amount to an unlawful act (see, for example, *Larkin* (1943)).

The requirement of dangerousness is satisfied on proof that all sober and reasonable people would recognise that striking Shifty with the umbrella was likely to subject him to the risk of some harm (*Church* (1966); *Goodfellow* (1986)). It is not necessary to show that there was a risk of serious harm, nor is it necessary to prove that the *defendant* was aware of any risk of harm (*Lipman* (1970)).[1]

There is some doubt as to the meaning of the requirement that the unlawful act was performed 'intentionally'. In *Newbury* (1977), the House of Lords held that the necessary *mens rea* for constructive manslaughter was an 'intention to do the acts which constitute the crime'. This is ambiguous. It may mean that all that is required is proof that the defendant's actions were voluntary. In the case of *Jennings* (1990), however, the Court of Appeal proceeded on the basis that *mens rea* in the full sense is required, in which case the prosecution would have to prove that Tippsy intended or was reckless with respect to the application of unlawful force (*Spratt* (1990)).

The facts do not disclose the degree of harm intended by Tippsy, but, in any case, whether he is charged with murder or manslaughter, it must be proved that he intended *unlawfully* to kill or cause grievous bodily harm or apply force.

It was decided in *Williams* (1983) and in *Beckford* (1988) that a mistaken but genuine belief in facts which, if true, would justify self-defence is an excuse to a crime of personal violence because the belief negatives the intent to act unlawfully. If the use of force would have been lawful had Shifty, in fact, been about to attack Tippsy, then Tippsy has a 'defence' to both murder and manslaughter. Furthermore, although it seems a mistaken belief in the need to use force may not be relied upon if it was a result of *voluntary* intoxication (*O'Grady* (1987)), the decision of the House of Lords in *Kingston* (1994) leads to the conclusion that mistakes resulting from involuntary intoxication may excuse.[2]

The exclusionary rules regarding voluntary intoxication and offences of basic intent are based on the principle of prior fault. The person who has made a mistake as a result of self-induced intoxication is regarded as being to blame for his condition. By contrast, the individual who, as a result of *involuntary* intoxication, makes a legally relevant mistake is not responsible for his condition. It is fair, therefore, that he be allowed to rely on the mistake as a defence (see *Majewski* (1977); *Hardie* (1984); *Kingston* (1994)).

Thus, whether charged with murder or manslaughter, Tippsy should be acquitted unless the prosecution prove that Tippsy did not use such force as was reasonable in the circumstances as he believed them to be (*Abraham* (1973); *Shannon* (1980); *Stripp* (1978); *Scarlett* (1994)).

It should be noted that force may be used to ward off an attack which the defendant anticipated (*Attorney General's Reference (No 2 of 1983)* (1984)).

Whether the force used was reasonable is a question solely for the judgment of the jury (*Owino* (1996)).

Smart – aggravated assaults: ss 18 and 20 of the Offences Against the Person Act 1861

Under s 20 of the Act, it is an offence to 'unlawfully and maliciously ... inflict grievous bodily harm upon any other person'. Under s 18, it is an offence 'unlawfully and maliciously to ... cause grievous bodily harm to any person by any means whatsoever ... with intent to do grievous bodily harm'.[3]

Until recently, it was generally believed that there could be no infliction of grievous bodily harm contrary to s 20 in the absence of an application of force to the body of the victim (see, for example, *Wilson* (1984)). But in *Ireland; Burstow* (1997), the House of Lords held that there was no 'radical divergence' between the meaning of 'inflict' in s 20 and 'cause' in s 18 and that psychiatric injury could be inflicted or caused without the application of force (see also *Mandair* (1995)).

Thus, the only significant difference in terms of the ingredients of liability for the two offences relates to their *mens rea* requirements. For s 20, it must be proved that the defendant was '*Cunningham* reckless' with respect to some harm (*Mowatt* (1967); *Savage; Parmenter* (1991)).

The *mens rea* requirement for s 18 is relatively high. The prosecution must prove that Smart intended to cause grievous bodily harm.

Maliciously administering a noxious thing

By virtue of s 23, it is an offence to maliciously administer a poison or other noxious thing to any person so as to endanger the life of such person or to inflict upon him any grievous bodily harm. The maximum punishment is a term of imprisonment not exceeding five years.

By virtue of s 24, it is an offence to maliciously administer a poison or other noxious thing with intent to injure, aggrieve or annoy such person. The maximum punishment is a term of imprisonment not exceeding five years.

In *Harley* (1830), it was held that an offence may be committed where, as in this case, the noxious thing is put into a drink taken by the victim.

The concept of a 'noxious thing' is wide enough to include anything which is even only slightly harmful or which disturbs either physiological or psychological function, bearing in mind not only the quality and nature of the substance, but also the quantity administered. In *Marcus* (1981), the Court of Appeal held that ordinary sleeping tablets administered in a normal dose without the knowledge of the victim were noxious.

For liability under s 23, the prosecution must prove, as an element of the *actus reus,* that either life was endangered or grievous bodily harm was inflicted.[4]

As far as the *mens rea* is concerned, the authorities are not absolutely clear.

In *Cunningham* (1957), it was held that the prosecution must prove that the defendant either intended or foresaw that the 'particular kind of harm' might result and went on to take the risk of it. In *Cato* (1976), the Court of Appeal interpreted this to mean that, although the prosecution had to prove that the defendant intentionally or recklessly administered the thing knowing at least that there was a risk that it would cause harm (that is, that it was 'noxious'), it was not necessary to prove that the defendant foresaw the risk that it would endanger life or cause grievous bodily harm. The crime is one of *'half mens rea'.*

It would seem, however, that the Court of Appeal intended that this restricted form of the *mens rea* would apply only if the noxious thing is applied directly (in *Cato,* heroin was injected). And, thus, if as in this case, the noxious thing is indirectly administered, the prosecution apparently must prove recklessness not only with respect to the administration of the noxious thing, but also with respect to the risk of endangering life or causing grievous bodily harm.[5]

For s 24, the *mens rea* consists of two elements: (a) intention or recklessness (*Cunningham*-type defined as above) with respect to the administration of a noxious thing; and (b) an intention to injure, aggrieve or annoy (see *Hill* (1985)).

If Smart is charged with the offence under s 23, but the prosecution fail to prove he had the necessary *mens rea*, he may be convicted of the offence under s 24 providing, as the facts imply, that he had the *mens rea* for that offence (s 25 of the Offences Against the Person Act 1861).

Road Traffic Act 1988

By virtue of s 4(1) of the RTA 1988, a person who drives a vehicle while unfit through drink or drugs commits an offence. The maximum punishment is six months' imprisonment or a £5,000 fine or both. And, unless there are special reasons, the offender must be disqualified from driving for at least 12 months.

By s 4(5) of the Act, a person is taken to be unfit to drive if his ability to drive properly was impaired. Whether a driver's ability was impaired is a question of fact. Medical evidence may be submitted to demonstrate that Tippsy was unfit before he parked the car and decided to walk.

Although the fact that his drink was laced does not absolve him of liability, it may amount to a special reason allowing the court, within its discretion, to refrain from imposing an order of disqualification (*Pugsley v Hunter* (1973)).

Smart, by virtue of s 8 of the Accessories and Abettors Act 1861, may be convicted of 'procuring' the commission of the offence under s 4(1) of the RTA 1988.

In *Attorney General's Reference (No 1 of 1975)* (1975), the Court of Appeal held, in a case involving similar facts to the present problem, that 'to procure means to produce by endeavour'. This implies that it is necessary to prove that the defendant intended to bring about the principal offence.

It seems, however, that recklessness will suffice as far as the circumstances of the offence are concerned (*Carter v Richardson* (1976)). In other words, it must be proved that Smart knew that Tippsy was going to drive and was aware that he was probably unfit as a result of the administered drug.[6]

Notes

1   The rule in *Watson* (1989) and *Dawson* (1985), to the effect that a peculiar vulnerability of the victim is not relevant to the issue of dangerousness unless it would have been apparent to a reasonable observer of the incident, does not

apply in this case. The rule applies only where the act of the accused would not otherwise be dangerous as defined.

2   Lord Mustill referred, with approval, to a number of Scottish decisions which state that involuntary intoxication is a defence if it results in an inability to form the necessary *mens rea*. Elsewhere, however, he stated that 'the excuse of involuntary intoxication ... is superimposed on the ordinary law of intent' and that 'in the absence of intention the involuntary nature of the intoxication would take a case such as the present outside *Majewski* and enable the defendant to rely on the absence of the necessary mental element'. This latter approach is surely the correct one. If D did not have the *mens rea*, he should be acquitted even though he was capable of forming it.

3   'Grievous bodily harm' means 'serious bodily harm'. It is a matter for the jury to decide whether the harm caused or inflicted is grievous (*DPP v Smith* (1961); *Saunders* (1985)). The Code for Crown Prosecutors, *Offences Against the Person*, June 1994, states, at para 2.15, that the prosecutor should regard injuries resulting in lengthy treatment or incapacity as amounting to grievous bodily harm.

4   Although the word 'inflict' is used in the section, there clearly can be no requirement of a direct application of force; cf s 20 and see *Wilson* (1984).

5   See Law Commission, *Codification of the Criminal Law – General Principles – the Mental Element in Crime*, Report No 89, 1989, p 15.

6   In *Blakely v DPP* (1991), Lord Bingham understood 'procuring' to involve intention or 'the willing acceptance of a contemplated result'. This implies that advertent recklessness with respect to the central conduct of the *actus reus* will suffice. Such an interpretation is far removed from the ordinary meaning of 'to procure' and, it is submitted, ought not to be followed.

Question 20

Tosh is a fanatical supporter of the England football team. He did not have a ticket for the match against Malta and so he jumped over the turnstile. He hid in the crowd and watched the match. England were beaten 6-0. Tosh was thoroughly shocked and depressed. As he walked home he passed by the office of the Malta Tourist Board. He jumped through the plate glass window of the office, smashing it. He claims that he was so shocked by the football result that he felt as though he were 'in another world' and that he did not know what he was doing.

Discuss Tosh's criminal liability.

Answer plan

This question raises issues concerning the distinction between sane and insane automatism and, in particular, the legal categorisation of conditions brought about by 'stress and disappointment'. In addition, it raises a question of liability for the offence of making off without payment contrary to s 3 of the Theft Act 1978.

The principal issues are:

- the distinction between sane and insane automatism; internal and external causes; conditions resulting from the 'ordinary stresses and disappointments of life';

- is there an offence of making off without payment contrary to s 3 of the Theft Act 1978 where payment is expected or required prior to the provision of the service?

The principal authorities are: *Caldwell* (1982); *Attorney General's Reference (No 2 of 1992)* (1992); *Sullivan* (1984).

Answer

Criminal damage

Tosh may be charged with the offence of criminal damage contrary to s 1(1) of the Criminal Damage Act 1971. By s 4, the maximum punishment for this offence is a term of imprisonment not exceeding 10 years.

The *actus reus* of the offence consists of damaging or destroying property belonging to another. Clearly, Tosh has committed the *actus reus*.

As far as the *mens rea* is concerned, the prosecution must prove that Tosh either intended to cause damage or was reckless with respect to damaging property.

The House of Lords decided in *Caldwell* (1982) that a person is reckless with respect to property being damaged if: (a) he does an act which in fact creates an obvious risk that property would be destroyed or damaged; and (b) when he does the act, he either has not given any thought to the possibility of there being any such risk or has recognised that there was some risk involved and has nonetheless gone on to do it.

Tosh may contend, however, that, at the relevant time, he was in a state of automatism, that is, that he had lost control of his actions. If he does wish to raise the 'defence', he is required to produce medical evidence supporting the claim that his actions were not voluntary. Provided he does so, the probative burden lies with the prosecution. In other words, the prosecution must satisfy the jury that, at the relevant time, Tosh did not lack conscious control of his actions (*Hill v Baxter* (1958); *Bratty* (1963); *Pullen* (1991)).

It is not clear from the facts of this case whether a plea of automatism would be successful. First, it should be noted that if Tosh knew what he was doing, in the sense that his conduct was within his immediate control but he acted without normal self-restraint, then the defence would not be available to him. There is no general defence of 'irresistible impulse' (*Isitt* (1977)). Secondly, the Court of Appeal held in *Attorney General's Reference (No 2 of 1992)* (1993) that the defence of automatism requires a total destruction of conscious control on the defendant's part. The court even seemed prepared to accept that *subconscious* control would be enough to preclude the 'defence'. There are, however, many authorities which support the view that a partial loss of control will suffice (see, for example, *Kemp* (1957); *Quick* (1973); *T* (1990)) and it is submitted that this approach is preferable. If the loss of control suffered by Tosh was of such a degree that he could not be said to be responsible for his actions in jumping through the window, then the defence of automatism should be available to him.[1] However, even if the loss of control was sufficient to found a plea of automatism, the judge may rule that Tosh has raised the defence of insanity (*Sullivan* (1984)).

The ingredients of the defence of insanity were laid down in the *M'Naghten Rules* (1843). These state that, to establish a defence on the ground of insanity, it must be proved that, at the time of committing the act, the party accused was labouring under such a defect of reason, from disease of the mind, as not to know the nature and quality of the act he was doing; or, if he did know that, that he did not know that what he was doing was wrong. Now, by definition, a person who was in a state of automatism was *labouring under such a defect of reason* as *not to know the nature and quality of his act.* The crucial issue, therefore, is whether the defect of reason resulted from a *disease of the mind.* It is this which determines whether the condition amounts to sane or insane automatism.

The significance of the distinction for the defendant is that, whereas sane automatism results in a complete acquittal, a verdict of not guilty by reason of insanity may be followed by an order committing the defendant to a hospital and may contain restrictions concerning the minimum period of time for detention. It may specify that the person may be detained until the Home Secretary orders release (s 5 of the Criminal Procedure (Insanity) Act 1964, as substituted by the Criminal Procedure (Insanity and Unfitness to Plead) Act 1991).

Tosh's condition – if it did result in an effective loss of conscious control – would be categorised as an instance of insane automatism. This is because only conditions caused by *external* factors are regarded as amounting to sane automatism and psychological states caused by the 'ordinary stress and disappointments of everyday life' are perceived to be a consequence of the predisposing *internal* factors.

The *legal* cause of Tosh's automatism, if that is what resulted, is his psychological or emotional make-up and not the 'ordinary disappointment' of his team's defeat, and, thus, if he lacked control at the time he caused the damage, the proper verdict is not guilty by reason of insanity.[2]

Making off without payment

Finally, it is proposed to consider whether Tosh committed the offence of making off without payment, contrary to s 3 of the Theft Act 1978. The offence is committed where D dishonestly makes off after having been supplied goods or having had some 'service done'.

There is no definition of 'service' for the purposes of s 3 but, even if it were interpreted to include the provision of the stadium facilities and the football match, the service was not done until the game was over and thus, as payment was neither required nor expected at the end of the football match, Tosh did not make off 'knowing that payment ... for a service done was required or expected from him'. Section 3 is worded such that it appears only to apply to situations where payment is expected or required *after* the service has been provided.

Notes

1   The decision of the Divisional Court in *Broome v Perkins* (1987), which implied that a total loss of control is required, was criticised by the Law Commission in its commentary to the Draft Criminal Code as being out of line with the authorities (Law Commission, Draft Criminal Code Bill 1989, Law Com No 177).

2   In *T*, the defendant's confused state was categorised as sane automatism. The immediate cause, that is, rape, was not an 'ordinary' stress. The condition was regarded as having been externally caused.

Question 21

Does English law recognise a general defence of necessity?

Answer plan

In criminal law, the term 'necessity' is sometimes used in a very general sense referring to a number of defences which excuse or justify otherwise criminal acts. For example, Lord Simon, in *DPP for Northern Ireland v Lynch* (1975), regarded duress by threats as a particular type of 'necessity' (see also *Martin* (1989); *Conway* (1989); *Bell* (1992)).

More commonly, 'necessity' is used in a narrower sense to describe those instances of compulsion where the defendant was compelled through force of circumstance to commit a criminal act. Used in this way, necessity is perceived as a species of compulsion comparable to but distinct from duress.

As this essay is concerned with the scope of the defence of necessity, it is proposed to adopt the former approach and to examine each of the recognised defences of compulsion and the areas of doubt.

The principal issues are:

- recognised defences of necessity;
- duress by threats;
- duress of circumstances;
- concealed defences of necessity.

The principal authorities are: *Howe* (1987); *Graham* (1982); *Willer* (1986); *Conway* (1988); *Dudley and Stephens* (1884); *Bourne* (1938); *Adams* (1957); *Gillick v West Norfolk and Wisbech AHA* (1985); *Bournewood Community and Mental Health NHS Trust* (1998); *Re A (Children) (Conjoined Twins: Medical Treatment) (No 1)* (2000).

Answer

Duress

It is well recognised that a defendant may be excused if he has committed a crime (other than murder, attempted murder or treason) because he was threatened by someone that, if he did not do so, he or another person would be killed or would suffer serious violence (see, for example, *Howe* (1987); *Gotts* (1991); *M'Growther* (1746)).[1]

The scope of this defence, duress, is fairly clear. Although in the past there was some uncertainty as to the types of threat which would suffice for the defence of duress, it now appears to be settled that only threats of death or grievous bodily harm will suffice (*Hudson and Taylor* (1971); *DPP v Lynch* (1975)). Furthermore, the defence is not available if the jury are sure that a person of reasonable firmness sharing the characteristics of the defendant would not have given way to the threats (*Graham* (1982); *Howe* (1987); *Martin* (1989)).

Duress of circumstances

In what Professor Smith has described as a 'happy accident', the Court of Appeal, in a series of recent decisions, has recognised a related defence.[2] In *Willer* (1986), D had driven along a pavement to escape from a gang of youths who intended violence towards him and his passengers. The Court of Appeal held that the judge had been wrong in refusing to let the defence of compulsion go to the jury and treated the case as one of duress. Clearly, the facts in this case did not raise the defence of duress of the traditional type discussed above. The youths did not say to Willer, 'drive recklessly or else we will beat up you and your passengers'. The real nature of the defence was explained by the Court of Appeal two years later in the case of *Conway* (1988). This case also concerned reckless driving. D had been urged by his passenger to drive off quickly to escape two youths running towards the car. D feared, apparently with good reason, that the two youths intended a fatal attack upon his passenger. The Court of Appeal held that it was bound by *Willer* to the effect that duress was available as a defence. However, it was stated that the defence was properly termed 'duress of circumstances' – a species of necessity analogous to duress in the traditional sense.

In *Martin* (1989), D was charged and convicted of driving whilst disqualified. At his trial, he put forward a plea of necessity asserting that his wife had threatened to commit suicide if he refused to drive their son to work. The trial judge decided that necessity was not a defence to the crime charged. On appeal, the Court of Appeal held that the defence of duress of circumstances should have been left to the jury. The Court of Appeal held that the ingredients of this defence were equivalent to those for 'duress by threats'. That is, the defence is available only if D has acted reasonably in order to avoid a threat of death or serious injury.

In *DPP v Bell* (1992), the Divisional Court held that the defence was available where D had driven a motor vehicle with excess alcohol to escape a group of youths who were pursuing him.[3]

The limits of duress

Both the defences of duress are limited in scope. They have no application in cases of murder or attempted murder (*Howe* (1987); *Gotts* (1992)), nor do they apply where the defendant was faced with 'threats' of less than serious physical harm (*Lynch* (1975); *Baker and Wilkins* (1997)).

What is not clear is whether, in addition to duress, the English courts recognise a general justifying defence of necessity applying to situations where, faced with a choice of two evils, a person commits an offence to avoid the greater evil.

Consider the following incident reported at the inquest into the deaths resulting from the *Herald of Free Enterprise* disaster.[4] Passengers attempting to escape found their route to safety obstructed by a petrified young man incapable of moving. One of the passengers pushed the man to his certain death. The passenger was not prosecuted for murder but, had he been, should he have been able to take advantage of a defence of necessity? Duress (of either type) would not have been available as it is no defence to murder and one of the few authorities in the area would suggest that the courts might be reluctant to acknowledge any other defence of necessity.

In *Dudley and Stephens* (1884), the defendants had been adrift in a small boat with very little food and water. After more than two weeks, they killed the cabin boy and fed on his body until they were rescued. They were convicted of murder. Lord Coleridge rejected the plea of necessity.

Professor Smith distinguishes the *Herald of Free Enterprise* incident from the facts of *Dudley and Stephens*. First, he says that whereas in *Dudley and Stephens* the appellants deliberately chose who was to be the victim, this element of choice was absent in the *Herald* case. Secondly, the immobile passenger was endangering the lives of other passengers, whereas the cabin boy was not. Pushing the young man was the lesser of two evils and was, in the circumstances, justified.[5] The passenger who pushed him out of the way was not morally blameworthy and it is arguable that the utilitarian objectives of punishment would not be served by denying a defence in such a case.[6] Thus, there are strong arguments for allowing a defence in these circumstances and it is arguable that it should be for the jury to determine whether the use of deadly force was justified in the circumstances by balancing the harm caused against the evil averted.[7]

On a number of occasions, however, the English courts have refused to recognise a general defence of necessity. For example, Lord Denning in *Southwark London Borough v Williams* (1971) expressed the view that hunger could never excuse theft and neither, in a civil context, could homelessness excuse trespass.[8] And in *Buckoke v Greater London Council* (1971), his Lordship stated, *obiter*, that the driver of a fire engine was obliged to stop at red traffic lights even if going to the rescue of a person in a blazing house.[9]

There are, on the other hand, a number of cases where the courts have, in effect, allowed a defence of necessity. One of the most celebrated is *Bourne* (1938), in which a doctor performed an abortion on a girl. The girl had become pregnant as a result of rape. He was charged with the offence of attempting to procure a miscarriage. MacNaghten J held that an attempt was not unlawful if it was done in good faith for the purpose of preserving the life of the mother and this might include protecting her from becoming a 'physical or mental wreck'. And, in *Newton and Stungo* (1958), Ashworth J directed the jury that an attempt to procure miscarriage would not be unlawful if it was done in good faith to preserve the life or health of the woman.[10]

Concealed necessity

There are, in addition, cases of 'concealed necessity' where the courts have in effect allowed a defence of compulsion by manipulating one or other of the constituent elements of criminal liability. In *Adams* (1957), for example, Devlin J held that a doctor is entitled to take measures to relieve the pain and suffering of a patient even if those measures might shorten life. Provided the steps taken are, from a clinical perspective, reasonable, they will not be regarded as a legal cause of death.

In *Gillick v West Norfolk and Wisbech Area Health Authority* (1985), the House of Lords held that a doctor who provides a girl under the age of 16 with contraception does not aid and abet unlawful sexual intercourse unless he intends to encourage the commission of the offence. If the doctor provides the advice and treatment because he believes it necessary for the physical mental or emotional health of the girl, then he lacks the necessary intent. This implies a very restricted meaning of intention out of line with authority.

As Professor Ashworth points out, the conclusions reached by the courts in *Adams* and in *Gillick* could have been arrived at by openly developing the defence of necessity. This, he argues, would have been preferable to distorting orthodox principles of causation and intention.[11]

A general defence of necessity?

A defence of necessity was recognised in *F v West Berkshire Health Authority* (1990). The House of Lords held that doctors were justified in carrying out a sterilisation operation on a woman who lacked the mental capacity to consent because there was a serious risk of her becoming pregnant which would have had grave psychiatric consequences for her. Lord Goff regarded the situation as falling within a general defence which applied where action is taken as a matter of necessity to assist another person without his consent (see also *R v Bournewood Community and Mental Health NHS Trust* (1998)).

Lord Goff's formulation of the defence is very limited; it would not have been available, for example, to the passengers on the *Herald of Free Enterprise*. There is, however, some recognition of a broader based defence of necessity justifying intentional homicides in certain circumstances in *Re A (Children) (Conjoined Twins: Medical Treatment) (No 1)* (2000). The issue facing the Court of Appeal was whether an operation to separate two conjoined twins should proceed where the inevitable result would be that one of the twins would die. If an operation were not performed, both twins were likely to die within months.

Both Brooke LJ and Ward LJ took the view that the operation was justified as the lesser of two evils. Walker LJ based his decision on the approach in *Gillick*, but was prepared to extend the defence of necessity to cover the case.[12] Brooke LJ expressly stated that the separation operation was lawful by reason of the operation of the doctrine of necessity. In his view, there were three requirements for the application of the defence:

(1) the act was needed to avoid inevitable and irreparable evil;

(2) no more would be done that was reasonably necessary for the purpose to be achieved;

(3) the evil inflicted was not disproportionate to the evil to be avoided.

He carefully considered the decision in *Dudley and Stephens* and identified two objections, based upon policy, that necessity might be available as a defence for the sailors. The first objection was: who is to be the judge of this sort of necessity? By what measure is the comparative value of lives to be measured? The second objection was that to permit such a defence would mark an absolute divorce of law from morality.

Neither of these objections applied to the present case. The weaker twin was 'self-designated for a very early death', her life could not be extended beyond a short span and the moral issues of saving one life at the expense of another were finely balanced.

Ward LJ, concerned that the decision could become authority for a wider proposition than he intended, formulated the defence in narrower terms reflecting the uniqueness of the case:

(1) it must be impossible to preserve the life of X without bringing about the death of Y;

(2) Y by his or her very continued existence will inevitably bring about the death of X within a very short period of time;

(3) X is capable of living an independent life but Y is incapable under any circumstances of viable independent existence.

Conclusion

While the judgment of Brooke LJ in *Re A (Children)* goes some way to recognising a general defence of necessity, broader in scope and application than either of the two well established forms of duress, Ward LJ's judgment suggests that the defence of necessity is extremely limited, as does that of Walker LJ. There is still some reluctance on the part of the English courts to recognise a justificatory defence based on a balancing of harms. Concern that a defence based upon principles of justification might be abused and that the law might lose much of its force if available continues to inhibit the recognition and development of a general defence of necessity.[13]

Notes

1   Where duress is raised, the burden of proof is on the prosecution (*Oyouncu* (2001); see also *Lyness* (2002)).

2   Smith, JC, *Justification and Excuse in the Criminal Law*, 1989, p 84.

3   In *DPP v Hicks* (2002), the respondent was charged with driving with an alcohol concentration in excess of the prescribed limit. At trial, he claimed that his 19 month old baby was very sick and that he had been driving to an all-night chemist in order to obtain some medicine. The respondent said he did not have access to a telephone and therefore could not have called for a doctor, and he did not wish to disturb the neighbours because of the lateness of the hour. His girlfriend gave evidence, stating that the child's condition was bad but she did not think it was sufficiently bad to warrant taking the child to hospital. The justices accepted his defence and acquitted him. The prosecution appealed by way of case stated. The appeal was allowed. The Divisional Court held that there was no basis on which the defence could be found established on the facts. The defence was only available, first, if the driving was done to avoid consequences that could not otherwise have been avoided; secondly, if those consequences were inevitable and involved serious harm either to the respondent or to some other person that he was bound to protect; thirdly, if the respondent did no more than was reasonably necessary to avoid the harm; and, fourthly, if the danger of driving a motor vehicle with excess alcohol in his system was not disproportionate to the harm that he sought to avoid.

4   Smith, JC, *Justification and Excuse in the Criminal Law*, 1989, p 73.

5   *Ibid*, p 77.

6   *Ibid*, p 89 and see Clarkson, CMV and Keating, HM, *Criminal Law: Text and Materials*, 4th edn, 1998, p 346.

7   Canadian criminal law recognises the defence in these circumstances. In *Perka et al v The Queen* (1984), the Supreme Court of Canada held that necessity excuses where in situations of emergency the harm inflicted by the defendant is less than the harm threatened.

8   Lord Denning said:

> If homelessness were once admitted as a defence to trespass, no one's house could be safe. Necessity would open a door which no man could shut. It would not only be those in extreme need who would enter. There would be others who would imagine they were in need, or would invent a need, so as to gain entry. ([1971] Ch 734, p 744.)

And Edmund Davies stated:

> [T]he law regards with the deepest suspicion any remedies of self-help, and permits those remedies to be resorted to only in very special circumstances. The reason for such circumspection is clear – necessity can very easily become simply a mask for anarchy. ([1971] Ch 734, pp 745–46.)

9   Duress of circumstances would now be available in this situation.

10 The 'defences' to abortion are now limited by s 5(2) of the Abortion Act 1967 to those conditions defined in s 1 of the Act.

11 Ashworth, A, *Principles of Criminal Law*, 3rd edn, 1999.

12 Walker LJ concluded that the operation would not be unlawful as:

> Mary's death would not be the purpose of the operation, although it would be
> its inevitable consequence. The operation would give her, even in death,
> bodily integrity as a human being. She would die, not because she was
> intentionally killed, but because her own body cannot sustain her life.

13 In *Shayler* (2001), Lord Woolf CJ, having referred briefly to Brooke LJ's
'thorough-ranging review of the development of the law on necessity' in *Re A*,
said:

> Nonetheless the distinction between duress of circumstances and necessity
> has, correctly (emphasis added), been by and large ignored or blurred by the
> courts. Apart from some of the medical cases like *West Berkshire* the law has
> tended to treat duress of circumstances and necessity as one and the same.
> ([2001] All ER (D) 99 (Sep), para 55.)

Question 22

Alfred was kidnapped by a terrorist organisation, SMERSH. Ugly, an agent
for SMERSH, contacted Barry, Alfred's brother, and informed him that,
unless he seriously injured Douglas, an agent for a rival organisation,
Alfred would be killed. Ugly told Barry not to contact the police and to
show that the threat was serious he sent Barry a toe severed from Alfred's
foot.

Barry knew that Douglas was very strong and would be difficult to deal
with on his own, so he approached Colin and asked him to assist him in
carrying out Ugly's order. Barry lied to Colin, telling him that SMERSH
also held Colin's mother captive. On the strength of this, Colin agreed to
help Barry.

They waylaid Douglas on his way home one night. As a result of the
attack, Douglas suffered severe injuries.

Discuss the liability of the parties.

How would your answer differ if:

(a) Douglas had died as a result of the attack?;

(b) Barry had himself been a member of SMERSH three years previously?

Answer plan

A fairly intricate question raising a wide range of issues. There are a number
of offences to discuss. Although one might not expect the prosecution to

charge incitement or conspiracy in these circumstances, they have been discussed for the sake of completeness. As the facts are fairly 'open' with respect to a number of issues, a number of possible resolutions must be considered.

The principal issues are:

- the ingredients of the defence of duress and its application;
- duress of circumstances;
- duress and murder;
- duress and membership of a criminal organisation;
- incitement where the incitee has a defence;
- conspiracy where one party may have a defence;
- the ingredients of the offence of kidnapping;
- threats to kill.

The principal authorities include: *Graham* (1982); *Howe* (1987); *Bowen* (1996); *Sharp* (1987); *Shepherd* (1988).

Answer

Barry and Colin

Causing grievous bodily harm with intent

As the facts of the problem state that Douglas suffered severe injuries, it is proposed, first, to consider Barry and Colin's liability for causing grievous bodily harm with intent, contrary to s 18 of the Offences Against the Person Act 1861. (The maximum punishment for this offence is a term of imprisonment for life.)

The facts of the problem imply the necessary intention to cause grievous bodily harm (*Belfon* (1976)).[1]

It is not clear from the facts of the problem whether both parties beat up Douglas. If they did, they may be charged as joint principals. They will be liable as joint principals (provided the relevant *mens rea* can be proved) if the injuries suffered were a result of the aggregate effect of their individual contributions to the attack, even if it could not be proved that their individual contribution would, on its own, have amounted to grievous bodily harm (*Macklin and Murphy's Case* (1838)).

If Colin did not attack Douglas but, say, held him while Barry struck him, he can be convicted as an accomplice (s 8 of the Accessories and Abettors Act 1861).[2]

Duress

Barry and Colin may, however, be able to take advantage of the defence of duress. This defence applies where D was compelled to act as he did because of threats of death or serious injury to him or someone for whose safety D would reasonably regard himself as responsible (see *Ortiz* (1986); *Martin* (1989); *Wright* (2000)). Once raised, the burden of negativing the defence rests on the prosecution (*Gill* (1963); *Bone* (1968)).[3]

In *Graham* (1982), Lord Lane CJ held that there were two questions to be considered by the jury:

(1) Was the defendant, or may he have been, impelled to act as he did because, as a result of what he reasonably believed X to have said or done, he had good cause to fear that if he did not so act, X would kill or cause serious injury?

(2) If so, would a sober person of reasonable person firmness sharing the characteristics of the defendant have responded, or might he have responded, to whatever he reasonably believed X said or did by doing as the defendant did?

With respect to the first of the questions above, it is not sufficient for the prosecution to prove that there was not in fact any threat or circumstance giving rise to duress; they must prove that the defendant did not believe, on reasonable grounds, in the existence of the threat or circumstance (*Safi* (2003); *Cairns* (1999)). Thus, the jury should be directed to consider whether Colin's mistaken belief that SMERSH had kidnapped his mother was, in the circumstances, reasonable.[4]

The second question is framed in objective terms, but allows for the attribution of certain characteristics of the defendant to the reasonable person. In *Bowen* (1996), it was said that, ordinarily, only the age and sex of the defendant will be relevant characteristics. Exceptional vulnerability, timidity or susceptibility to threats are not in themselves characteristics to be imputed to the reasonable person, but physical disability which inhibits self-protection or a recognised psychiatric illness (provided persons generally suffering from such a condition may be more susceptible to pressure and threats) are.

The issue for the jury is whether the threat of imminent death or serious injury was operating on the minds of the defendants so as to overbear their will at the time they attacked Douglas. It is not necessary that the execution of the threat was immediately in prospect. The jury should consider what the likely reaction of the reasonable person would have been to the threat, taking into account the relevant characteristics of the defendants, the circumstances in which they found themselves, the opportunities which existed to avoid it and the risks that they faced (see *Hudson and Taylor* (1971); *Abdul-Hussain and Others* (1999); *Z* (2003)).

Alternative facts

Part (a)

An intention to do grievous bodily harm is sufficient *mens rea* for murder (*Moloney* (1985); *Cunningham* (1982)). According to the House of Lords in *Howe* (1987), duress is no defence to murder, whether as a principal or an accomplice. Consequently, had Douglas died, Barry and Colin would be guilty of murder.

Part (b)

In *Z* (2003), the Court of Appeal held that the defence is denied if D, by joining a criminal organisation, had anticipated that the group might try to coerce him by violence or threats of violence into committing offences of the type with which he is charged (*Sharp* (1987) and *Baker and Ward* (1999) followed; *Heath* (2000) and *Harmer* (2002) not followed). In *Fitzpatrick* (1977), the Court of Criminal Appeal in Northern Ireland held that D could not avail himself of the defence of duress for a robbery carried out whilst a member of the IRA, despite the fact that he had tried, unsuccessfully, to leave the organisation. The court said that D could not rely on the duress to which he had voluntarily exposed himself as an excuse, *either* in respect of the crimes he committed against his will, *or* in respect of his continued, but unwilling, association with those who exercised duress upon him (see also *Ali* (1995)).

In this case, however, Barry left the organisation three years previously. It cannot realistically be argued that he has submitted himself to illegal compulsion. He had broken his links with the organisation before the offence was contemplated and therefore the defence ought to be available to him.

Incitement

Might Barry be guilty of inciting Colin to commit the offence under s 18 of the 1861 Act?

The essence of incitement is intentionally encouraging another to commit a crime and may be committed whether or not the crime incited is in fact committed (*Higgins* (1801)). But the act incited must be one which, if performed by the person incited, would be a crime. Could Barry be convicted of inciting Colin if Colin himself escaped liability because he was compelled to act as he did?

A person cannot be convicted of incitement unless he intended that the person incited would act with *mens rea*.[5] Duress is a defence independent of the *mens rea* and it was held in *Bourne* (1952) that a person might be convicted as an *abettor*, despite the fact that the 'principal' – a victim of duress – was acquitted. It is arguable, by analogy with that case, that a person may be guilty of incitement, even though the other party would have or does have a defence to liability.

Barry could not be convicted of incitement, however, if his intention was that Colin was merely to assist him while he beat up Douglas. There cannot be a conviction for incitement to aid and abet the commission of an offence (*Bodin and Bodin* (1979)).

With respect to alternative facts (a), if Douglas died, Barry could not be convicted of incitement to murder. Like attempt, incitement is defined by reference to the inciter's intention (see *Whybrow* (1951)).

Duress of circumstances

Barry could not rely on duress *by threats* to the charge of incitement. He was not ordered to incite Colin (*Cole* (1994)). He might, however, be entitled to avail himself of the defence known as 'duress of circumstances'. This defence applies in situations where objective dangers other than threats of the form 'do this or else ...' compel criminal action (see *DPP v Rogers* (1998); and *Pommell* (1995)).

It is subject to the same limiting conditions as duress by threats (see *Graham*, above). Thus, it is available if, from an objective standpoint, the accused acted reasonably and proportionately in order to avoid a threat of death or personal injury (*Martin* (1989); *Conway* (1989); *Abdul-Hussain* (1999)).

Conspiracy

Barry and Colin may be charged with conspiracy to cause grievous bodily harm contrary to s 1(1) of the Criminal Law Act 1977.[6]

The sub-section provides that a person is guilty of conspiracy if he agrees with another to pursue a course of conduct which, if carried out as intended, will necessarily amount to the commission of an offence by at least one of the parties.

The defence of duress may, of course, be available to both Barry and Colin, in which case, there could be no liability for conspiracy. But if, for whatever reason, only one of them, D1, was successful in his plea of duress, then the other, D2, is guilty of conspiracy, as long as the plan was that D2 would perpetrate the offence. The agreed course of conduct would, in that case, amount to the commission of an offence by D2.[7]

Note that, with respect to alternative facts (a), if Douglas had died, Barry and Colin could not be convicted of conspiracy to murder. The *agreed* course of conduct did not include killing Douglas.

A person convicted of statutory conspiracy to commit an offence for which a maximum of imprisonment for life is provided (for example, as in this case, the offence under s 18 of the Offences Against the Person Act 1861) shall be liable to imprisonment for life (s 3(2)(b) of the Criminal Law Act 1977).

Ugly *et al*

Kidnapping, etc

SMERSH and Ugly may be convicted of the common law offence of kidnapping. The ingredients of the offence consist of: (a) the taking or carrying away of one person by another; (b) by force or fraud; (c) without the consent of the person taken; and (d) without lawful excuse.

The offence is punishable with a fine or imprisonment at the discretion of the court (*D* (1984)) (for sentencing guidelines, see *Spence* (1983)).

In addition, they would be guilty of the less serious offence of false imprisonment. See also s 1 of the Taking of Hostages Act 1982, which provides that it is an offence punishable with imprisonment for life if anyone detains a person and threatens to injure or kill the person detained in order to compel another to do some act. For this offence, proceedings may only be instituted with the approval of the Attorney General.

Aggravated assaults

Those responsible for cutting off Alfred's toe can be convicted of the offence under s 18 of the 1861 Act (see discussion above).

In addition, Ugly can be convicted of the offence under s 16 of the Act. It is an offence to threaten another that he *or a third party* will be killed. The *mens rea* requirement for the offence (that is, an intention to cause the other to fear that it would be carried out) appears to be satisfied in this case.

The maximum penalty for this offence is a term of imprisonment not exceeding 10 years.

Notes

1   In this problem, the facts clearly imply an intention to cause grievous bodily harm and so the lesser offence under s 20 is not discussed.

2   Section 8 of the Accessories and Abettors Act 1861 provides that:

> ... whosoever shall aid, abet, counsel or procure the commission of any indictable offence ... shall be liable to be tried indicted and punished as a principal offender.

If it could not be established whether they both took part in the attack, or who had perpetrated the injuries, they could both be convicted if the prosecution could prove they both participated and that they had the relevant *mens rea*. If it was unclear whether Colin perpetrated the offence or acted as an accomplice, he could be indicted for causing the injuries to Douglas (or, in the second part, with his murder), instead of alleging that he aided and abetted Barry to cause those injuries or kill Douglas (*Swindall* (1846)).

3   In *Shayler* (2001), a case concerning duress of circumstances, Lord Woolf CJ stated that an evil directed at a person or persons for whom the defendant has responsibility or the situation makes him responsible would suffice.

4   Although occasionally referred to as 'the subjective test', the first question is expressed in terms of the defendant's 'reasonable belief' and whether or not he had 'good reason' to fear death or serious injury. In *DPP v Rogers* (1998), however, Lord Brooke stated that the reference to 'reasonable belief' was a mistake. In *Martin (David Paul)* (2000), the Court of Appeal held that the test in *Graham* should be approached subjectively. D admitted that he carried out two robberies, but put forward a defence of duress. A consultant psychiatrist gave evidence that D suffered from a schizoid-affective disorder, which meant that he was more likely than others to regard things said to him as threatening and to believe that such threats would be carried out. The Court of Appeal held that the trial judge was wrong to rule that the defendant was to be judged against the standard of a reasonable man not having the particular condition from which D suffered. These decisions, it is submitted, are clearly out of line with authority. The decision in *Graham* was considered to be correct by the House of Lords in *Howe* and, in *Martin*, it was held that the same principles applied to duress of circumstances.

5   Insofar as *Curr* (1968) appears to require proof that persons incited actually possess [the] *mens rea*, it is manifestly erroneous; a person incited need not actually commit the offence at all, so it cannot be necessary to prove his *mens rea* [Murphy, P *et al* (eds), *Blackstone's Criminal Practice*, 1998, para A6.7, p 81].

6   Although counts of conspiracy and related substantive charges may be brought together, the prosecution would be required to satisfy the judge that the count alleging conspiracy was demanded by the interests of justice (*Practice Note* (1977)).

7   Professors Smith and Hogan cogently argue that 'commission of offence' in s 1(1) means commission as a principal in the first degree – Smith, JC and Hogan, B, *Criminal Law*, 7th edn, 1992, p 280; and see *Hollinshead* (1985).

Question 23

With reference to the rationale of the defence and its parameters, consider critically the English courts' unwillingness to accept duress as a defence to murder.

Answer plan

This question requires a critical evaluation of the rule that duress is no defence to murder by reference to the rationale of the defence and the limits on its availability.

The principal points to be discussed are:

- the rationale of the defence of duress;
- the distinction between excuses and justifications;
- the objective limiting criteria;
- the arguments for/against allowing duress as a defence to murder.

The principal authorities are: *DPP v Lynch* (1975); *Howe* (1987); *Graham* (1982).

Answer

The defence of duress operates where the accused has committed the *actus reus* of an offence with the appropriate *mens rea* but was compelled to act as he did because of threats made by another. Where the defence applies, it is a complete defence.

What are the parameters of the defence?

First, the accused's will must be overborne by threats of death or serious bodily harm (*DPP v Lynch* (1975)).[1] This includes threats to kill or seriously harm a third party for whose safety D would reasonably regard himself as responsible (see *Ortiz* (1986); *Martin* (1989); *Wright* (2000); *Shayler* (2001)).

Secondly, the Court of Appeal in *Graham* (1982) held that there are two elements to the defence, the burden of proof being on the prosecution. The jury should consider whether:

(a) the accused was, or may have been, impelled to act as he did because, as a result of what he reasonably believed X had said or done, he had good reason to fear that, if he did not so act, X would kill him or cause him serious injury; and

(b) a sober person of reasonable firmness, sharing the characteristics of the accused, would have responded to whatever he reasonably believed X said or did by acting as the accused did.[2]

What is the rationale of the defence?

Duress, when it applies, excuses the defendant's conduct. It does not justify the commission of the offence. The distinction is an important one. There is an element of approval or, indeed, encouragement in the case of justifications. Thus, for example, a person who uses force to prevent crime is justified in what he does. He has a 'right' to use force. An excuse, on the other hand, whilst an acknowledgment that the defendant does not deserve to be punished, does not exist to promote the behaviour in question. The victim of duress does not have a 'right' to commit the offence. Duress excuses the conduct of the defendant because he was effectively denied a 'fair opportunity' to choose between obeying or disobeying the law.[3] Lord Morris in *DPP v Lynch* (1975) explained that the law would be 'censorious and inhumane' were it not to recognise the 'powerful and natural' instinct of self-preservation.

In addition, not only would it be unfair to punish the accused for failing to resist the threat if the person of reasonable steadfastness would have done likewise but, also, it is arguable that punishment would serve no rational purpose. If the defendant acted as a person of reasonable steadfastness would in the circumstances, then it is reasonable to suppose that the threat of punishment would not influence his decision, nor the decision of the ordinary person, to observe the law in the same situation in the future.

The defence is not available, however, either to murder (*Howe* (1987)) or attempted murder (*Gotts* (1992)). Prior to *Howe*, a distinction had been drawn between principals and accomplices to murder. Whilst the defence was not available to the actual perpetrator (*Abbott* (1977)), it was available to the accomplice (*Lynch* (1975)).

The distinction drawn between accomplices and perpetrators of murder was criticised as illogical and unsatisfactory. Professors Smith and Hogan pointed out that it is not always true that the perpetrator is more blameworthy than an accomplice. There may be little or no moral difference between them.[4] Professor Williams agreed and pointed out that there is no moral distinction between, for example, the individual who is forced to drive a bomber to a pub and the person who is forced to carry the bomb into the pub.[5] When the matter came before the House of Lords in *Howe*, their Lordships agreed that there was no valid distinction between the perpetrator of murder and an accomplice to it and overruled the decision in *Lynch*, holding that duress was not a defence to murder, irrespective of the degree of participation.

Why should the defence not be available to a person accused of murder?

Lord Hailsham regarded it as neither good law nor good morals nor, perhaps more importantly, good policy to suggest that the ordinary man of reasonable fortitude is not capable of heroism. He added that the object of the criminal law was to protect ordinary lives and to set a standard of conduct which ordinary men and women are expected to observe if they are to avoid criminal liability. In his Lordship's opinion, it was not 'just or humane' to withdraw the protection of the criminal law from an innocent victim and in the name of 'a concession to human frailty' to offer protection to the 'coward'.

It is submitted, with respect, that this appears to require unrealistic heroism and overlooks the fact that an appropriate standard is set by the second limb of the defence. Only if the jury believe that a person of reasonable fortitude would have or might have yielded to the threat will the defence succeed. As Lord Morris pointed out in *Lynch*, standards of heroism should not be demanded – in the 'calm of the courtroom' – when they could not have been expected of the reasonably resolute person when the threat was made.[6] Furthermore, the argument advanced by Lord Hailsham would apply equally to other crimes of violence, for example, wounding with intent – a crime for which his Lordship accepted the defence of duress would, in appropriate circumstances, be available.

Some of the 'policy' reasons for denying the defence in cases of murder were explained by Lord Salmon in *Abbott* (1977). Allowing the defence would invite the danger of providing a 'charter for terrorists, gang leaders and kidnappers'. D, if he were allowed to go free, might be approached again by the terrorist group and, having gained relevant experience and expertise, commit a further murder.

The Court of Appeal in *Gotts* gave a further reason for restricting the availability of the defence: Lord Lane thought that the defence was easy to raise and difficult for the prosecution to disprove beyond reasonable doubt.

Again, however, these arguments are arguments against the defence generally and do not justify the special treatment of murder and attempted murder. In any case, is there reason to suppose that the jury would be any less capable of recognising a bogus claim of duress than one in respect of, say, self-defence?

Lord Hailsham in *Howe* advanced a further argument. He stated that where the accused faced the choice between the threat of death or serious injury and deliberately taking an innocent life, a reasonable man might reflect that one innocent life is at least as valuable as his own or that of his loved one. In such a case, if the man chooses to kill, he cannot claim that he is choosing the lesser of two evils.

There are two objections to this point.

First, and most importantly, the defence of duress is not based upon the idea that the defendant chose the lesser of two evils. The error lies in regarding duress as a justification. As explained above, duress is a defence because, if D was subject to immediate threats which were so powerful that the reasonable man would have acted in a similar fashion, the law would lack deterrent force and it would be unconscionably harsh to punish D.

As Lord Edmund Davies correctly observed in *Lynch*, to allow a defence is not necessarily to approve of the defendant's conduct, but simply to recognise that it is not deserving of punishment.

Secondly, to give way to the threat might amount to choosing the lesser of two evils, where, for example, the threat is to kill a large number of people, say, the defendant's family, unless he kills one individual.

Two additional arguments were put forward to justify the refusal of the defence in cases of murder.

Lords Bridge and Griffiths said that Parliament's failure to enact the recommendation of the Law Commission made 10 years previously was an indication that Parliament had rejected the proposal. However, as Professors Smith and Hogan have pointed out, the matter has not been put before Parliament for its consideration.[7]

Lords Griffiths and Hailsham felt that the interests of justice would be served in hard cases, especially those involving secondary participation in murder under duress, by leaving issues relating to the culpability and punishment of those involved to administrative discretion. It would be 'inconceivable', according to Lord Griffith, that, for example, a woman who was forced to act as a getaway driver for the principal offender would be prosecuted. In other cases, the Parole Board might be expected to weigh fairly the relative culpability of the defendant and, where appropriate, advise the Home Secretary that an early release would be justified.

However, leaving the fate of the defendant to discretionary executive action is unacceptable, as the outcome is by no means certain and neither early release nor the granting of a royal pardon would remove the stigma of a criminal conviction for what most people regard as the most heinous crime.

The decisions in *Howe* and *Gotts* mean that, when charged with murder or attempted murder, it is no excuse that, in the face of threats, the accused behaved with what a jury would consider to be reasonable fortitude. The law seems to require suicidal heroism.[8]

Notes

1   In *Baker and Wilkins* (1997), the Court of Appeal held that the defence was not available in cases where the defendant believed the criminal act was necessary to avoid serious psychological harm.

2   For an analysis of the relevant characteristics which the jury should consider in applying this test, see *Bowen* (1996):

> ... the mere fact that the accused is more pliable, vulnerable, timid or susceptible to threats than a normal person are not characteristics with which it is legitimate to invest the reasonable/ordinary person for the purpose of considering the objective test [*per* Stuart-Smith LJ in *Bowen* [1996] 2 Cr App R 157, p 161].

3   Hart, HLA, *Punishment and Responsibility*, 1968, p 22.

4   Smith, JC and Hogan, B, *Criminal Law*, 8th edn, 1996, p 241.

5   Williams, G, *Textbook of Criminal Law*, 2nd edn, 1983, p 629.

6   In *Horne* (1994), the Court of Appeal expressed approval of the trial judge's description of the reasonable person as an average member of the public; neither a hero nor a coward, just an average person.

7   Smith, JC and Hogan, B, *Criminal Law*, 8th edn, 1996, p 236.

8   A compromise solution would be for duress, in cases of murder, to operate as a partial defence, reducing liability, when successfully pleaded, to manslaughter. Recognising duress as a partial defence to murder would allow the gravity of the duress and its effect on the culpability of the accused to be taken into account at the sentencing stage, rather than to convict of murder and leave it to executive discretion to order early release.

This compromise was, however, rejected in *Howe*. Lord Griffiths said that it would be 'anomalous' for the defence of duress to operate as a form of mitigation for the crime of murder alone, but this is precisely the effect of a successful plea of the analogous defence of provocation.

Question 24

In what circumstances will a mistake relieve a defendant of criminal liability?

Answer plan

The principal issues are:

- the effect of mistakes negativing *mens rea*;
- the inconsistent treatment of mistakes relevant to defences;
- mistakes induced by voluntary intoxication;
- mistakes resulting from 'a defect of reason caused by a disease of the mind';
- mistakes of law.

The principal authorities are: *DPP v Morgan* (1976); *Williams* (1983); *Howe* (1987); *Majewski* (1977); *M'Naghten* (1843).

Answer

In discussing the effect of mistake upon criminal liability, it is important to appreciate that there are different types of mistake. The mistake may be such that it negatives the *mens rea* for the offence charged. Alternatively, the mistake may relate to an issue of relevance to a particular defence. Thirdly, the accused may make a mistake of law. In addition, the causes of the mistake must be examined. Mistakes caused by the voluntary consumption of alcohol or drugs, for example, are subject to special legal treatment.

Mistakes negativing *mens rea*

For most crimes, the prosecution must prove not only that D performed the *actus reus* of the offence, but that he did so with the appropriate *mens rea*. For example, a person is guilty of murder if he kills a human being, intending to kill or cause grievous bodily harm (*Moloney* (1985)). Thus, if a person, whilst hunting, shoots and kills what he believes to be a bear, he cannot be convicted of murder if it transpires that he has killed a human being. His mistake as to the nature of his target negatives the appropriate *mens rea*.

In *DPP v Morgan* (1976), the House of Lords held that, where the law requires intention, knowledge or recklessness with respect to the *actus reus*, a mistake, *whether reasonable or not*, which negatives the *mens rea* will excuse.[1]

The case concerned the offence of rape, the *mens rea* for which is an intention (or recklessness) to have sexual intercourse with a woman without her consent. The trial judge, however, had informed the jury that only a reasonable mistake as to whether the woman was consenting would excuse.

The House of Lords disapproved of the trial judge's direction and held that 'as a matter of inexorable logic', any mistake which negatives the *mens rea* requirement of the offence must result in an acquittal. Since an honest mistake clearly negatives the *mens rea*, the reasonableness or otherwise of that mistake is no more than evidence for or against the view that the mistake was made.

From the above, it should be clear that mistake is not really a 'defence'. The burden of proving *mens rea* lies with the prosecution (*Woolmington v DPP* (1935)). The accused does not even bear an evidential burden in respect of mistakes going to the *mens rea* (*DPP v Morgan, per* Lord Hailsham).

In *Kimber* (1983), D was charged with indecent assault contrary to s 14(1) of the Sexual Offences Act 1956. He alleged that he thought the woman was consenting. The Court of Appeal held that the *mens rea* for indecent assault is an intention to apply unlawful personal violence. As violence would not be unlawful if the woman consented to it, D should be acquitted if he mistakenly believed she was consenting. Observing the logic of the House of Lords judgment in *Morgan*, the Court of Appeal in *Kimber* held that the burden lay with the prosecution to prove that D did not believe she was consenting.

Where negligence is the basis of liability (see, for example, s 25 of the Firearms Act 1968), only a reasonable mistake will excuse. This follows because an unreasonable mistake is a negligent mistake which, clearly, cannot excuse a crime based on negligence (see also *Tolson* (1889)).

A crime of strict liability is one for which neither *mens rea* nor negligence need be proved with respect to one or more of the elements in the *actus reus*. It follows that no mistake with reference to that element will excuse, even if it is a reasonable mistake. For example, in *Cundy v Le Cocq* (1881), the defendant was convicted of selling intoxicating liquor to a drunken person contrary to s 13 of the Licensing Act 1872. The Divisional Court held, as a matter of construction, that the offence was one of strict liability and, therefore, it was unnecessary to prove that D knew the customer to be drunk. Logically, then, it was legally irrelevant that he mistakenly believed that the person served was sober, and this was true even though D's mistake was a reasonable one.

Thus, whether a mistake will excuse depends on the *mens rea* requirement of the particular crime with which the accused has been charged. In *Ellis, Street and Smith* (1987), the defendants were charged with an offence contrary to s 170(2) of the Customs and Excise Management Act 1979, under which there are a number of offences of being knowingly concerned in the fraudulent evasion of a prohibition on the importation of various types of contraband, including controlled drugs and obscene material. The defendants imported drugs, mistakenly believing that they were importing prohibited obscene material. The Court of Appeal held that they had sufficient *mens rea* – knowledge that they were importing a prohibited good – despite their mistake as to the nature of the prohibited goods.

In *R v Forbes* (2001), the appellant had flown from Amsterdam to Heathrow airport where he was stopped by customs officers and found to be in possession of two video tapes, falsely labelled as 'Spartacus' and 'The Godfather Part 2'. On inspection by the officers, it was found that both tapes contained footage of indecent photographs of teenage boys under the age of 16. The appellant gave evidence to the effect that a man he met in a bar in Amsterdam had asked him to take the videos to London and to deliver them to another man in London. The appellant claimed that he was told when given the videos that they were recordings of two films called 'The Exorcist' and 'Kidz' and that he had assumed they were prohibited films. That belief, he explained, was the reason he had behaved suspiciously upon his arrival in the UK. In fact, neither 'The Exorcist' nor 'Kidz' is indecent or obscene and their importation is not prohibited.

The trial judge directed the jury that if an accused person knew that the activity he was engaged in was the evasion of a prohibition against importation and he knowingly took part in that operation, his conviction would be justified under s 170(2) even if he did not know precisely what kind of goods were being imported. In addition, he explained to the jury that unless they were sure that the defendant's explanation that he believed the films were 'The Exorcist' and 'Kidz' was untrue, they should acquit. The defendant appealed. He contended that the trial judge ought to have directed the jury that the prosecution were required to prove that the appellant knew that the videos contained indecent photographs of young persons under 16.

The House of Lords dismissed the appeal. It was not necessary to prove that the defendant knew that the goods were indecent photographs of children; indeed, it was not even necessary to prove that he knew they were photographs.

The appellant's defence was based on the decision in *R v Taaffe* (1984). In that case, the defendant was charged with having been knowingly concerned in the fraudulent evasion of the prohibition on the importation of cannabis resin. His defence was that he believed the goods to be currency, which he wrongly believed to be subject to a prohibition on importation. The judge ruled that those facts afforded no defence. His conviction was quashed. The House of Lords held that being 'knowingly concerned' involved not merely knowledge of a smuggling operation, but also knowledge that the substance in question was one the importation of which was prohibited and thus he was to be judged on the facts as he believed them to be.

The judge in *Forbes* directed the jury in accordance with *Taaffe*, but the jury clearly did not believe the appellant's account. Having rejected his explanation, the only issue for the jury was whether the appellant was aware that the goods which he was transporting were subject to a prohibition. The prosecution were not required to prove that the accused knew what the goods were; it was sufficient to prove that he knew that they were prohibited goods.

Where *Caldwell* recklessness applies, a person acts recklessly if either he has recognised that there is some risk involved in his actions or he fails to consider the possibility of a risk that would have been obvious to a reasonable man (*Caldwell* (1982)). If D considered whether there was a risk, but mistakenly concluded there was none, it follows that he was not reckless.

This analysis was accepted, *obiter*, by the Court of Appeal in *Reid* (1990). In the House of Lords, however, the speech of Lord Browne-Wilkinson suggests that it is only where D, *on reasonable grounds*, dismisses the risk that he is not reckless. Lord Ackner, on the other hand, expressed the view that *Caldwell* recklessness concerned the state of mind of the defendant himself. It is submitted that this is the correct view and that the reasonableness of the defendant's mistake is relevant only to the question whether it was honestly held. This was the view taken by Lord Goff, who stated that D is not reckless if he, in good faith, mistakenly concluded that there was no risk.[2]

Mistake as to a defence element

There is another type of situation where the accused may have made a relevant mistake and that is where, if the facts had been as he believed them to be, he would have been entitled to a defence. For example, imagine that D intentionally wounded another because he *mistakenly* believed that the other was attacking him. If D claims that he was acting in self-defence, is it sufficient that he honestly held that belief, or will only a 'reasonable mistake' excuse?

In *Albert v Lavin* (1981), the Divisional Court held that a mistaken belief in the necessity for self-defence will only excuse if it was reasonable. The court proceeded on the basis that the *mens rea* for assault was an intent to apply force and drew a distinction between the case where D's mistake relates to a defence element and the situation where the mistake relates to an element of the *actus reus*, as, for example, in *DPP v Morgan*.

The decision in *Albert v Lavin* was disapproved in *Williams* (1983). D was charged with an assault occasioning actual bodily harm to a man whom he mistakenly believed was unlawfully assaulting another man. The Court of Appeal held that the mental element necessary for an assault is the intent to apply unlawful force to the victim. Force used in defence of oneself or others or to prevent crime is not unlawful force (s 3 of the Criminal Law Act 1967). Therefore, as D acted to prevent what he mistakenly believed to be an unlawful attack on another, he did not *intend* to apply *unlawful* force.

In these circumstances, the reasonableness or unreasonableness of D's mistake is material only to the credibility of the assertion that he made the mistake. If the mistaken belief was, in fact, held, its unreasonableness is irrelevant. In *Beckford* (1988), the Privy Council endorsed this approach in a case where D, having mistakenly believed that his life was in danger, acted in self-defence. By treating unlawfulness as a definitional element of the *actus reus* to which the accused must have *mens rea*, the distinction drawn in *Albert v Lavin* disappears.[3]

This approach has not been adopted with respect to all defences. In *Graham* (1982), the Court of Appeal held that the defence of duress is available only where D *reasonably* believed that he was being subjected to duress. It was stated that, where D has committed the *actus reus* of the offence with the requisite *mens rea,* a mistake relating to a defence must be reasonable. The court did not treat duress as relating to the element of unlawfulness in the *actus reus.*

The approach in *Graham* was subsequently endorsed by the House of Lords in *Howe* (1987) and the Court of Appeal in *Martin* (1989) adopted the same approach to the defence of duress of circumstances.[4]

The courts are prepared, however, to allow the defence of provocation where the accused mistakenly believed, without reasonable grounds, that he was being provoked (*Letenock* (1917); *Luc Thiet Thuan* (1996)).

This lack of consistency has been criticised. Professors Smith and Hogan argue that, as far as crimes of *mens rea* are concerned, the accused should always be judged on the basis of what he actually believed without a requirement of reasonableness. It is argued that the effect of the rule in *Graham* is to convict D on the basis of negligence and not on the basis of subjective fault, even where the offence may be one requiring *mens rea.*[5]

Mistakes and voluntary intoxication

If a relevant mistake of the defendant was induced by alcohol or drugs voluntarily consumed, then the treatment of the mistake varies depending upon whether the mistake negatives the *mens rea* or relates to a defence element:

(a) Intoxicated mistakes which negative the *mens rea*:

In this case, although a mistake induced by *voluntary* intoxication will excuse, it will only do so for crimes of 'specific intent' (for example, murder) but not crimes of 'basic intent' (for example, manslaughter) (*Majewski* (1977)). In cases of *involuntary* intoxication, however, a lack of *mens rea* will excuse all crimes (*Kingston* (1994)).

In *Richardson and Irwin* (1999), the defendants, after a drinking session, went with a friend to a flat belonging to one of the defendants. As a prank, the defendants lifted their friend over the edge of the balcony. He fell about 10 or 12 ft and sustained serious injuries. The defendants were convicted of inflicting grievous bodily harm contrary to s 20 of the Offences Against the Person Act 1861. The defendants claimed that their friend had consented to the horseplay and that his fall was an accident.

The Court of Appeal allowed their appeal on the grounds that the trial judge had not directed the jury to take account of the evidence that the defendants' minds were affected by alcohol when considering whether they believed their friend was consenting. This is a very strange decision. The offence under s 20 is an offence of basic intent. The decision means that an intoxicated mistake relieves the prosecution of having to prove foresight that some harm might result, but not that the defendant believed that the victim consented.[6]

(b) Intoxicated mistakes and defences:

In *O'Grady* (1987), the Court of Appeal held that in relation to self-defence, a mistake of fact which has been induced by voluntary intoxication cannot be relied upon by the defendant even for crimes of specific intent. The court held that the decision in *Williams* was of no application where the mistake was caused by voluntary intoxication. Although *obiter*, this decision was regarded as binding by the Court of Appeal in *O'Connor* (1991).[7]

In the case of those defences for which only reasonable mistakes will excuse, for example, duress, an intoxicated mistake cannot excuse.

There is, however, some authority for the proposition that, where a statute provides that a belief shall afford a defence to a particular offence, a mistake induced by intoxication may be considered. This is a matter of statutory construction. Thus, for example, in *Jaggard v Dickinson* (1981), the court held that the defendant could rely on the 'lawful excuse' defence in s 5(2) of the Criminal Damage Act 1971 even though she had made a drunken mistake. Section 5(3) of the statute provides that 'it is immaterial whether a belief is justified or not if it is honestly held'. The court was of the opinion that, as a matter of statutory construction, no exception could be made to this rule even where the mistake was caused by voluntary intoxication.

Mistakes resulting from a 'defect of reason caused by disease of the mind'

If the defendant's mistake is a result of a 'defect of reason due to disease of the mind', and the mistake is such that the defendant either did not know the 'nature and quality' of his act or did not know that 'he was doing wrong', then, in legal terms, the defendant is not guilty by reason of insanity and entitled only to a qualified acquittal (*M'Naghten Rules* (1843)).

Mistakes of law

It is no excuse that the defendant mistakenly believed his conduct to be lawful (for example, *Esop* (1836); *Attorney General's Reference (No 1 of 1995)* (1996); *Hipperson v DPP* (1996); *Lee* (2000)). However, where a mistake as to law is such that the defendant lacks the *mens rea* for the offence charged, then it is, generally, an excuse (see, for example, s 2(1)(a) of the Theft Act 1968).[8]

Notes

1   This is true of crimes requiring *Cunningham*-type recklessness. See p 127, above, for an analysis of the position where *Caldwell*-type recklessness will suffice.

2   [1992] All ER 673. See the speeches of:
  • Lord Ackner, pp 683f–g and 684c–d;
  • Lord Browne-Wilkinson, pp 695f–g and 696f;
  • Lord Goff, pp 690f–h.

  Clause 41(1) of the Draft Criminal Code Bill proposed that:

  ... a person who acts in the belief that a circumstance exists has any defence that he would have if the circumstances existed [Law Commission, *Draft Criminal Code*, Law Com No 177, 1989].

3   Whilst a mistake as to the necessity for force is legally relevant, a mistake as to what constitutes reasonable force in the circumstances is not. A person may use such force as is *objectively* reasonable in the circumstances as he subjectively believes them to be (*Owino* (1996)).

4   In *Baker and Wilkins* (1997) and *Rogers* (1998), it was held that duress of circumstances would be available if the defendant knew or believed that it is immediately necessary to avoid death or serious injury. But these decisions are out of line with the previous authorities and are probably best ignored.

5   Smith, JC and Hogan, B, *Criminal Law*, 7th edn, 1992, p 240.

  The correspondence between 'unreasonableness' and 'negligence' was actually recognised by Hodgson J in *Albert v Lavin* [1981] 1 All ER 628, pp 633a, 639e.

6   In *McKnight* (2000), the Court of Appeal held that the test was whether drunkenness had rendered the defendant *incapable* of forming the necessary specific intent. This is inconsistent with authority (see, for example, *Pordage* (1975)). The issue is not whether D was *capable* of forming the intent, but whether the necessary *mens rea* was in fact formed.

7   This part of the decision of the Court of Appeal in *O'Connor* was also *obiter dicta*.

8   Where D makes a mistake of law as a result of a defect of reason caused by a disease of the mind, then D is legally insane (*Windle* (1952)).

Question 25

Jeremy is a well known practical joker. One day, he went into the office of a colleague, Robin, and pointed a water pistol at him. He was about to fire it in Robin's face when Robin, irritated by Jeremy's constant joking, threw an ashtray at him which hit Jeremy in the face, resulting in the loss of an eye. The water pistol was found to contain ammonia and Jeremy has admitted that he intended to injure Robin, by spraying it in his face.

Discuss the criminal liability of Jeremy and Robin.

Answer plan

This question concerns the availability of self-defence where the defendant is unaware of the justifying circumstances. There is an almost total lack of authority as far as this issue is concerned.

The principal issues are:

- the *Dadson* principle;
- liability for attempts;
- the ingredients of liability for burglary under s 9 of the Theft Act 1968;
- possession of an offensive weapon – the meaning of 'public place'.

Answer

Robin

As the facts of the problem state that Jeremy lost an eye, it is proposed to consider Robin's liability for causing grievous bodily harm with intent, contrary to s 18 of the Offences Against the Person Act 1861, and maliciously inflicting grievous bodily harm, contrary to s 20 of the same Act. 'Grievous bodily harm' means 'serious bodily harm' (*DPP v Smith* (1961); *Saunders* (1985)).[1]

To establish liability under s 18, the more serious offence, the prosecution would have to prove that Robin intended to cause serious harm. Recklessness will not suffice (*Belfon* (1976)).

If it was Robin's aim or purpose to cause serious harm, then he intended grievous bodily harm. In addition, even if Robin did not desire to cause serious harm, the intention is established if he knew that serious harm was a virtually certain result of his actions (*Bryson* (1985); *Purcell* (1986)).[2]

If intention cannot be proved, then liability under s 20 should be considered.

The *mens rea* requirement for the offence under s 20 is (advertent) recklessness with respect to some harm. This means that it must be proved that Robin was aware when he threw the ashtray that Jeremy might suffer some harm, albeit not serious harm (*Savage*; *Parmenter* (1991)).

The maximum penalty for the offence under s 20 is a term of imprisonment not exceeding five years and, under s 18, life imprisonment.

Now, it would appear that, had he acted in response to Jeremy's intended attack upon him, Robin would have been able to avail himself of the defence of self-defence. Robin, however, was not aware of the facts which would have justified his conduct and, thus, it is necessary to consider whether a defence is available where the defendant is unaware of the facts which form the basis of that defence.

In the 19th century case of *Dadson* (1850), the defendant was a constable whose duty was to guard a copse from which wood had been stolen. P emerged from the copse carrying stolen wood. Dadson shouted at him to stop. P refused to do so and started to run away. Dadson shot him in the leg.

Dadson was convicted of unlawful wounding with intent to cause grievous bodily harm. It was not unlawful to wound an escaping felon, but stealing wood was not in itself a felony, unless the thief had at least two previous convictions. In fact, P had numerous previous convictions for theft. Dadson, however, did not know of the circumstances making P a felon and it was held that, as a consequence, he could not take advantage of the defence.

The decision has been criticised. Professor Williams, for example, argues that Dadson did not *unlawfully* wound P. In his view, the element of unlawfulness which appears in the definition of most offences against the person is a component of the *actus reus* and, therefore, the lawfulness or otherwise of the defendant's behaviour may be assessed without reference to the defendant's beliefs or knowledge. Thus, he argues, if a person assaults or wounds or, indeed, kills another in unknown circumstances of justification, the assault or wounding or killing is lawful.[3]

Professor Smith, on the other hand, maintains that the word 'unlawfully' in the definition of a crime means simply 'in the absence of a recognised defence', but does not imply anything about the requirements of any particular defence. It is a matter of policy whether any given defence requires knowledge of the relevant circumstances. In *Dadson*, the court came to the 'perfectly reasonable conclusion', according to Professor Smith, that the particular defence in that case should not be available unless the defendant was aware of the circumstances justifying his actions.[4]

Should self-defence be subject to the *Dadson* principle?

Professor Smith clearly believes that it should be and has argued that the existing law as expressed in *Williams* (1983) and *Beckford* (1988) supports this conclusion.

Those cases dealt with the situation where D mistakenly believed that he was justified in using force and, therefore, they were not directly concerned with the matter currently under discussion. However, in both cases, the court expressed the opinion that a person may use such defensive force as is reasonable in the circumstances *as he believes them to be*. It would appear to follow that, if the defendant does not believe it is necessary to use defensive force – if he does not intend to defend himself – then the defence is not available to him. If this analysis is correct, Robin would not be able to take advantage of self-defence.

Professor Williams disagrees with such a conclusion. He draws a distinction between 'justifications' and 'excuses'. There is an element of approval or indeed encouragement in the case of the former. For example, a person who uses force to prevent crime is justified in what he does. An 'excuse', on the other hand, whilst an acknowledgment that the defendant does not deserve to be punished, does not exist to promote the conduct in question. Duress, for example, excuses. It does not justify.[5]

In Professor Williams' view, as justifications are concerned with the promotion of particular consequences, they should be available, even if the defendant is unaware of the justifying circumstances.

Self-defence is a justification. Thus, if Professor Williams' analysis is correct and, provided that the force used was, in the circumstances, reasonable, Robin will escape liability for the injuries inflicted on Jeremy.[6]

However, even if self-defence is available in this case, Robin might be guilty of an attempt to cause grievous bodily harm contrary to s 1(1) of the Criminal Attempts Act 1981. This is because s 1(2) of the Act provides that a person can be convicted of an attempt to commit an offence even though the facts are such that the offence is impossible to commit. This is reinforced by s 1(3) which provides that the question whether the defendant has the necessary intent for an attempt is to be answered by reference to the facts as he believed them to be (see *Shivpuri* (1987)).

For attempt, the prosecution must prove an intention on the part of the accused as to the consequence defined in the *actus reus*. Thus, for an attempt to commit the offence under s 18, it must be proved that the defendant intended grievous bodily harm (*Millard and Vernon* (1987)). Intention in this context bears the same meaning as discussed above (*Walker and Hayles* (1990)) (but see note 2).

If Robin intended to cause harm but not serious harm, then he may be convicted of an attempt to commit the offence under s 47 of the Offences Against the Person Act 1861.

Professor Smith argues that Professor Williams' analysis leads to an absurd conclusion, that is, that the defendant was justified in causing grievous bodily harm, but may be convicted of an attempt unlawfully to cause grievous bodily harm![7]

It is submitted that Professor Smith's analysis is preferable to that of Professor Williams and that, as it is sound in principle to limit defences justifying or excusing the use of force to those occasions where the defendant is aware of the justifying or excusing circumstances, the defence of self-defence ought not to be available to Robin.

Jeremy's liability

Jeremy may be convicted of an attempt to cause grievous bodily harm contrary to s 1(1) of the Criminal Attempts Act 1981.[8]

The facts of the problem indicate that he had the requisite intent. Thus, the only issue is whether he has done 'an act which is more than merely preparatory' to the commission of the offence (s 1(1)).

Provided there is sufficient evidence of acts capable in law of amounting to an attempt, the question whether those acts are more than mere preparation is a question to be left to the jury (s 4(3)).

It is submitted that, in this case, there is clear evidence of an attempt. In *Jones* (1990), the defendant jumped into P's car and pointed a loaded sawn off shotgun at his face. P managed to grab hold off the gun and throw it out of the window. Although the safety catch of the gun was on, and D had to put his finger on the trigger and pull it, the Court of Appeal upheld his conviction for attempted murder.

Burglary

Jeremy may be guilty of an offence contrary to s 9(1)(a) of the Theft Act 1968.

This provides that a person is guilty of burglary if he enters a building, or part of a building, as a trespasser, intending to commit therein one of a number of offences including the infliction of grievous bodily harm (s 9(2)).

A person enters as a trespasser if he enters without the occupier's consent.

The facts of the problem do not state whether Jeremy had permission to enter Robin's office. However, even if he did, presumably the permission granted, expressly or impliedly, was limited to particular (lawful) purposes. As Jeremy entered the office intending to cause grievous bodily harm, he entered in excess of that permission and thus entered as a trespasser (*Jones and Smith* (1976)) and, consequently, since he was aware of the facts that made his entry trespassory, he may be convicted of burglary (*Collins* (1973)).

He also committed burglary contrary to s 9(1)(b). This section provides that a person is guilty if, having entered a building or part of a building as a trespasser, he attempts to inflict grievous bodily harm on any person therein.

For this form of burglary, the prosecution have to prove, in addition to the elements of attempt (discussed above), that D entered as a trespasser (as above) and that, at the time of the attempt, he knew of, or at least was reckless with respect to, the facts that made his entry trespassory (*Collins*).

As he intended to cause grievous bodily harm when he entered the office, the above criteria are satisfied.

Jeremy may be convicted and sentenced to a term of imprisonment not exceeding 14 years for each offence of burglary.

Possession of an offensive weapon

Section 1 of the Prevention of Crime Act 1953 provides that any person who has with him in a public place any offensive weapon is guilty of an offence punishable with up to two years' imprisonment. 'Offensive weapon' is defined to include things intended to cause injury and thus the water pistol would qualify (s 1(4), as amended by s 40(2) and Sched 2 of the Public Order Act 1986).

The only unclear issue is whether Jeremy had the offensive weapon with him *in a public place*.

By s 1(4), this includes any highway and any premises to which the public have access.

The facts do not state whether or not the public have access to this workplace but, even if it is not a public place, the jury are entitled to draw the inference, if the evidence permits, that Jeremy brought the ammonia filled water pistol to work and that he necessarily had it with him on the public highway (*Mehmed* (1963)).

Notes

1 The Code for Crown Prosecutors, *Offences Against the Person,* June 1994, para 2.15, advises prosecutors to treat any injury 'resulting in permanent disability or permanent loss of sensory function' as grievous bodily harm.

2 In *Woollin* (1998), the House of Lords held that, for the purposes of murder, a consequence foreseen as virtually certain is intended. Whether the same approach will be adopted in respect of other crimes is not yet clear.

3 Williams, G, *Criminal Law: the General Part,* 1961, p 22.

4 Smith, JC, *Justification and Excuse in the Criminal Law,* 1989, p 31.

5 Williams, G, *Criminal Law: the General Part,* 1961, p 25.

6 The question whether the force used was, in the circumstances reasonable, is a matter for the jury (*Attorney General for Northern Ireland's Reference (No 1 of 1975)* (1977)).

7 Smith, JC, *Justification and Excuse in the Criminal Law,* 1989, p 43.

8 The Code for Crown Prosecutors (see note 1) additionally advises prosecutors to treat 'permanent, visible disfigurement' as grievous bodily harm.

Question 26

Bodie and Doyle, two armed plain clothes policemen, saw someone they believed to be Budgie, a dangerous escaped criminal, driving through the town. In fact, the occupant of the car was Hilton, who bore a remarkable resemblance to Budgie.

Bodie and Doyle stopped the car. As they knew Budgie was a very ruthless man, and that he was often armed, Bodie and Doyle approached the car with their guns drawn.

Hilton made to get his driver's licence from the glove compartment. Doyle, mistakenly believing that he might be reaching for a weapon, fired at the car. He aimed to miss the driver, but hoped to frighten him.

The bullet smashed the windscreen and struck Hilton's arm.

Hilton, fearing for his life, drove the car at Bodie and Doyle. The car struck Doyle who was seriously injured. It then collided with a lamp-post. Hilton was slightly injured.

Bodie ran to the car and pulled Hilton out. Hilton, fearing attack, punched Bodie. Bodie, still believing him to be Budgie, hit Hilton over the head with his gun, intending to incapacitate him. Hilton suffered serious injuries.

Discuss the liability of the parties.

Would your answer differ had Hilton been aware that he resembled Budgie and had realised, as he drove at them, that Bodie and Doyle were plain clothes policemen who had mistakenly thought him to be the dangerous criminal?

Answer plan

A fairly complex question involving issues relating to the lawful use of defensive force. A wide variety of offences under the Offences Against the Person Act 1861 provides the context for the defence. The bases of liability for these offences must be discussed before tackling the defence issues.

The principal issues are:

- ss 47, 20, 18 and 38 of the Offences Against the Person Act 1861; s 89 of the Police Act 1996;
- force used in self-defence and in effecting a lawful arrest;
- the effect of a mistake upon the defences;
- force used against an attack known in the circumstances to be lawful.

Answer

Bodie and Doyle

It is proposed to consider the liability of Bodie and Doyle for a number of aggravated assaults and then to examine whether they are entitled to take advantage of any defences.

By virtue of s 47 of the Offences Against the Person Act 1861, it is an offence to 'assault another occasioning actual bodily harm'.

The *actus reus* of common assault consists of unlawfully causing another to apprehend the application of immediate and unlawful force. The *mens rea* requirement is intention or recklessness (subjectively defined) with respect to the elements of the *actus reus* (*Venna* (1976); *Spratt* (1991)).

In addition to the requirement of a common assault, as defined above, it must be shown for the s 47 offence that the victim suffered actual bodily harm as a result of the assault. Any harm or injury which interferes with the health or comfort of the victim is 'actual bodily harm' (*Miller* (1954); *Chan-Fook* (1994); *Burstow; Ireland* (1997)). There is, however, no requirement that the defendant intended, or was reckless as to, the occasioning of actual bodily harm. The *mens rea* for this offence is the same as for common assault (*Savage; Parmenter* (1991), confirming *Roberts* (1971) and overruling *Spratt* on this point).

It is clear from the facts of the problem that Bodie and Doyle intentionally caused Hilton to apprehend the application of force (although they thought he was Budgie, the offence requires only that '*any person*' is intentionally or recklessly put in fear, etc).

The question whether bodily harm was occasioned by the assault is one for the jury. In *Williams* (1992), the Court of Appeal stated that, where V takes evasive action to escape a threat, the chain of causation between the assault and the harm is not broken if the reaction of the victim was within the range of responses which one might reasonably expect from a person in his situation. In applying the test, the jury should bear in mind that the victim, in the agony of the moment, might act without proper reflection.

With respect to the bullet injury sustained by Hilton, if the continuity of the whole skin was broken, that is, if the injury amounted to a 'wound', then Doyle may be charged with the offence under s 20 of the 1861 Act (*Moriarty and Brookes* (1834)).[1]

For this offence it must be shown that the defendant was 'malicious'; that is, that he was at least reckless with respect to some harm resulting. In this context, recklessness bears a subjective meaning. Thus, the prosecution would be required to prove that, although aiming to miss, Doyle foresaw a risk that some harm might result (*Savage*; *Parmenter* (1991)).

(If the injury does not amount to a 'wound', then Doyle may be charged with the s 47 offence (above), in respect of any actual bodily harm caused.)

However, for assault, there is no liability unless the defendant intentionally caused the other to apprehend *unlawful* force and, in the case of s 20, a person is only liable if he '*unlawfully* and maliciously ... wounds ...'. Similarly, although Bodie intentionally caused Hilton grievous bodily harm, his liability for the offence under s 18 of the 1861 Act will depend upon whether there was an intentional use of *unlawful* force.[2]

By virtue of s 24 of the Police and Criminal Evidence Act 1984, a police constable may arrest without warrant anyone whom he, with reasonable cause, suspects to have committed, be in the act of committing or be about to commit an arrestable offence. And, by virtue of s 3 of the Criminal Law Act 1967, 'a person may use such force as is reasonable in the circumstances in the prevention of crime, or in effecting the lawful arrest of offenders or suspected offenders or of persons unlawfully at large'. Similarly, the common law defence of 'private defence' allows the use of reasonable force in defence of one's person or that of another.

Whether the force used was reasonable is essentially an objective question, but if, as in this case, the defendant mistakenly believed that the circumstances were such as required the use of force to effect arrest, or to defend against in attack – present or imminent – the jury must decide whether the force used was reasonable by reference to the circumstances as the defendant believed them to be (*Williams* (1983); *Beckford* (1988); *Owino* (1996)).[3]

If the jury believed that, in the heat of the moment, Doyle and Bodie did what they honestly believed to be necessary, then that would be 'potent evidence' (but no more than that) that the force used was reasonable (*Palmer* (1971); *Attorney General for Northern Ireland's Reference (No 1 of 1975)* (1977)). In addition, although there is no duty to retreat, a failure to do so is a factor that might be taken into account when assessing the reasonableness of the defendant's actions.[4]

Hilton

There are a number of offences with which Hilton may be charged:

(a) assault with intent to resist arrest contrary to s 38 of the 1861 Act;

(b) assault on a police constable in the execution of his duty contrary to s 89 of the Police Act 1996;

(c) the offence under s 18 of the 1861 Act in respect of the 'serious injuries' caused to Doyle.

(It shall be assumed that the attempted arrest was lawful, that is, that Bodie and Doyle had reasonable grounds for suspicion.)

As far as s 38 is concerned, it must be shown that there was an intent to resist arrest and, as Hilton did not know they were police officers (nor, presumably, did he believe that they were individuals making a citizen's arrest!), he should, on that basis alone, be acquitted (see *Brightling* (1991)).

A police officer making a lawful arrest is acting in the execution of his duty for the purposes of s 89 (*Waterfield* (1964)). According to *Forbes and Webb* (1865), the only *mens rea* required for this offence is that required for a common assault. As explained above, however, a defendant may rely upon a mistaken belief in circumstances which, if true, would render the use of force lawful (*Gladstone Williams*). This 'defence' applies to all offences and thus, provided the use of force was reasonable, Hilton should, despite his mistake, be acquitted of all three offences.

Alternative facts

Although Hilton knew that the men were police officers who suspected he was a dangerous criminal, he may have mistakenly believed that the arrest was unlawful. This mistake, however, being a mistake of *law*, would not excuse him (*Bentley* (1850); *Lee* (2000); *Hewitt v DPP* (2002)).[5]

Is he entitled, however, to take advantage of self-defence even though he knows the officers are acting in circumstances that make their use of force lawful? May one use force lawfully against a *lawful* attack?

(Clearly, Hilton cannot rely on s 3 of the Criminal Law Act 1967 – force used 'in the prevention of crime' – if he knows that Bodie and Doyle are acting lawfully.)

In *Browne* (1973), the Court of Appeal in Northern Ireland stated, *obiter*, that when an officer is using lawful force in effecting the arrest of a suspect, self-defence against him is not lawful. It was said that this was the case, even if, as in the present problem, according to the true facts, the police were acting unjustifiably.

In *Fennell* (1971), on the other hand, Lord Widgery implied that where a person honestly believes that he, or another person, is in imminent danger of injury from an arresting officer, he may use reasonable force in defence. This statement was *obiter*. It is also ambiguous – it is not clear whether it was meant to apply to the situation where the defendant, as in Hilton's case, knows of the circumstances making the police officer's behaviour lawful.

Professor Smith argues that the wide *dicta* in *Browne* should not be followed. He points out that, although an innocent person must submit to arrest, it is unreasonable to expect him to do nothing in the face of a serious attack. Thus, he suggests that an otherwise innocent person should not be convicted of an offence for taking reasonable defensive action, even though he knows that the police officer he assaults or injures has reasonable grounds for suspicion and is, therefore, acting lawfully.[6]

It is submitted that this view is preferable to that expressed in *Browne* and that Hilton should be acquitted if the force used was, in all the circumstances, reasonable.

Notes

1   The Code for Crown Prosecutors, *Offences Against the Person*, June 1994, para 2.14, advises that:

> ... s 20 should be reserved for those wounds considered to be serious [equivalent to the offence with the infliction of grievous, or serious, bodily harm under the other part of the section]. Although legally a wound, a minor cut or laceration will more appropriately be charged under s 47.

2   In *Finch and Jardine* (1983), the trial judge agreed with the submission of the prosecution that force that is reasonable in self-defence may be excessive if done in order to effect an arrest. Thus, Bodie and Doyle might be advised to rely on self-defence.

3   Force may be used, as in this case, to ward off an attack which the defendant anticipated. Again, if the defendant mistakenly believed he was in imminent danger, the mistake need not be a reasonable one (*Beckford*).

4   It is generally accepted, however, that police officers attempting to effect an arrest may advance, using such defensive measures as are reasonable, as they do so (*McInnes* (1971); *Finch and Jardine* (1983)).

In *Finch and Jardine*, the trial judge agreed with the submission of the prosecution that force that is reasonable in self-defence may be excessive if done in order to effect an arrest.

5   In *Lee*, it was said that a mistaken belief that the victim was not a police officer might afford a defence in relation to assault with intent to resist arrest or assaulting an officer in the execution of his duty; in *McKoy*, it was held that the trial judge had erred when instructing the jury that a defendant who mistakenly believed he was being arrested was not entitled to use force to free himself.

6   Smith, JC, *Justification and Excuse in the Criminal Law*, 1989, p 26.

CHAPTER 4

MODES OF PARTICIPATION, INCHOATE OFFENCES AND VICARIOUS LIABILITY

Introduction

In this chapter will be found questions where the principal issues relate to one or more of the following topics: accessorial liability; attempts; conspiracy; incitement; and vicarious liability. (These topics also arise as subsidiary matters in a number of other questions.)

Checklist

The following issues are covered in this chapter:

- modes of participation: liability as an accomplice; s 8 of the Accessories and Abettors Act 1861; aiding, abetting, counselling, procuring; joint unlawful enterprises; the *mens rea* requirement of accessorial liability; the offence of aiding and abetting a suicide contrary to s 2 of the Suicide Act 1961;

- attempts: the Criminal Attempts Act 1981; the rationale for the punishment of attempts; the *actus reus* of attempt – an act more than merely preparatory to the commission of the full offence; the *mens rea* for attempts; attempting the impossible;

- conspiracy: statutory conspiracy – the Criminal Law Act 1977; the *mens rea* for conspiracy; exemptions from liability for conspiracy; common law conspiracy to defraud; conspiring to do the impossible;

- incitement: the ingredients of liability;

- vicarious liability: the 'delegation' principle and the principle of 'extensive construction'; corporate liability; the liability of unincorporated associations.

Question 27

Why do we punish attempts? Should they be punished as severely as the full offence?

Answer plan

A straightforward question concerning the policy underlying the punishment of attempts.

The principal issues are:

- the distinction between 'complete' and 'incomplete' attempts;
- the justification for the punishment of attempts – 'utilitarian' and 'desert' theories;
- arguments for and against the equal punishment of attempts and the full offence.

Answer

By virtue of s 1(1) of the Criminal Attempts Act 1981, a person is guilty of an attempt if, with intent to commit an offence triable on indictment, he does an act which is more than merely preparatory to the commission of that offence. The maximum penalty for an attempt is generally the same as for the complete offence (s 4(5) of the 1981 Act). However, normally, a person convicted of attempt receives a lesser sentence than he would have had he been successful. A 'discount' of 50% is not uncommon.

The question whether an act is more than merely preparatory is a question of fact for the jury and not a question of law for the judge (s 4(3)). If, however, there is insufficient evidence or it would be unsafe to leave the evidence to the jury, the judge can rule that there was no attempt and direct a verdict of not guilty (*Campbell* (1991)). In *Gullefer* (1987), it was held that, if there is evidence on which a jury could reasonably arrive at the conclusion that the defendant had gone beyond preparation by having 'embarked on the crime proper', then it is for the jury to decide whether the defendant did, in fact, go beyond mere preparation. Lord Lane added that there may be evidence of an attempt, even though the defendant had not performed the last act prior to the commission of the substantive offence (see also *Jones* (1990); *Geddes* (1996)).

As far as the *mens rea* requirement for an attempt is concerned, the prosecution must prove that the accused intended the result defined in the *actus reus* of the full offence (s 1(1) of the 1981 Act; *Pearman* (1985); *Walker and Hayles* (1990)). It would appear, however, that, if recklessness as to circumstances in the *actus reus* will suffice for the full offence, it will also be sufficient for an attempt (*Khan* (1990); *Attorney General's Reference (No 3 of 1992)* (1994)).

Before discussing the justifications for the punishment of attempts, a distinction must be drawn between two types of attempt, both of which attract criminal liability.

First, there are those attempts where the person has done all that he believes is necessary to achieve the intended object but fails for some reason. These may be termed 'complete attempts'. An 'incomplete attempt', on the other hand, occurs where, although he has done an act that is more than merely preparatory, the defendant has not yet taken the step which would amount to the commission of the full offence.

Complete attempts

An example of a complete attempt is where the defendant has detonated a bomb, intending to kill, but the bomb fails to explode. In such a case, the defendant has engaged in conduct with a manifestly blameworthy intent. Clarkson and Keating point out that such a person is as much in need of rehabilitation or restraint or deterrence as if he had been successful. There is a danger that, if unpunished, he might try to commit the offence again (and, perhaps, with some success the next time).[1]

From a utilitarian standpoint, the punishment of an attempt is justified in terms of general deterrence just as it is where the full offence is committed. Others who might be more successful should be discouraged from attempting to commit the crime.

Should the person who is guilty of a 'complete' attempt be punished to the same extent as he would had he been successful, or does the fact that no 'harm' was caused justify a lower penalty?

Clarkson and Keating argue that the fact that the specific harm intended has not occurred does not mean that no harm at all has been caused by the behaviour of the defendant. The 'complete attempt' is a threat to the general security of the members of society and to that extent is harmful. Brady claims, however, that the social consequences of criminal activity which results in specific harm are qualitatively different from the situation where no specific harm results (even if by accident) and that no theory of 'equal harm' could justify the equal treatment of attempts and consummated crimes.[2] He suggests that the equal treatment of the failed attempt and the completed offence may, however, be justified on the basis that a person who attempts to cause harm but fails is as *culpable* as the person who succeeds. According to this 'subjectivist' view, the influence of morally neutral chance elements is minimised. The failed attempt 'deserves' the same degree of punishment as the complete offence.[3]

Indeed, as the *mens rea* for attempts is based upon an intention to commit the *actus reus*, it is arguable that, in some cases, the degree of culpability of the attempter is greater than that of the person who commits the full offence. For example, whereas a person may be guilty of murder 'merely' on proof of an intention to cause grievous bodily harm, attempted murder requires proof of an intention to kill (*Cunningham* (1982); *Whybrow* (1951)).

Professor Williams, on the other hand, cautions that the equal treatment of attempts and consummated crimes might result in the law losing public support. He argues that, from the crudely retributive perspective adopted by much of the general public, according to which punishment should relate to the harm done, the equal treatment of attempts and consummated crimes might appear harsh.[4]

There may be additional 'emotional' reasons justifying a lesser punishment for attempts. Professor Hart, for example, argues that a greater punishment is necessary to deprive the successful offender of the 'illicit satisfactions' and gratification that follows success. And, he argues, the retributive 'instinct' of the victim is stronger and the demand for revenge is greater where harm has actually been caused than in cases where the intended victim has escaped harm.[5]

Incomplete attempts

An example of an 'incomplete' attempt is where the defendant has planted a bomb and is apprehended as he is about to detonate it.

The requirement of acts that are more than 'merely preparatory' should ensure that attempts of this sort are not simply 'thought crimes'. The law insists upon some conduct because an individual who has taken steps to achieve the prohibited result has manifest a 'firm resolve' and may be regarded as more disposed to criminal activity than one who merely expresses an intention to commit a crime without acting on that intent.[6] In addition, there is a greater degree of psychological commitment to completing the crime concerned as one approaches its actual commission. The person who sets out to commit an offence becomes progressively less likely to change his mind the more steps that he takes.

Many of the arguments in favour of punishing complete attempts apply, with equal force, to this type of attempt. In addition, the criminalisation of the incomplete attempt enables and justifies law enforcement officials to intervene before any real harm has been caused.

Does the person who makes an 'incomplete attempt' deserve equal punishment to the person who consummates the crime?

Arguments in favour of relative leniency may be advanced in the case of incomplete attempts that do not apply to completed attempts. As it is conceivable that the interrupted attempter might have changed his mind and not gone through with his intentions to the point of consummation, his 'moral blameworthiness' may be less than that of either the complete attempter or the person who commits the full offence. As liability for an attempt attaches before the commission of the last act, there must always be some doubt that the accused had the necessary firm resolve. In addition, the less severe punishment of incomplete attempts may provide some incentive to stop at the last moment.[7]

In conclusion, therefore, it may be said that although the punishment of attempts is justified, there are utilitarian arguments in favour of relative leniency, especially in the case of 'incomplete' attempts.

Notes

1   Clarkson, CMV and Keating, HM, *Criminal Law: Text and Materials,* 4th edn, 1998, pp 464–76.

2   Brady, J, 'Punishing attempts' (1980) 63 Monist 264.

3   Ashworth, A, *Principles of Criminal Liability,* 1991, p 399.

     And note s 1(2) of the 1981 Act: a person may be guilty of attempting to commit an offence even though the facts are such that the offence is *impossible*. Does the degree of incompetence of the individual who sets out to achieve an event which fails through impossibility justify a lesser punishment than that given to the successful offender or the chance failure? Does the person who attempts to kill by poisoning, but who uses a substance which he does not realise is innocuous, present the same danger as the person who administers a poisonous substance but fails in his attempt to kill due to the intervention of a doctor?

4   Williams, G, *Textbook of Criminal Law,* 2nd edn, 1983, p 405.

5   Hart, HLA, *Punishment and Responsibility,* 1968, p 1314.

6   Morris, N, 'Punishment for thoughts', in Summers, RS (ed), *Essays in Legal Philosophy,* 1968.

7   If a person gives up after having done an act that is more than merely preparatory, then, although this does not affect his liability, it may affect the level of punishment that the court imposes (*Taylor* (1859)).

Question 28

Part (a)

Although Paula did not consent, Cliff, who was drunk, tried unsuccessfully to have sexual intercourse with her.

Part (b)

Anson had sexual intercourse with Hilda. He was not sure whether or not she had consented. In fact, she had consented.

Part (c)

Sam and Dave agreed to sell a necklace left to them by their grandmother. They agreed to advertise the necklace as being made of pure gold. In fact, as Sam knew, it was gold plated. Dave suspects that it was not pure gold but is not sure.

Consider the criminal liability of Cliff, Anson, Sam and Dave.

Answer plan

The three parts of this question involve issues of attempt and conspiracy. There is a lack of authority regarding some of the issues.

The principal issues are:

- 'reckless' attempts and intoxication;
- 'reckless' attempts and impossibility – s 1(3) of the Criminal Attempts Act 1981;
- 'recklessness' and statutory conspiracy – s 1(2) of the Criminal Law Act 1977;
- 'recklessness' and common law conspiracy to defraud.

Answer

Part (a): attempted rape

Cliff may be convicted of attempted rape contrary to s 1(1) of the Criminal Attempts Act 1981. This provides that if, with intent to commit an offence, a person does an act which is more than merely preparatory to the commission of the offence, he is guilty of attempting to commit the offence.

By s 1 of the Sexual Offences Act 1956, as substituted by s 142 of the Criminal Justice and Public Order Act 1994, a man commits the *actus reus* of rape if he has unlawful sexual intercourse with a man or woman who at the time of the intercourse does not consent to it.

Section 4(3) of the 1981 Act provides that, where there is evidence that the defendant had done something that was more than 'merely preparatory', the question whether it does or does not amount to an attempt is to be left to the jury (*Jones* (1990)). We are not told exactly what Cliff did, but it shall be assumed that his acts were more than 'merely preparatory'.

As far as the *mens rea* of attempt is concerned, the prosecution must prove that the acts of the defendant were intentional, that is, he was not an automaton and, as far as so called result crimes are concerned, it must be proved that the defendant intended the appropriate result even if proof of recklessness will suffice for the full offence (*Pearman* (1985)).

However, where recklessness as to *circumstances* will suffice for the full offence, it would appear from the decision of the Court of Appeal, in *Khan* (1990) that recklessness as to those circumstances will suffice for an attempt to commit the offence. As rape may be committed where the man is reckless with respect to the lack of the woman's consent, so may attempted rape.[1] The Court of Appeal explained that the attempt related to the physical activity and, thus, the intent that had to be proved was an intention to have sexual intercourse with a woman, the defendant either being aware that she was not consenting or being reckless with respect to that fact.

For the complete offence of rape, recklessness bears a 'subjective' meaning. The same, presumably, is true for attempted rape, that is, the prosecution must prove that the defendant was aware there was a possibility that the woman was not consenting (*Satnam and Kewal S* (1983); *Breckenridge* (1984)).

The facts of the problem state that Cliff was drunk. It is not clear, however, whether he was so drunk that he lacked the *mens rea* for an attempt. If, despite his intoxicated state, he had the *mens rea*, as defined above, then, of course, he is guilty of attempted rape. What is the position if, due to his drunkenness, he lacked the *mens rea* for attempted rape?

The House of Lords in *DPP v Majewski* (1977) held that self-induced intoxication negativing *mens rea* is a defence to a crime requiring a 'specific intent', but not to a crime of 'basic intent'.

Although the authorities are not consistent, it is submitted that a crime of basic intent is one for which recklessness is enough to constitute the necessary *mens rea* (*DPP v Majewski*, *per* Lords Elwyn-Jones, Edmund Davies and Russell).

Rape is a crime of basic intent (*Woods* (1982)). What, then, of attempted rape?

There are authorities which suggest that attempts to commit an offence are crimes of specific intent (see, for example, *Majewski*; *Mohan* (1976)). However, the Court of Appeal decided in *Khan* that the *mens rea* for attempted rape is no different from that for rape – that is, recklessness with respect to the woman's consent – and thus, logically, attempted rape must also be a crime of basic intent.[2]

If convicted of attempted rape, Cliff will face a maximum penalty of life imprisonment (s 4(1) of the Criminal Attempts Act 1981).

Part (b): attempted rape

Clearly, Anson cannot be convicted of rape. Although he had the *mens rea*, he did not commit the *actus reus* of rape, that is, he did not have sexual intercourse with a woman without her consent.

Can he be convicted of attempted rape?

He was reckless with respect to Hilda's consent and, as the discussion to Part (a) points out, there can be liability for attempted rape where the defendant is reckless (*Khan*).

Furthermore, according to s 1(2) of the Criminal Attempts Act 1981, a person may be guilty of attempt even though the facts are such that the commission of the offence is impossible. Thus, it is submitted that Anson may be convicted of attempted rape although he was merely reckless and the commission of rape was, in the circumstances, impossible.

Professors Smith and Hogan have argued that such a conclusion is neither desirable nor inevitable. They suggest that s 1(3) requires us to assess the defendant's liability by reference to the facts 'as he believed them to be'. The reckless defendant does not believe that the woman is not consenting; he merely believes she *might* not be consenting. Thus, they conclude that the rules relating to impossibility do not apply to the reckless defendant.[3]

With respect, it is submitted that their argument is fallacious. Section 1(3) only applies where, otherwise, a person's intention would not be regarded as having amounted to an intent to commit an offence. Anson's intention in this case is to have sexual intercourse with a woman who, as far as he is concerned, may not be consenting. That is sufficient *mens rea* for rape and attempted rape and thus there is no need to rely upon s 1(3).[4]

Part (c): statutory conspiracy

The offence of statutory conspiracy is defined in s 1 of the Criminal Law Act 1977, as amended by s 5 of the Criminal Attempts Act 1981. It provides that a person is guilty of conspiracy if he agrees with any person or persons to pursue a course of conduct which, if carried out as intended, will necessarily amount to the commission of an offence by one or more of the parties to the agreement.

In this case, it is proposed to consider Sam and Dave's liability for conspiracy to obtain property by deception.

It is an offence contrary to s 15(1) of the Theft Act 1968 to dishonestly obtain property belonging to another intending to permanently deprive the other of it. By virtue of s 15(4), a deception may be made 'deliberately or recklessly'. Thus, had they continued with the representation and induced someone to buy the necklace on the strength of it, both would have been guilty of the s 15 offence.

However, D cannot be guilty of a statutory conspiracy to commit an offence where he is merely reckless as to a relevant circumstance. This is the effect of s 1(2) of the 1977 Act. The sub-section provides that, even when the full offence does not require knowledge of a circumstance, conspiracy requires that the defendant and at least one other party to the agreement know that any relevant circumstance will exist when the conduct constituting the offence is to take place.

Thus, clearly, Dave cannot be convicted of conspiracy. Neither can Sam, despite the fact that he *knows* that the necklace is not made of solid gold. There is no conspiracy.

Common law conspiracy to defraud

In *Scott v Metropolitan Police Commissioner* (1975), the House of Lords stated that an agreement by two or more by dishonesty to deprive a person of something which is his constitutes a conspiracy to defraud.

Dishonesty is an issue to be determined in accordance with the *Ghosh* (1982) test. That is, if what the accused did was in accordance with the ordinary standards of reasonable people or he mistakenly believed that it was, then he is not dishonest.

The law is not clear, however, as to whether a reckless deception will suffice for common law conspiracy to defraud. In *Wai Yu-Tsang* (1991), the House of Lords, whilst stating that they did not wish to become enmeshed in a distinction between intention and recklessness said, *obiter*, that it is enough that the conspirators have dishonestly agreed to bring about a state of affairs which they realise will *or may* result in the victim being deceived.

Furthermore, as recklessness sufficed for attempt at common law, it would be remarkable were it not sufficient for common law conspiracy (see *Pigg* (1982)).

The maximum punishment for a common law conspiracy to defraud is a term of imprisonment not exceeding 10 years (s 12 of the Criminal Justice Act 1987).

Notes

1   See also *Attorney General's Reference (No 3 of 1992)* (1994).

2   It would seem from the speeches of Lord Elwyn-Jones and Lord Simon in *Majewski* that the rule regarding self-induced intoxication is a rule of substantive law which relieves the prosecution from the burden of proving *mens rea*, where the accused, as a result of voluntary intoxication, lacked a basic intent. The Court of Appeal in *Woods*, however, took a different approach as far as the offence of rape is concerned. Section 1(2) of the Sexual Offences (Amendment) Act 1976 provides that where the jury are required to consider whether the defendant had the necessary *mens rea*, they should have regard to the reasonableness of the defendant's belief and 'any other relevant matters'. The court held that self-induced intoxication was not a legally relevant matter and should be ignored by the jury, but that they should consider all the other relevant evidence before deciding whether the defendant had the necessary *mens rea*. Where a defendant introduces evidence that he was so intoxicated that he lacked the *mens rea* for rape, the jury should be directed to consider whether he was reckless *disregarding the evidence that he was drunk*.

If this approach were followed in the present case, the jury would, in effect, be directed to consider whether Cliff would have had the *mens rea* if he had not been drunk! (See also note 6 to Question 24, p 131.)

3   Smith, JC and Hogan, B, *Criminal Law*, 7th edn, 1992, p 323.

4   As Professors Smith and Hogan acknowledge elsewhere, sub-s (3) 'does nothing'. It simply spells out what is obvious from sub-ss (1) and (2), that is, that liability for attempts depends upon the intent of the defendant even if founded upon some mistake or misunderstanding.

Question 29

Part (a)

Criminal law regards a person as responsible for his own crimes only ... *Qui peccat per alium peccat per se* is not a maxim of criminal law [*per* Lord Diplock in *Tesco v Nattrass* (1972)].

What are the exceptions to this 'rule'?

Part (b)

Matthew sold Chump a gun and ammunition. Although nothing was said, Matthew thought that Chump intended to use it to shoot his neighbour, Funny. Matthew was aware that Chump and Funny had had a series of disputes. In fact, Chump had bought the gun as he intended to kill himself. His girlfriend, Chagrin, had left him. He returned home, put the gun to his head, and pulled the trigger. The gun jammed. He decided to hang himself.

He tied a rope to the ceiling and stood on a chair. Just as he was about to jump, Funny peered through the window. He smiled to himself when he realised that Chump was about to commit suicide. Chump, who had not seen Funny, jumped from the chair. The rope broke. Funny was disappointed. Later that evening he gave Chump a leaflet, published by an organisation called JUMP (an unincorporated association), which explained tried and tested methods of suicide. He hoped that this would strengthen Chump's resolve to kill himself. Chump, however, was no longer interested in committing suicide. Chagrin had realised that Chump was the most lovable man in the world and had decided to marry him.

Discuss the liability of Matthew, Funny and JUMP.

Answer plan

The first part of this question concerns the exceptions to the general rule of English law that one person is not liable for the criminal acts of another. These exceptions define vicarious liability and the liability of corporations. The second part relates to the offence of aiding and abetting a suicide contrary to s 2 of the Suicide Act 1961. It also raises the issue of criminal liability of an unincorporated association.

The principal issues are:

- vicarious liability;
- the delegation principle;
- the 'extensive construction' principle;
- liability of corporations;
- aiding and abetting a suicide;
- attempting to aid and abet (s 1(4)(b) of the Criminal Attempts Act 1981);
- criminal liability of an unincorporated association.

Answer

Part (a): vicarious liability

The general rule in criminal law that a person is not liable for the unauthorised acts of another is subject to two major exceptions. The first is the 'delegation principle'. This applies where a statutory offence imposes liability on a person occupying a particular position, for example, the owner or licensee of premises, who has delegated the management of the premises to another. The owner or licensee will be vicariously liable for the acts of the delegate.

For example, in *Allen v Whitehead* (1930), the licensee of a cafe employed a manager to run the premises. Despite instructions from the licensee not to allow prostitutes to enter, the manager permitted women he knew to be prostitutes to meet on the premises. The licensee was convicted of 'knowingly suffering prostitutes' to meet on the premises, contrary to s 44 of the Metropolitan Police Act 1839. The licensee was liable on account of the manager's acts and knowledge.

Were it not for the principle allowing vicarious liability, in such a case, the legislation would be devoid of effect, as it (in common with many other statutory offences applying to licensed premises) creates an offence which applies only to the licensee or keeper and not to the manager. But, even in the case of offences which impose personal liability upon the manager, vicarious liability may, additionally, be imposed on the delegator (see, for example, *Howker v Robinson* (1972)).

The delegate need not be an employee of the licensee. The licensee will be vicariously responsible for the acts of a partner or co-licensee committed in his absence (*Linnett v MPC* (1946)).

The principles whereby delegation will be found to have taken place are not totally clear. The absence of the licensee is, however, of great importance as this is consistent with delegation of authority. In *Vane v Yiannopoullos* (1965), a licensee was charged with an offence contrary to s 161(1) of the Licensing Act 1964 of 'knowingly selling or supplying alcohol' contrary to the conditions of his licence. A waitress, contrary to the licensee's instructions, served drinks illegally while he was in the basement of the restaurant. The House of Lords held that the licensee was not guilty of the offence. Lord Hodson held that the principle imposing vicarious liability applies only where there is a complete delegation of authority which had not occurred in this case. Lord Reid based his decision on the fact that the licensee had not left the premises in the charge of the waitress.

In *Howker v Robinson* (1972), the Divisional Court held that whether or not there has been delegation is a question of fact. In that case, a licensee who was serving in the public bar was found to have delegated authority to a barman in the lounge bar. There was complete delegation as far as that part of the premises was concerned.

In *Winson* (1969), Lord Parker pointed out that the delegation principle applies only where the statutory offence requires *mens rea*. In cases of strict liability, the second of the two exceptions to the general principle of personal liability may come into play.

This second exception is based on the construction of certain verbs used in penal statutes. For example, where the *actus reus* of an offence consists of 'selling' goods of some description then, as the legal transaction of sale is made by the owner of the goods, the employer and not the assistant commits the offence (*Coppen v Moore (No 2)* (1898)).

The principle has been held to apply to statutes imposing liability for, among other things, 'supplying goods' (s 1 of the Trade Descriptions Act 1968) and 'using a motor vehicle' (Motor Vehicles (Construction and Use) Regulations).

Vicarious liability based on this construction principle does not allow for the attribution of the employee's *mens rea* to the employer. The principle is limited to offences of strict liability unless it can be proved that the employer has the appropriate *mens rea* (*Winson*). For this reason, there can generally be no vicarious liability for aiding and abetting an offence nor for an attempt to commit the offence (*Ferguson v Weaving* (1951); *Gardner v Ackroyd* (1952)).

The justification for vicarious liability is pragmatic. The offences concerned are of a regulatory nature concerned with the sale and supply of food, drugs and alcohol. Were it not for the principle of delegation, a licensee could avoid responsibility for an offence requiring *mens rea* by turning the management over to an employee. The manager himself would escape liability where the offence strikes at the licensee.

Furthermore, by imposing liability on the employer for the acts of an employee, it is hoped that the employer will be encouraged to take steps to prevent the commission of offences by his staff.

This solution, however, involves, in the case of the delegation principle at least, interpreting statutes in clear contradiction of the words used. A licensee may be convicted of an offence of 'knowingly allowing, etc' even though he neither allowed it nor was aware of it, and despite expressly instructing his employee to observe the legislation. A fairer solution would be to impose liability on the employer for the unauthorised acts of an employee only where the employer was negligent and that, in general, ineffectual legislation should be redrafted rather than applied by imposing a fictitious interpretation on it.[1]

There is one further situation in which one person may be responsible for the acts of another, and that concerns the liability of corporations. A corporation is, in English law, a legal person distinct from its members or directors.

Corporate liability

In addition to those situations where a company might attract liability vicariously for the acts of its employees, there is a more direct form of liability which may be imposed on a corporation for the unlawful acts of an employee or officers. In this situation, the corporation is regarded as having primary responsibility for the offence.

For whose acts might the corporation be criminally liable?

In *Lennard's Carrying Co Ltd v Asiatic Petroleum Co Ltd* (1915), it was held that criminal liability may be attributed to the corporation for the acts of those individuals who could be identified with the company itself – those employees and officers who individually or collectively constituted the 'directing mind and will' of the company.

In *Tesco Supermarkets Ltd v Nattrass* (1972), Lord Reid explained that a corporation, although a separate entity, acts through living individuals. The controlling officer is an embodiment of the company. His acts are the acts of the company and his mind is the mind of the company. This would include directors and others to whom management authority has been delegated. Lords Diplock and Pearson stated that the constitution and organisation of the corporation should be considered.

This rule has a fairly restricted range of application. Liability will only be attributed if a senior manager committed the *actus reus* of the offence with *mens rea*.

In *Meridian Global Funds Management Asia Ltd v Securities Commission* (1995), the Privy Council examined the authorities including *Tesco Supermarkets* and *Lennard's Carrying Co*, and concluded that there had been 'some misunderstanding of the true principles' upon which they were decided. In his advice, Lord Hoffmann stated that whether criminal acts of an employee should be attributed to a company is a matter of interpretation of the particular substantive rule and, in particular, the policy underlying it. The fundamental question is:

> ... whose act (or knowledge, or state of mind) was for this purpose intended to count as the act of the company?[2]

For which offences might a corporation be criminally liable?

Criminal liability for most offences may be attributed to a company. This includes serious offences carrying heavy penalties. In *ICR Haulage Ltd* (1944), the company's conviction for common law conspiracy to defraud was upheld. It is also now clear that a corporation can be convicted of manslaughter provided an identified individual's conduct, characterisable as gross criminal negligence, can be attributed to the corporation (*Attorney General's Reference (No 2 of 1999)* (2000)). See the Law Commission's Report No 237, *Involuntary Manslaughter* (HC 171 (1996)) and the Home Office Consultation Paper of May 2000, *Reforming the Law of Involuntary Manslaughter*.

The exceptions to this rule consist of crimes, like murder, where the forms of punishment are inappropriate, and crimes like bigamy and rape which, because of their personal nature, cannot be committed by a company.

It is sometimes argued that holding a corporation criminally liable is pointless or unjust. The expense is either borne by the shareholders or employees or passed on as a cost to the consumer. On the other hand, it is arguable that the behaviour of the officers of the corporation may be shaped by the subculture of the organisation as a whole and that, in order to influence the behaviour of the group, it may be necessary to punish the corporation. In addition, the potential of bad publicity resulting from a conviction might encourage good practice. In any case, the officers of the company can, as an alternative, be convicted personally as perpetrators or, if the company is convicted as perpetrator, the officers can be convicted as accessories. Further, offences of omission – where there is a duty on the company to perform some act – may not attach to individual officers. If the company could not be convicted, the law would be ineffective.[3]

Part (b): Matthew

Section 2 of the Suicide Act 1961 provides that it is an offence to aid, abet, counsel or procure the suicide of another or the attempt by another to commit suicide. The maximum punishment is a term of imprisonment not exceeding 14 years.

The words 'aid and abet', etc, have the same meaning for this offence as they do for the general law relating to the liability of accomplices to crime (*Reed* (1982)).

Has Matthew intentionally helped the attempted suicide by Chump?

Supplying a gun is clearly capable of amounting to assistance (*NCB v Gamble* (1959)), but Matthew mistakenly believed that Chump was going to murder Funny. In *Bainbridge* (1960), the Court of Criminal Appeal held that a person may be liable as an accomplice even if he did not know the particular crime intended. It was enough that he knew *the type* of crime intended. This decision was referred to with approval in *Maxwell v DPP for Northern Ireland* (1979).

However, although murder and suicide both involve the intentional killing of a human being, they are not similar types of crime. This is because, although aiding a suicide is an offence, neither suicide nor attempted suicide is an offence (s 1 of the Suicide Act 1961). Thus, the principle in *Bainbridge* does not apply in this case and, therefore, Matthew cannot be convicted of the offence under s 2.

Nor can Matthew be convicted of *attempting* to aid and abet murder (s 1(4)(b) of the Criminal Attempts Act 1981).

Funny

Funny's deliberate failure to attempt to save Chump's life when he saw him about to hang himself does not amount to aiding and abetting his attempted suicide. It is only where a person has a duty to act, or controls the actions of another, that he can be regarded as assisting through inactivity (*Russell* (1933); *Tuck v Robson* (1970)).

However, when Funny gave Chump the JUMP leaflet, intending unsuccessfully to encourage Chump to commit suicide, Funny committed an offence contrary to s 1(1) of the Criminal Attempts Act 1981.

Section 1(4) of the 1981 Act states that a person may be convicted of attempting to commit any offence which, if it were completed, would be triable on indictment.

Section 1(4)(b) (mentioned above in relation to Matthew's liability) does not apply in this case because 'aiding, etc, a suicide', triable on indictment, is the principal offence.

In *Attorney General v Able* (1984), it was held that, although the distribution of a book explaining methods of suicide is not in itself an offence, an offence would be committed if the distributor intended that the booklet would encourage or assist someone who was contemplating suicide and that the person was in fact assisted or encouraged by the book.

JUMP

In *Attorney General v Able*, Woolf J stated that an unincorporated association could not be guilty of an offence. However, unincorporated associations are 'persons' as far as statutory offences passed since 1889 are concerned (s 19 of the Interpretation Act 1889 and Sched 1 to the Interpretation Act 1978).

Section 2 of the 1961 Act imposes liability on any 'person', as does s 1 of the Criminal Attempts Act 1981 and, it is submitted therefore, that JUMP may be prosecuted for the full offence provided someone has, in fact, committed or tried to commit suicide, having been assisted or encouraged by the leaflet, or an attempt to commit that offence if it cannot be proved that anyone has committed or tried to commit suicide.

The prosecution would have to prove, of course, that a 'controlling official' was responsible for the distribution of the leaflet and had the appropriate *mens rea* defined and explained above.[4]

Notes

1   See Card, R, *Cross and Jones: Criminal Law*, 12th edn, 1992, p 558.

2   See also *Re Supply of Ready Mixed Concrete (No 2)* (1995).

3   See Clarkson, CMV and Keating, HM, *Criminal Law: Text and Materials*, 4th edn, 1998, pp 244–46.

4   Although the question does not raise the issue, members or controlling officials of JUMP may, of course, be personally responsible either as perpetrators or accessories depending on their involvement in the production of the leaflet and their own *mens rea*.

Question 30

Charles was angry at his girlfriend, Josephine, as she had been unfaithful. Charles asked Andrew, who had recently discharged himself from a psychiatric hospital, to rape Josephine. Andrew agreed. He lay in wait for her near her house. He saw a woman approach and, believing her to be Josephine, he attacked and raped her. In fact, the woman attacked was not Josephine, but her neighbour, Kathy. When arrested, Andrew maintained that he did not think that rape was against the law.

Discuss the criminal liability of Andrew and Charles.

Answer plan

This question raises the defence of insanity and issues concerning conspiracy, incitement and accessorial liability where one of the parties is insane.

The principal issues are:

- the defence of insanity and the requirement that D knew the act was wrong;
- liability for conspiracy where one of the parties is insane;
- accessorial liability where the perpetrator is not guilty by reason of insanity;
- incitement where the incitee would escape liability on the grounds of insanity.

The principal authorities are: *Sullivan* (1984); *Windle* (1952); *Bourne* (1952); *Cogan* (1975); *DPP v K and C* (1997); *Whitehouse* (1977).

Answer

Rape

Rape is an offence contrary to s 1 of the Sexual Offences Act 1956 as substituted by s 142 of the Criminal Justice and Public Order Act 1994. The maximum punishment is life imprisonment (s 37 of and Sched 2 to the 1956 Act).

Although ignorance of the law is no excuse (*Esop* (1836)), Andrew may be able to take advantage of the common law defence of insanity. The criteria of the defence are set out in what are known as the *M'Naghten Rules* (1843). These were accepted by the House of Lords in *Sullivan* (1984) as providing the authoritative definition of insanity in English criminal law.

The *M'Naghten Rules* provide that, to establish a defence on the ground of insanity, it must be proved that, at the time of committing the act, D was:

> ... labouring under such a defect of reason, from disease of the mind, as not to know the nature and quality of the act he was doing or if he did know that, he did not know that what he was doing was wrong.

A person is presumed sane unless the contrary is proved to the jury's satisfaction on 'a balance of probabilities' (*Bratty v Attorney General for Northern Ireland* (1963)).

There is no suggestion in this case that Andrew did not know the nature and quality of his act and, thus, it is proposed to consider the alternative limb: that, at the time he 'raped' Josephine, he was labouring under a defect of reason caused by disease of the mind such that he did not know that what he was doing was wrong.

Whether Andrew suffers from a condition amounting to a 'disease of the mind' is not a medical question, but a question of law (*Kemp* (1957); *Bratty*). Any disease, whether organic or functional, that results in a malfunctioning of the faculties of the mind is a disease of the mind. It matters not whether it is temporary or permanent, curable or incurable (*Kemp*). Lord Denning in *Bratty* said that any condition which has 'manifest itself in violence and is prone to recur' is a disease of the mind.

The requirement that the defendant experienced a defect of reason means that it must be proved that there was a deprivation of cognitive ability (*Clarke* (1972)).

Turning finally to the requirement that the defendant did not know that the act he was doing was wrong, we are told that Andrew maintained that he did not realise rape was a crime. Provided that he can prove this to the jury's satisfaction, it would seem, on the strength of *obiter* statements made by the Court of Criminal Appeal in *Windle* (1952), that the requirement is satisfied even if he believed that it was *morally* wrong to commit an act of rape.

If the defence is successful, Andrew will be found not guilty by reason of insanity (s 1 of the Criminal Procedure (Insanity) Act 1964) and, by virtue of the Criminal Procedure (Insanity and Unfitness to Plead) Act 1991, the court may make a hospital order with or without a restriction as to discharge, a guardianship order, a supervision and treatment order, or an order of absolute discharge.

Conspiracy

It is now proposed to consider Charles' liability for conspiracy to rape contrary to s 1 of the Criminal Law Act 1977.

The central issue here is whether a person can be guilty of conspiracy where the alleged co-conspirator is insane within the *M'Naghten Rules*.

Section 1(1) of the Act provides that a person is guilty of conspiracy if he agrees with another to pursue a course of conduct which, if carried out as intended, will necessarily amount to the commission of an offence by at least one of the parties.

In this case, the agreement was that Andrew should rape Josephine. If he was insane, the agreement was not one which, if carried out as intended, would 'necessarily amount to the commission of an offence' by him. And, as it appears to have been accepted that 'commission of an offence' in s 1 means commission of an offence as a principal, and not as a secondary party, neither would it have amounted to an offence by Charles (see the decision of the Court of Appeal in *Hollinshead* (1985); the House of Lords did not consider it necessary to decide the matter).

There is, therefore, no conspiracy between Andrew and Charles.

Secondary liability

Section 8 of the Accessories and Abettors Act 1861 provides that a person who aids, abets, counsels or procures the commission of an offence is liable to be tried and punished for that offence as a principal offender.

Charles has 'counselled', that is, encouraged the commission of the offence (*Calhaem* (1985)). The fact that he asked Andrew to rape Josephine and he mistakenly raped Kathy has no effect upon Charles' liability. It would be different if Andrew had *intentionally* deviated from the agreed plan to rape Josephine (see, for example, *Saunders and Archer* (1573)).

The principal issue concerns whether Charles may be convicted as an accomplice if the alleged principal offender, Andrew, is not guilty by reason of insanity.

The traditional view is that accessorial liability is derived from the liability of the principal and that, unless there was a perpetrator responsible for the offence, there is no basis for the conviction of the accomplice (*Thornton v Mitchell* (1940)).

In *Bourne* (1952), however, the Court of Appeal held that a person may be guilty as a secondary party even though the 'principal offender' is excused. In that case, the principal was excused as she had been the victim of duress. The Court of Appeal stated that, despite the duress, there had been an offence committed to which the other party could be an accessory.

The decision has been criticised by the supporters of the traditional view as being based on the conceptually improper notion of an 'excused offence'. However, in *Cogan* (1975), the Court of Appeal gave some support to the decision in *Bourne* by holding, *obiter*, that a man could be convicted as an accessory to rape even though the 'perpetrator' was acquitted due to a lack of *mens rea*. And in *DPP v K and B* (1997), the Divisional Court held that a person could be convicted of rape as a procurer, despite the fact that the prosecutor had failed to rebut the presumption of *doli incapax* in respect of the alleged principal (see also *Millward* (1994)).[1]

Although there are difficulties with the reasoning in these cases, it is submitted that the outcome is correct and that, despite Andrew's lack of capacity, Charles may be convicted of rape as a procurer.[2]

Alternatively, there is some authority to suggest that Charles might be convicted as the principal offender acting through the innocent agency of Andrew.

The doctrine of innocent agency states that a person may be regarded as the perpetrator of an offence where he intentionally causes the *actus reus* of an offence to be committed by a person who is himself innocent because of a lack of *mens rea* or lack of capacity (*Anon* (1634)). Indeed, the main ground for the decision in *Cogan* was that a man might be convicted of rape through an innocent agent.

However, this reasoning has been strongly criticised. It is generally accepted that the doctrine of innocent agency applies only where it is possible to say that the defendant performed the *actus reus* and that there is no room for its application where, as in the case of rape, the offence is specified in terms implying personal conduct on the part of the offender (see, for example, *Thornton v Mitchell* (1940) and *DPP v K and B*).[3]

Incitement

Charles may be guilty of inciting Andrew to rape.[4]

The essence of the offence is intentionally encouraging another to commit a crime. Incitement may be committed whether or not the offence incited is in fact committed (*Higgins* (1801)).

In *Curr* (1968), it was held that a person could not be convicted of incitement to commit an offence unless it could be proved that the persons 'incited' had acted with the requisite *mens rea* for that offence. The case has been criticised. It is argued that it should not be necessary to prove that the individual incited acted with *mens rea*. It should suffice that the accused intended the incitee would so act.[5]

In any case, in this problem, Andrew, despite his defence of insanity, did apparently rape with *mens rea* and thus the narrow rule in *Curr* presents no obstacle to the conviction of Charles.

However, there is some authority for the view that a person may not be convicted of incitement where the person incited is, in law, incapable of committing that offence. In *Whitehouse* (1977), for example, it was held that it was not an offence for a man to incite a girl of 15 to permit incestuous intercourse as the girl committed no offence by permitting it.

Whitehouse is, however, distinguishable from the present problem on the basis that *Whitehouse* would not have committed the *actus reus* of an offence had she allowed sexual intercourse to take place, whereas Andrew committed the *actus reus* of rape and did so with *mens rea*. There is no good reason why Andrew's lack of personal capacity due to insanity should exempt Charles from liability – whether or not Charles was aware of Andrew's disability. It is submitted, therefore, that Charles is guilty of incitement.

Incitement is a common law offence, the penalty for which depends upon whether the offence incited is triable summarily or on indictment. Incitement to rape, an indictable offence, is itself an offence triable on indictment and Charles if found guilty may receive a sentence of imprisonment at the discretion of the court (*Morris* (1951)).

Notes

1   The Divisional Court treated the concept of *doli incapax* as a 'presumption concerning *mens rea*'. It is, more accurately, a presumption of incapacity.

2   The principle in the cases would appear to be that, if D1 induces D2 to commit the *actus reus* of an offence, he may be convicted as an accomplice provided he has the necessary intent even though D2 is not guilty of an offence because, for example, he lacks *mens rea*.

Consider the following view of the Law Commission (*Assisting and Encouraging Crime*, Consultation Paper No 131, 1993, para 4.207):

A prime danger of such a rule is that, in its anxiety to meet cases of the type just discussed [including *Bourne* and *Cogan*], it will reach too far. For that reason, we doubt whether it can be right (though we invite views on the point) to adopt a general rule for the abetting or counselling of a mere *actus reus*.

3   See Williams, G, *Textbook of Criminal Law*, 2nd edn, 1983, p 371.

4   Where the substantive offence has been committed, it is not normal practice to charge with incitement – the inciter will be charged as an accomplice. However, the fact that the crime was committed is no defence to a charge of incitement and so Charles' liability for incitement is discussed in answer to this question.

5   In *DPP v Armstrong* (2000), the Divisional Court, distinguishing *Curr*, held that the *mens rea* of the incitee was irrelevant.

Question 31

Dougal had been persistently making advances to Susan, Simon's girlfriend. He had phoned her up on a number of occasions to invite her out. When Simon found out, he was extremely angry and decided to visit Dougal. He asked his brother, Peter, to accompany him. They decided they would 'warn' Dougal that, if he did not agree to stop making advances toward Susan, they would smash up his flat and they agreed that, if Dougal 'gave them lip', they would beat him up.

They visited Dougal and told him that they wanted him to stop making advances towards Susan, and that, if he did not agree to stop visiting her, they would smash up his flat. Dougal responded by saying that he would not be intimidated and had no intention of changing his behaviour. He said that Susan preferred him to Simon and that she would be happier if Simon left her alone. At this, Simon flew into a rage. He pulled out a knife and, intending serious injury, stabbed Dougal in the right eye.

Dougal fell to the floor, unconscious. He was taken to hospital where it was discovered he had suffered severe brain damage. In addition, a medical examination revealed that he had a duodenal ulcer. The doctors decided that because of the brain damage they could not operate on the ulcer. Two weeks later, while still unconscious, Dougal died when the ulcer burst.

Discuss the criminal liability of Simon and Peter. (Ignore offences under the Prevention of Crime Act 1953 and the Criminal Justice Act 1988.)

Answer plan

A fairly complicated question raising a variety of issues, including those relating to the effect of provocation upon the liability of an accessory.

The principal issues are:

- principles of causation where injuries prevent medical treatment;
- the defence of provocation: cumulative provocation;
- accessorial liability: the effect upon secondary liability where the principal is provoked to kill;
- conspiracy and conditional intention.

The principal authorities are: *McKechnie* (1992); *Pearson* (1992); *Ahluwalia* (1992); *Camplin* (1978); *Powell; English* (1997).

Answer

Simon

It is proposed to consider Simon's liability for murder.

First, the prosecution must prove that Simon's actions were a legal cause of Dougal's death.

In *McKechnie* (1992), the Court of Appeal held that it must be proved to the jury's satisfaction that the injuries significantly contributed to the victim's death and, where they prevent life saving medical treatment, injuries will be regarded as a significant contribution if the prosecution prove that the decision not to operate was reasonable and competent. It is unnecessary for the prosecution to prove that the decision not to operate was the only decision that a competent doctor might arrive at, nor that it was necessarily the correct one.

It shall be assumed, for the purposes of further analysis, that Simon's actions were a legal cause of death. The next issue to consider is his *mens rea* at the time he administered the blow.

The facts state that he intended to cause serious injury and thus he will be convicted of murder unless he can take advantage of the defence of provocation (*Moloney* (1985)).

Provocation is a common law defence modified by s 3 of the Homicide Act 1957, which, if successfully pleaded, reduces liability from murder to manslaughter.

The defence is available where:

(a) at the time of the fatal attack the defendant had, as a result of provocation, lost his self-control; and

(b) the reasonable man in the same circumstances would have done as the defendant did.

Although the defendant bears an evidential burden in support of his plea that he was provoked to lose his self-control, the burden of disproving provocation lies with the Crown (*Woolmington v DPP* (1935); *McPherson* (1957)).

Only a 'sudden and temporary' loss of self-control as a result of provocation will suffice (*Duffy* (1949); *Thornton* (1992); *Ahluwalia* (1992); *Acott* (1997)).

In deciding this issue, the jury may consider not only things said and done immediately prior to the fatal act (that is, in this case, Dougal's statement that he would continue his advances towards Simon's girlfriend), but also the effects of earlier provocative behaviour which may have contributed to the loss of control (Dougal's prior advances) (*Pearson* (1992)). In other words, the jury are entitled to conclude that the comments of Dougal immediately prior to the attack upon him amounted to 'the straw that broke the camel's back' (*Pearson*). It would appear that Simon acted spontaneously to the perceived insults and this is good evidence that he suddenly lost his self-control (*Ahluwalia*).

Although there is no authority on the point, it is submitted that if, as a result of provocation, the defendant loses his self-control and kills with malice aforethought, the fact that the defendant had a conditional intention to cause grievous bodily harm prior to the provocation should be no bar to the defence. The prior intention may not have been carried out. Provided the jury are satisfied that the murderous attack was a result of a sudden and temporary loss of self-control, the causal nexus between the provocation and the fatal attack is satisfied. And, in *Johnson* (1989), the Court of Appeal held that a person may avail himself of the defence of provocation even if the attack was a foreseeable result of his own conduct.

The second issue mentioned above is a matter exclusively for the jury.

In *Smith* (2000), the House of Lords held that the question for the jury is whether a person of ordinary self-control would have reacted as the accused reacted if he were similarly placed. It is not necessary for the judge to direct the jury in terms of the 'highly artificial' and potentially misleading image of the reasonable man. In Lord Hoffmann's view, the judge may direct the jury in simple language to consider whether the circumstances were such as to make the loss of self-control sufficiently excusable to reduce the gravity of the offence from murder to manslaughter. In deciding what should count as a sufficient excuse, they should be instructed to apply what they consider to be appropriate standards of behaviour; on the one hand, making allowances for human nature and the power of the emotions but, on the other hand, not allowing someone to rely upon his own violent disposition.

Simon may also be convicted of the offence, contrary to s 2 of the Criminal Damage Act 1971, of making threats to destroy or damage property belonging to another. It is unnecessary to prove that Dougal actually feared Simon would damage his property. It is sufficient that Simon *intended* Dougal to fear that his property would be damaged. The maximum penalty for this offence is 10 years' imprisonment.

Peter – liability as a secondary party

Section 8 of the Accessories and Abettors Act 1861, as amended by the Criminal Law Act 1977, provides that a person who aids, abets, counsels or procures the commission of an indictable offence is liable to be tried, indicted and punished as a principal offender.[1]

Now where, as in this case, two persons embark on a joint unlawful enterprise, each of the parties is equally liable for the consequences of such acts of the other as are done in the pursuance of that joint enterprise and also for the unforeseen consequences of the other's acts done in pursuance of their agreement (*Anderson and Morris* (1966)). If an accomplice lends himself to a criminal enterprise on the understanding that grievous bodily harm should, if necessary, be inflicted, he will be guilty of murder if the principal kills in accordance with the plan (*Hyde, Sussex and Collins* (1990)). So, if Dougal had died as a result of the intended beating, Peter would have been guilty of murder as an accomplice.

What difference might it make that death resulted from the use of the knife?

The issue has been discussed in the recent decisions of the House of Lords in *Powell; English* (1997) and the Court of Appeal in *Uddin* (1998) and *Greatrex* (1998) (see also *Hyde* (1991); *Hui Chi-Ming* (1992); *Roberts* (1993); *Cairns* (2002); *McCarthy* (2003)). In these cases, the courts identified a number of principles, the relevance of which depends upon elements of the secondary party's *mens rea*. As Peter's *mens rea* is not fully disclosed, there are a number of possible outcomes in this case. The following summary deals with the most likely:

(a) a secondary party is not responsible for an act which is of a fundamentally different type from that foreseen by the secondary party. It is outside the scope of the common enterprise. It would appear that the question whether one attack is different in type from another is a matter for the jury and they might conclude that an attack by using a knife is different from an attack with fists;

(b) if the jury conclude that the use of the knife was outside the scope of the joint enterprise, no responsibility for the homicide attaches to Peter. He is guilty of neither murder nor manslaughter (*English*; *Anderson and Morris*);[2]

(c) if Peter knew that Simon had the knife and that he might use it with an intention to do grievous bodily harm, then he is guilty of murder unless, perhaps, the contemplated use of the knife was fundamentally different from the way in which it was in fact used.[3]

How might a finding that Simon was provoked affect Peter's liability?

In *McKechnie* (1992), the principal killed having been provoked whilst carrying out the joint enterprise. The Court of Appeal held that the provocation was incompatible with a joint enterprise to cause grievous bodily harm to the deceased. Thus, although the principal was guilty of voluntary manslaughter, the other parties were neither guilty of homicide nor of causing grievous bodily harm with intent.

Professor Smith suggests that this implies that the loss of self-control brings a prior joint enterprise to an end. But, it is submitted that it is not at all clear that this is what the court intended.[4]

The Court of Appeal appeared to take the view that the jury's finding that the principal was provoked ruled out the possibility that there was, *prior to the provocation*, a joint enterprise to cause grievous bodily harm to which the other defendants could have been parties. The court added that, if the principal had been labouring under long term provocation and the parties had agreed upon a joint enterprise to do serious harm prior to the final act of provocation, then, although the principal would have been guilty of manslaughter, the other parties would have been guilty of murder.

In *Pearson* (1992), the Court of Appeal, distinguishing *McKechnie*, held that the existence of provocation does not necessarily terminate a joint enterprise. In that case, both parties were provoked prior to undertaking the joint enterprise and, although it is not clear from the judgment, it is submitted that the possible basis of the distinction is that, in *Pearson*, there was evidence that both parties intended to kill or cause serious harm from the outset (and see *Uddin* (1998)).

Moreover, it was said in *Hui Chi-Ming* that if, for example, two men embark upon a robbery and the principal is carrying a weapon which he intends to use merely to frighten if they meet resistance, but, through panic at the scene, changes his mind and uses it with malice aforethought, then the secondary party will be guilty of murder if he foresaw *at the outset* that the principal might use the weapon with malice aforethought.

It is submitted, therefore, that the question of secondary liability where the principal is provoked to kill depends primarily upon whether the secondary party had the appropriate *mens rea* prior to the provocation. If Peter was aware that Simon carried a knife and foresaw that he might use it with an intention to do grievous bodily harm, then he may be convicted of murder, although Simon might be guilty only of manslaughter.[5]

In addition, Peter may be convicted as an accomplice to the offence, perpetrated by Simon, of making threats contrary to s 2 of the Criminal Damage Act 1971.

Conspiracy

Did Peter and Simon conspire to cause grievous bodily harm? It is submitted that they did not.

By virtue of s 1(1) of the Criminal Law Act 1977, a person is guilty of statutory conspiracy if he agrees with another that a course of conduct shall be pursued which, if the agreement is carried out as intended, will necessarily amount to the commission of an offence by at least one of the parties to the agreement. As their agreed course of conduct would not *necessarily* involve the infliction of grievous bodily harm, they did not conspire to commit that offence (*Reed* (1982)).[6]

They are, however, guilty of a conspiracy to make threats to damage property belonging to another.[7]

Notes

1   In *Concannon* (2001), it was held that a conviction for murder and the resulting imposition of a mandatory life sentence where the offender was a secondary party was not in breach of Art 6 of the European Convention on Human Rights.

2   See also *Dunbar* (1988) and *Mitchell and King* (1999); cf *Stewart and Schofield* (1995) and *Roberts, Day and Day* (2001). In *Uddin*, it was said that if D2 continues to participate in an attack after becoming aware that D1 has produced a weapon, he will be guilty of murder if the weapon is used to kill V: see *Cairns* (2002).

3   See Professor Smith's commentary to *Powell* in [1998] Crim LR 48, p 51:

   B has agreed that A should use the shotgun he carries to 'kneecap' V. A deliberately uses the gun to shoot V through the head, killing him instantly. If B did not foresee a real risk of such use of the gun, he should not be liable for murder or manslaughter: the act causing death is one for which he is not responsible.

4   See Professor Smith's commentary to *McKechnie* in [1992] Crim LR 197.

5   Cf Williams, G, *Textbook of Criminal Law*, 2nd edn, 1983, p 429.

6   If, however, Professor Smith's analysis of *McKechnie* is correct and provocation of one party terminates the joint enterprise, then Peter will incur no liability for

the homicide or for grievous bodily harm with intent, even if he foresaw the possibility that Simon might use the weapon with malice aforethought.

7   Where the defendants have been charged with a substantive offence, the prosecution may not also proceed with a charge of conspiracy to commit it, unless they can satisfy the judge that the interests of justice demand it (*Practice Note* (1977)).

Question 32

Husband and wife, Bonnie and Clyde, decided to manufacture a controlled drug. Clyde approached Darrow and, explaining to him the plan, asked him to supply certain chemicals. Although he knew that it was not possible to manufacture the drug from the process that Bonnie and Clyde intended, Darrow agreed to supply the chemicals.

Darrow supplied the chemicals. Clyde went to his basement laboratory with the chemicals to begin the process of manufacture. He was arrested a short time later.

Discuss the criminal liability of the parties.

Answer plan

This question raises issues relating to liability for conspiracy and attempt and liability as an accessory.

The principal issues are:

•   whether D can be convicted of conspiracy when he does not believe that the agreed plan will succeed;

•   agreements between spouses;

•   when an act is 'more than merely preparatory' for the purposes of an attempt;

•   attempting the impossible;

•   the *mens rea* of an accomplice.

The principal authorities are: *Gullefer* (1990); *Campbell* (1991); *Anderson* (1986); *Yip Chiu-Cheung* (1994); *NCB v Gamble* (1959); *DPP v Lynch* (1975).

Answer

Conspiracy

The offence of statutory conspiracy is defined in s 1 of the Criminal Law Act 1977, as amended by s 5 of the Criminal Attempts Act 1981. It provides that a person is guilty of conspiracy if he agrees with any other person or persons to pursue a course of conduct which, if carried out as intended, will necessarily amount to the commission of an offence by one or more of the parties to the agreement or would do so but for the existence of facts which render the commission of the offence impossible.

The production of a controlled drug is an offence under s 4 of the Misuse of Drugs Act 1971.

By virtue of s 2(2)(a) of the Criminal Law Act 1977, a person cannot be convicted of conspiracy if the only other person with whom he or she agrees is his or her spouse. Bonnie, however, may be convicted of conspiring with Darrow, even though her agreement is with Clyde, if she knows of the existence of Darrow and that he has agreed to play some part in the unlawful object. It is neither necessary that she knows the identity of Darrow, nor that she has met him (*Chrastny* (1991)).

The fact that it is impossible to produce the drug does not preclude liability for conspiracy. The decision of the House of Lords in *Nock* (1978) has been overruled by s 1(1)(b) of the 1977 Act.

Further, there is some authority for the proposition that Darrow may be convicted of conspiracy, even though he *knew* that the production of the drug was impossible. In *Anderson* (1986), the defendant had agreed with others to take part in a plan to effect the escape of one of them from prison by providing cutting equipment, etc. He said that he did not intend that the escape plan be put into effect and that he believed that it had no chance of succeeding. It was held that this was not a defence. Lord Bridge, in a speech with which the other Lords concurred, said that it was not necessary to prove that the defendant intended that the substantive offence be committed.

The case has been criticised. It has been argued that, as s 1(2) requires proof of knowledge of the circumstances necessary for the commission of the offence, it would seem to follow that intention as to the consequences is a requirement of liability.[1]

Anderson was not cited in *Edwards* (1991), where it was held that the defendant could not be convicted of conspiracy to supply amphetamine, as agreed, unless it could be proved that he intended to carry out the agreement. In *Yip Chiu-Cheung* (1994), the Privy Council held that the crime of conspiracy requires an agreement between two or more persons *with the intention of carrying it out.* Lord Griffith stated that it is the intention to carry out the crime that constitutes the necessary *mens rea* for the offence of conspiracy. This is in direct contradiction to the opinion expressed by Lord Bridge in *Anderson*.[2]

If Lord Griffith's approach is followed, and it is submitted that it ought to be, then, as a result of the rule regarding spouses, there is no conspiracy to produce a controlled drug in this case.[3]

Attempt – Clyde

Section 1(1) of the Criminal Attempts Act 1981 provides that a person is guilty of attempting to commit an offence if, with intent to commit the offence, he does an act which is more than merely preparatory to the commission of the offence.

Clearly, Clyde acted with the *mens rea* for the offence, but the facts of the problem do not disclose whether Clyde had performed an act which was more than merely preparatory to the process of production.

The question is a question of fact for the jury and not a question of law for the judge (s 4(3)). If, however, there is insufficient evidence or it would be unsafe to leave the evidence to the jury, the judge can rule that there was no attempt and direct a verdict of not guilty (*Campbell* (1991)).

In *Gullefer* (1990), Lord Lane identified 'two lines of authority' prior to the statute. One line endorsed what came to be known as the 'last act' or 'Rubicon' principle, where only acts immediately connected with the offence could be attempts. The alternative test was that an attempt was an act done with intent which formed part of a series of acts which, if not interrupted, would amount to the commission of the offence (see, for example, *Eagleton* (1855); *DPP v Stonehouse*; *Robinson* (1915)).

Lord Lane rejected both tests: the former was too restrictive, the latter too vague and, possibly, too broad. He preferred a 'midway course'. In his Lordship's opinion, an attempt begins when it can be said that the defendant has embarked on the crime proper. This approach was endorsed in *Jones* and *Campbell* (1991).[4]

Thus, only an inconclusive answer can be offered to the question whether Clyde may be convicted of an attempt. Provided there is sufficient evidence that he was engaged in the commission of the offence of production of a controlled drug, it is a question of fact for the jury whether what he did was more than merely preparatory.

It should be noted that, even though production of the drug was impossible, Clyde can be convicted of an attempt to produce it (s 1(2) and (3) of the Criminal Attempts Act).

Accessorial liability

A person can be convicted as an accomplice to an attempt and, therefore, Bonnie will be liable for any help or encouragement which she has given to Clyde, provided that he has done an act which is 'more than merely preparatory' (*Dunnington* (1984); s 8 of the Accessories and Abettors Act 1861).

With respect to Darrow, the position is less clear.

In *NCB v Gamble* (1959), it was held that, although it must be proved that the secondary party intended to do acts of assistance, it is not necessary to prove that he intended that the crime be committed. Devlin J said that indifference to the result of the crime does not negative aiding. Similarly, in *Lynch v DPP for Northern Ireland* (1975), it was said that, if the accused *knowingly* assisted another in a criminal purpose, he aided the offence.

These decisions suggest that Darrow is guilty of aiding the commission of the attempt. He knowingly assisted Clyde in his (futile) attempt to produce a controlled drug. But, in this case, Darrow was not merely indifferent as to whether the controlled drug was produced. He knew that it was impossible to produce it by the process Clyde had chosen.

Clyde, if he did acts that were more than merely preparatory, is guilty of an attempt because he intended to commit the full offence. The 'real mischief' is, of course, the production of a controlled drug, but there is no difference, in terms of *culpability*, between an unsuccessful attempt at production and a successful one. The attempt is punished to discourage the offender from trying again, perhaps with more success.

Darrow, on the other hand, did not intend the full offence to be committed because he knew that, in the circumstances, it could not be. In terms of Clyde's real purpose, Darrow gave no assistance nor did he intend to and, therefore, it is submitted that he ought not to be convicted as an accomplice.

Being concerned in the management of premises, etc

Section 8 of the Misuse of Drugs Act 1971 provides that an occupier of premises commits an offence if he knowingly permits or suffers the production or attempted production of a controlled drug in contravention of s 4(1) of the same Act.

The facts do not reveal Bonnie and Clyde's domestic arrangements but, assuming they are co-occupiers, Bonnie may be convicted of the offence (*Ashdown, Howard and Others* (1974)).

The maximum punishment for this offence is dependent on the drug which Clyde attempted to produce. If a Class A or Class B drug, the maximum is a term of imprisonment not exceeding 14 years; if a Class C drug, the maximum is five years.

Notes

1   The Law Commission disapproved of *Anderson*: Draft Criminal Code, Law Com No 177, 1989. And see Smith, JC and Hogan, B, *Criminal Law*, 8th edn, 1996, pp 281–82, where it is suggested that Anderson should have been convicted as an accomplice to the conspiracy. That would not be possible in this case as, by virtue of s 2(2)(a), there is no conspiracy between Bonnie and Clyde; see Card, R, *Cross and Jones: Criminal Law*, 12th edn, 1992, p 487.

2   In *McPhillips* (1989), the defendant was not guilty of conspiracy to murder as he intended to issue a warning to the authorities explaining the location of a bomb that he and others had planted. In *Giu* (1992), the Court of Appeal held that the appellant had been properly convicted of conspiring with M to offer to supply a controlled drug (Ecstasy) contrary to s 4(1)(b) of the Misuse of Drugs Act 1971 *even though* he had no intention to supply Ecstasy and had been cheating his customers by actually supplying Vitamin C. The decision rested on the fact that it had previously been decided that a mere 'offer' to supply a controlled drug constituted an offence under s 4(1). The belief of the offerer as to what he was offering was irrelevant. On this analysis of s 4(1), which the court did not question, a 'conspiracy to offer' does not require 'an intention to supply'.

3   Is there a conspiracy to *attempt* to produce a controlled drug in this case?

Section 1 of the Criminal Law Act 1977 applies to agreements to commit *any* offence. The parties have agreed a course of conduct which, if carried out in accordance with their intentions, will necessarily amount to the commission of an attempt by Clyde.

Clyde and Bonnie intend the attempt to produce the drug, but does Darrow?

As Darrow presumably does not care whether or not Clyde carries out the planned process, he lacks the necessary intent and, thus, it is submitted there is no conspiracy.

4   See also *Leather* (1993). In *Geddes* (1996), the Court of Appeal acknowledged that the line of demarcation between acts which were merely preparatory and acts which could amount to an attempt was not always obvious or easy to recognise. There would always be a need for an exercise of judgment by the judge before leaving the matter to the jury (see also *Tosti* (1997)).

Question 33

Part (a)

James, Chris and Mike planned to kill John. They arranged to meet later in the evening, then proceeded to John's house where it was intended that James and Chris would restrain John while Mike stabbed him. At the appointed time, Chris and Mike met but James did not turn up. He had changed his mind. He had tried to telephone Chris and Mike to inform them of his decision, but had been unable to make contact. James telephoned John to warn him that Chris and Mike were on their way and that they planned to attack him. As James was explaining the danger, Chris and Mike arrived. Chris grabbed hold of John, whereupon Mike, following the plan, stabbed John in the heart. John died instantly.

Discuss the criminal liability of James, Chris and Mike.

Part (b)

Maxwell, walking Sweet home, pushed her to the ground. He told her that he intended to have sexual intercourse with her and warned her that he would hurt her severely if she resisted. He told her to undress. Sweet was extremely frightened and so did as she was told. Maxwell was about to have sexual intercourse with Sweet when suddenly he felt extremely guilty. He decided not to have sexual intercourse with her. He dressed himself and set off to church to pray for forgiveness.

Discuss the criminal liability of Maxwell.

Answer plan

Part (a)

This part raises issues concerning accessorial liability, conspiracy and incitement.

The principal issue concerns whether James' failed attempt at informing the other parties that he no longer wished to carry out their agreed plan and/or his telephone conversation with John amounted to an effective 'withdrawal' absolving James of liability for the murder.

In addition, the liability of the parties for conspiracy is discussed. For this offence, 'withdrawal' does not negative liability.

Part (b)

This part involves analysing whether Maxwell is guilty of attempted rape. The principal issue concerns whether or not his acts were 'more than merely preparatory' to the commission of the full offence. For reasons given below, it is not possible to come to a conclusive answer on this point. In addition, his liability for assault and indecent assault is discussed.

The principal authorities are: *Becerra and Cooper* (1975); *Whitefield* (1984); *Attorney General's Reference (No 1 of 1992)* (1993); *Haughton v Smith* (1975).

Answer

Part (a)

Murder

It would appear that both Chris and Mike are guilty of murder; Mike as principal and Chris as a secondary party. Murder consists of the killing of a human being with either an intention to kill or an intention to cause grievous bodily harm (*Moloney* (1985)) and, by virtue of s 8 of the Accessories and Abettors Act 1861, as amended by the Criminal Law Act 1977, anyone who assists or encourages the commission of an offence is liable to be tried and punished as a principal offender.

The mandatory sentence for those convicted of murder is a term of imprisonment for life (Murder (Abolition of Death Penalty) Act 1965).

Whether James is also guilty of murder is less clear. A person can escape secondary liability for an offence by withdrawal before the offence is committed, but what amounts to effective withdrawal depends on the circumstances of the case. Where the mode of participation consists merely of counselling or encouraging the commission of the offence, it is generally accepted that communication of the intention to abandon the common purpose to the other parties will suffice. The communication must be timely and must serve unequivocal notice to the others that, if they proceed, they do so without the assistance or encouragement of the party seeking to withdraw (*Whitehouse* (1941); *Whitefield* (1984)). Even where the mode of participation consists of giving material assistance, communication of withdrawal may be effective (*Grundy* (1977)).

James tried but failed to communicate his intention to the other parties, but it is arguable that an attempted communication is sufficient.[1] In any case, his telephone call to John might amount to an effective withdrawal. In *Becerra and Cooper* (1975), the Court of Appeal quoted with approval a passage from the decision of the Court of Appeal of British Columbia in *Whitehouse*, in which it was stated that communication to the other parties is essential only where it was 'practicable and reasonable'. It has also been suggested that, where it is either not practicable or not reasonable, timely notification of the proposed offence to the police would suffice.[2] Presumably, timely notification to the intended victim would also suffice.

If so, the question then is whether James' telephone call to John was 'timely'.

That may depend on the nature of James' participation. It has been suggested that where material assistance has been given and, particularly, where 'withdrawal' is attempted at a relatively late stage, it will only be effective if the defendant took all reasonable steps or at least did his best to prevent the commission of the offence.[3] If that is the correct principle, then presumably it is a question of fact for the jury taking into account the nature of James' participation, the timing of the 'withdrawal' and all other relevant circumstances whether what he did was sufficient to amount to an effective withdrawal.

Conspiracy

Even if James' withdrawal is adjudged to be effective such that he attracts no criminal liability for the murder of John, it would appear that he is guilty of conspiring to murder him. An agreement between two or more persons to commit a crime is a statutory conspiracy defined in s 1(1) of the Criminal Law Act 1977. As conspiracy is complete the moment the parties agree to commit an offence, subsequent 'withdrawal' does not negative liability (*Barnard* (1979)). It may, however, be a relevant factor in mitigation (*Gortat and Pirog* (1973); *Davies* (1990)).

By virtue of s 3(2)(a), the maximum penalty for a conspiracy to murder is a term of imprisonment for life.

Chris and Mike could also be charged with conspiracy in addition to murder. However, such a practice is discouraged and the prosecution is required to satisfy the judge that the interests of justice demand charging with both offences (*Practice Note* (1977)).

Incitement

If James encouraged the others to commit the murder, he is guilty of incitement. In common with conspiracy, subsequent withdrawal has no effect on liability for incitement.

Incitement to commit an offence is a common law crime punishable, on indictment, with a fine and imprisonment at the discretion of the court (*Higgins* (1801)). In addition, by s 4 of the Offences Against the Person Act 1861 (as amended by the Criminal Law Act 1977), it is an offence, punishable with life imprisonment, to encourage a person to commit murder. Any persuasion or encouragement will suffice.

Part (b)

Attempt

Maxwell may be guilty of attempted rape contrary to s 1(1) of the Criminal Attempts Act 1981. The sub-section provides that a person is guilty of an attempt if, with intent to commit an indictable offence, he does an act which is more than merely preparatory to the commission of that offence.

Section 1 of the Sexual Offences Act 1956, as substituted by s 142 of the Criminal Justice and Public Order Act 1994, provides that:

(1) It is an offence for a man to rape a woman or another man; [and]

(2) a man commits rape if:

    (a) he has sexual intercourse with a person (whether vaginal or anal) who at the time of the intercourse does not consent to it; and

    (b) at the time he knows that the person does not consent to the intercourse or is reckless as to whether that person consents to it.

Had Maxwell had sexual intercourse with Sweet, he would have been guilty of rape. Sweet's decision to submit to sexual intercourse would not have amounted to consent (*Olugboja* (1982)) and Maxwell had the appropriate *mens rea* for attempted rape – he intended to have sexual intercourse with a woman knowing that she did not consent. But, as far as the *actus reus* of attempted rape is concerned, it is not clear that his acts were more than merely preparatory.

In *Gullefer* (1990), it was held that if there is evidence on which a jury could reasonably arrive at the conclusion that the defendant had done acts which were more than merely preparatory and had 'embarked on the crime proper', then it is for the jury to decide whether the defendant did in fact go beyond mere preparation. Lord Lane added that there may be evidence of an attempt even though the defendant had not performed the last act prior to the commission of the substantive offence.[4] Following this approach, the Court of Appeal in *Attorney General's Reference (No 1 of 1992)* (1993) held that, in the case of attempted rape, it is not necessary to prove that the defendant had gone as far as to attempt physical penetration of the vagina. It is sufficient if there is evidence of acts which a jury could properly regard as more than merely preparatory to the commission of the offence. In that case, the evidence that the defendant had dragged the woman up some steps, lowered his trousers, got on top of her and interfered with her private parts, together with his statements to the police and the evidence that she was partly undressed and in a state of distress, was thought to be sufficient to justify leaving the question to the jury. It was a matter then for the jury to decide whether they were sure that those acts were more than merely preparatory.

The facts of Maxwell's case are, of course, different from the facts involved in the *Attorney General's Reference*. There is no suggestion, for example, that Maxwell touched Sweet. Might there nonetheless be sufficient evidence of an attempt to rape to leave the matter to the jury? Unfortunately, the expression 'embarking on the crime proper' is not sufficiently clear to allow one to answer that question with certainty.[5]

Provided that there is sufficient evidence and the jury conclude that Maxwell's acts were more than merely preparatory, he may be convicted of attempted rape. The fact that Maxwell changed his mind about raping Sweet has no effect upon his liability. Withdrawal is not possible after the stage where a more than merely preparatory act has been performed (*Taylor* (1859); *Lankford* (1959); *Haughton v Smith* (1975)).[6] The fact that his decision to abandon the attempt was voluntary may, however, mitigate the penalty imposed.

The maximum penalty for attempted rape is a term of imprisonment for life (s 4(1) of the Criminal Attempts Act 1981).

Assault and indecent assault

Maxwell is guilty of an assault contrary to s 39 of the Criminal Justice Act 1988. He intentionally caused Sweet to apprehend the application of immediate, unlawful force (*Venna* (1976)).[7] Indeed, owing to the nature of the assault on Sweet, he is guilty of the more serious offence of indecent assault contrary to s 14 of the Sexual Offences Act 1956 (*Rolfe* (1952)). This offence is punishable with a term of imprisonment not exceeding 10 years.

Notes

1 See, for example, Smith, JC and Hogan, B, *Criminal Law*, 8th edn, 1996, p 155.

2 Card, R, *Cross and Jones: Criminal Law*, 12th edn, 1992, p 552.

  On the other hand, in *Rook* (1993), the Court of Appeal stated that communication of withdrawal to the other parties was 'the minimum necessary'. In that case, however, the defendant had not made any attempt to tell the others that he no longer wished to take part in an agreed murder nor did he do anything to stop them carrying out the agreement. He simply failed to turn up at the appointed place.

3 See, for example: Williams, G, *Textbook of Criminal Law*, 2nd edn, 1983, p 363; Smith, JC and Hogan, B, *Criminal Law*, 8th edn, 1996, p 154; *Becerra and Cooper* (1975).

  It is obviously not necessary that the defendant successfully prevents the commission of the offence. The issue of secondary liability would not arise at all if the offence were prevented. In *Rook* (1993), Lord Lloyd was not prepared to endorse the view that aid already afforded had to be neutralised. He stated, *obiter*, that it might be enough that the defendant 'did his best' to prevent the commission of the offence.

4 See also *Jones* (1990).

5 Lord Lane thought his formulation of the test was 'perhaps as clear a guidance as is possible in the circumstances'. It is true that the nature and variety of attempts and the complex and sometimes conflicting reasons for their

punishment makes precise formulation difficult. However, other than the obscure requirement that the defendant must have 'embarked on the crime proper', the law as it is currently formulated gives the judge very little positive guidance. The decisions of the Court of Appeal give illustrations of what is *not* necessary for liability. There is, however, no precise explanation of the type of evidence that is necessary and/or sufficient. Each case is 'merely an example' (Lord Taylor in *Attorney General's Reference (No 1 of 1992)* (1993)). It is up to the judge, therefore, to decide intuitively whether or not he feels there is sufficient evidence to allow the matter to go the jury. If he is 'wrong' – that is, if the intuitions of the Court of Appeal do not correspond with those of the trial judge – an appeal will be successful (see *Geddes* (1996) and commentary thereto).

It might be thought that the problem is not a major one as the judge is simply concerned with the threshold question of whether there is *prima facie* evidence of attempt and the jury have the task of deciding whether the acts were in fact more than merely preparatory. It is worth noting, however, that in most of the leading cases in this area, the jury found the defendant guilty of attempt, but the Court of Appeal held that there was not sufficient evidence from which a reasonable jury could conclude that there was an attempt.

6   For the recommendations of the Law Commission, see *Criminal Law: Attempts and Impossibility in Relation to Attempts, Conspiracy and Incitement*, Law Com No 102, 1980, paras 2.131–2.133.

7   The maximum penalty for this offence is a term of imprisonment not exceeding six months or a fine not exceeding level 5 on the standard scale or both.

CHAPTER 5

OFFENCES AGAINST PROPERTY

Introduction

Questions of liability for property offences occupy a considerable part of most examinations in criminal law. There are many such offences and they often overlap. Consequently, most of the questions in this chapter require discussion of the defendant's potential liability for a number of offences. Occasionally, questions raise additional issues concerning offences against the person.

The principal statute in this area is the Theft Act 1968. In addition, this chapter deals with offences created by the Theft Act 1978, the Theft (Amendment) Act 1996 and with the major offences of criminal damage under the Criminal Damage Act 1971.

Checklist

Theft and related offences

One of the major current issues concerns the meaning of an appropriation for the purposes of theft and, in particular, the question whether there can be an appropriation of property belonging to another if the owner consents to what D does in relation to the property. It is important that you have a good understanding of the decisions of the House of Lords in *Gomez* (1992) and *Hinks* (2000).

Also, as most of the offences in this section are offences of 'dishonesty', it is most important that you are well acquainted with the decision of the Court of Appeal in *Ghosh* (1982) and later cases concerning the meaning of that concept.

Issues of civil law – for example, rules concerning the passing of ownership – are of relevance to the law of theft and the basic principles should be learnt.

The following offences are dealt with (references are to the Theft Act 1968 unless otherwise stated):

- theft: s 1;
- robbery: s 8; assault with intent to rob: s 8(2);
- blackmail: s 21;
- burglary: s 9(1);

- offences involving deception: ss 15 and 16 of the 1968 Act and ss 1 and 2 of the Theft Act 1978;
- making off without payment: s 3 of the 1978 Act;
- handling stolen goods: s 22;
- aggravated burglary: s 10;
- taking a conveyance: s 12; aggravated vehicle-taking: s 12A;
- abstracting of electricity: s 13;
- false accounting: s 17;
- going equipped: s 25;
- obtaining a money transfer by deception: s 15A;
- dishonestly retaining a wrongful transfer: s 24A.

Offences of damage: the Criminal Damage Act 1971

With regard to criminal damage, you should be familiar with:

- 'simple' damage: s 1(1);
- 'dangerous' damage: s 1(2);
- arson: s 1(3);
- threats to destroy or damage property: s 2;
- the defences of 'lawful excuse' in s 5(2).

A number of the problem questions raise issues dealt with in earlier chapters.

Question 34

One day, Colin visited his friend Tom. When Colin was about to leave, he discovered that he had lost his car keys. After searching for them, he decided to take the train home, where he kept a spare set. When Colin had gone, Tom found the keys and decided to use Colin's car to go into town.

He drove into town and had lunch at the Snappers restaurant. He left the restaurant without paying for the meal.

He noticed an advertisement in a local newspaper from a minicab firm seeking 'drivers with clean cars and clean licences for immediate work with good pay'. He decided to apply and went to the minicab office. Harry, the owner of the firm, asked Tom whether the car was his. Tom responded that it was. Harry told Tom that he could start work immediately. He was supplied with radio equipment for which he was required to pay a daily fee.

His first customer was Franco, a foreign visitor, who ha airport and wished to be conveyed to the town centre. Prio car, Franco asked Tom what the fare would be. Tom lied, saying would be 'reasonable'. When they arrived at Franco's destination, Tom asked for £180. Franco expressed surprise that it was so expensive. Tom said that it was the proper fare and said that he would call the police if Franco did not pay. Franco felt that he was being overcharged but, having just arrived in England, he was not sufficiently confident to protest. He reluctantly paid the fare.

Tom worked for a few hours and then decided that he had had enough. He returned the radio equipment to the minicab firm.

He drove home.

Colin returned the following morning to collect his car. Tom did not tell him that he had used it.

Discuss Tom's criminal liability.

Answer plan

A fairly typical question about a rogue who commits a variety of property offences – mainly those involving deception. There is a lot to discuss in this type of question but none of the points are very complex. The answer has been structured according to the various 'scenes'. This is a useful technique when the question consists of a number of distinct incidents, each involving questions of liability for a number of offences.

The principal issues are:

- the meaning of 'dishonesty';
- obtaining by deception – the requirement of a causal link;
- the relationship between theft and obtaining property by deception;
- the meaning and application of 'menaces' for the purposes of blackmail.

Answer

Colin's car: taking a conveyance; theft of the petrol; abstraction of electricity – s 13

Section 12(1) of the Theft Act 1968 provides that it is an offence for a person who, without having the consent of the owner or other lawful authority, takes any conveyance for his own or another's use.

According to s 12(6), there is no offence if the accused believed, at the time of the taking, that the owner would have consented had he known of the circumstances.[1]

The test is subjective and, of course, is a matter for the jury. The facts, however, imply that Tom did not believe he would have had Colin's consent and, as there is no requirement of an 'intention to permanently deprive' for s 12, it would appear that he is guilty of the offence.

Tom may also be convicted of theft of the petrol contrary to s 1 of the 1968 Act. And, perhaps, he may be convicted of the 'dishonest use without authority of electricity (in the car battery)' contrary to s 13 of the 1968 Act. The jury may conclude, however, that, as there was no intention to cause loss, the use was not 'dishonest' (see the discussion of dishonesty below).[2]

Lunch at Snappers: theft; obtaining by deception; making off without payment

It would appear that Tom has committed the offence of 'making off without payment' contrary to s 3 of the Theft Act 1978.

There is no suggestion in the facts of the problem that he was not dishonest but, as the facts are 'open' – there is no indication given as to the reason he left without paying – it should be pointed out that, if there is evidence that Tom was not dishonest, the jury should be directed with respect to the meaning of the term and informed that the issue is a matter of fact for their determination (*Feely* (1973); *McVey* (1988); *Price* (1989)).

For the purposes of s 3, a person who makes off is not dishonest if the jury consider that what he did was not dishonest according to the ordinary standards of reasonable people or he mistakenly believed that it was not dishonest according to those standards (*Ghosh* (1982)).

Whether Tom may be convicted of obtaining the meal by deception contrary to s 15 of the Theft Act 1968 will depend upon whether the prosecution can prove, to the jury's satisfaction, that he intended not to pay for the meal prior to consuming it.

When a person orders a meal in a restaurant, he impliedly represents that he intends to pay for it on presentation of the bill and this representation continues until the bill is paid. Thus, if the customer does not intend to pay, he practises a deception (*DPP v Ray* (1974); s 15(4) of the 1968 Act).

If Tom formed the intention not to pay for the meal only after having consumed it, then he is not guilty of the s 15 offence. By that stage, he would, as a matter of civil law, have obtained ownership and possession of the meal, and thus, it would not be possible to say that he had obtained the meal *by* deception. Put simply, the deception must precede the obtaining (*Collis-Smith* (1971); *Coady* (1996)).

The fact that he left the restaurant without paying is evidence, but no more than that, of his prior dishonest intention when he ordered the meal (see *Aston* (1970)).

The same issues are relevant to the question whether he can be convicted of obtaining services (that is, the production of the meal, etc) by deception contrary to s 1 of the Theft Act 1978.

Can Tom be convicted of stealing the meal contrary to s 1 of the Theft Act 1968?

If Tom formed the dishonest intention not to pay *after* having consumed the meal then, it is submitted, he could not be convicted of stealing it. The ownership in the meal having previously transferred to him, he could not be said to have 'dishonestly appropriated property belonging to another' on leaving the restaurant.[3]

If, however, he had intended not to pay from the outset, he is guilty of theft as well as obtaining by deception (*Gomez* (1992)).

Prior to *Gomez*, although the law was not clear, the balance of authority supported the conclusion that, if a cheat deceived another into selling him something, the victim intending to transfer his entire proprietary interest, the cheat got a voidable title and could not be convicted of theft because he was the owner of the thing.[4] In addition, Lord Roskill in *Morris* (1984) stated that a person did not appropriate property unless he did something in relation to it that he was not authorised to do. If the owner had consented to the act, there could be no appropriation, even where that consent was obtained by fraud.

The House of Lords in *Gomez* disagreed. Lord Keith stated that, although the actual decision in *Morris* was correct, it was unnecessary and erroneous to suggest that an authorised act could never amount to an appropriation. His Lordship quoted with approval a passage from the judgment of Lord Parker in *Dobson v General Accident Fire and Life Assurance Corp plc* (1990), in which it was stated that appropriation can occur even if the owner consents, and it is no defence to say that the property passed under a voidable contract. It was felt to be wrong to introduce, into this branch of criminal law, questions of whether particular contracts are voidable on the ground of fraud.

This decision means that practically all cases of obtaining by deception also amount to theft. Thus, if Colin, prior to consuming the meal, intended not to pay for it, he is guilty of both offences.

By s 7 of the 1968 Act, as substituted by s 26 of the Criminal Justice Act 1991, the maximum penalty for theft is seven years' imprisonment. The maximum punishment for obtaining property by deception is a term of imprisonment not exceeding 10 years (s 15(1)); and, for obtaining services by deception, a maximum of five years and/or a fine (s 4 of the 1978 Act).[5]

The minicab office: obtaining a pecuniary advantage by deception contrary to s 16

Section 16(2) of the Theft Act 1968 defines the situations in which a pecuniary advantage is to be regarded as having been obtained and these include where the defendant is given the opportunity to earn remuneration in an office or employment.

In *Callender* (1992), the Court of Appeal held that the term 'office or employment' in s 16 was not restricted to contracts of service and would cover situations, such as the present one, where the defendant enters into a contract for services.

It must be proved, of course, that the opportunity was obtained *by deception*. Tom falsely stated that the car was his. There is, however, no deception if the prosecution fail to prove that Harry believed that representation or at least accepted it as the truth (*Hensler* (1870)). Nor would it amount to an obtaining *by* deception if Harry was indifferent as to the truth or falsity of the representation (see, for example, *Clow* (1978)).

In addition, it must be proved that Tom's obtaining was *dishonest*.[6] In *Clarke* (1996), the Court of Appeal pointed out that it is not *necessarily* dishonest to tell lies to obtain employment. The issue is one for the jury who should be directed in accordance with the test in *Ghosh*. They should consider all the relevant facts, including the defendant's beliefs and intentions in respect of the employment.

The offence under s 16 carries a maximum punishment of imprisonment not exceeding five years (s 16(1)).

Minicab office: obtaining services by deception

The supply of the radio equipment to provide information regarding customers is a 'service' for the purposes of s 1 of the Theft Act 1978. Providing the deception was operative and the obtaining was dishonest, Colin may be convicted of this offence.

(Tom's obtaining of the services may be regarded as dishonest despite the fact that he has paid for them as required (see *Potger* (1970)). The issue of dishonesty would be a matter for the jury directed in accordance with *Ghosh* (above).)

Franco: obtaining property by deception, theft

It would appear from the facts of the problem that, although initially deceived as to Tom's intention to charge a 'reasonable' fare (see *Silverman* (1987)), Franco was aware at the end of the trip that the fare requested was not the proper fare for the journey. Thus, it might be argued that Franco did not part with the money as a result of a deception practised on him; when he parted with the property, Franco was not deceived. As explained above, there is no deception unless the victim believes that the representation made is false.

However, in *Miller* (1992), a case involving similar facts to the present problem, the Court of Appeal held that the question whether there has been a deception is one for the jury to decide and, in coming to their decision, they are entitled to look to the whole course of events to determine whether the deception induced the victim to hand over the money.

The decision may be criticised. The Court of Appeal overlooked the requirement of a causal link between the obtaining and the deception. It is submitted that the accused should be convicted of an *attempt* to obtain property by deception contrary to s 1(1) of the Criminal Attempts Act 1981 if, at some stage in the proceedings, he knew that the victim was deceived or was reckless with respect to that fact (*Khan* (1990); *Attorney General's Reference (No 3 of 1992)* (1994)).

Blackmail

Colin might also be guilty of blackmail, contrary to s 21 of the 1968 Act. The *actus reus* of the offence is the making of a 'demand with menaces'.

Even though he may have expressed himself in the *form* of a request, Colin made a 'demand' for the £180 (*Studer* (1915)). It is the presence of a threat or a menace – explicit or implicit – which determines whether a statement couched in terms of request is, in reality, a demand.

In this case, Colin's statement that he would call the police probably amounted to a menace.[7] The general rule is that a menace is a threat of any action which might influence the ordinary person of normal stability to accede unwillingly to the demand (*Clear* (1968)). Where, however, the threats would not have affected the ordinary person, they may still be regarded as amounting to menaces if the person addressed was influenced and D was aware of the likely effect of his threats upon V (*Garwood* (1987)). Thus, even though a person of 'normal stability' might not ordinarily be expected to give way to a threat to call the police, Colin was aware of the special circumstances that rendered Franco – a newly arrived foreigner – more vulnerable to the threat.

There is no suggestion in the facts of the problem that Colin believed his demand with menaces to be 'warranted'. It is inconceivable that he believed he had reasonable grounds for making the demand and that the menaces were a proper means of reinforcing the demand (s 21(1)(a) and (b)) and, as he made the demand with the necessary view to gain (s 34(2)(a)), he is guilty of blackmail.

The penalty for blackmail is a term of imprisonment not exceeding 14 years (s 21(3)).

Theft

Colin may be convicted of stealing the money he received from Franco. Although Franco agreed to paying the fare, Colin appropriated it and did so with a dishonest intent (*Gomez* (1992); *Hinks* (2000)).

Notes

1   The defendant has an evidential burden in relation to a s 12(6) defence, but the prosecution have the burden of proving that he did not have the specified belief (*Gannon* (1987); *MacPherson* (1973)).

2   As Professor Smith points out, it would be strange were a person to be convicted of the offence under s 13 in these circumstances as they would have committed a more serious offence in switching the car on than driving it. The offence under s 13 carries a maximum punishment of five years, whereas taking a conveyance contrary to s 12 is punishable with a term of imprisonment not exceeding six months and/or a fine of £2,000 (s 12(2) of the Theft Act 1968; s 37 of the Criminal Justice Act 1988).

3   It is submitted that this analysis is unaffected by the decision of the House of Lords in *Hinks* (2000). When Tom received the meal, he was not dishonest and it stretches credulity to suggest that he appropriated the meal when, having consumed it, he left the restaurant.

4   See, for example: Smith, JC, *Law of Theft*, 8th edn, 1997, p 30; *Corcoran v Whent* (1977).

5   In *Gomez*, counsel for the respondent pointed to the difference in maximum terms for the offences under ss 1 and 15 in support of his submission that the offence of obtaining by deception was not submerged in theft. However, bearing in mind that the offence under s 15 carries the greater maximum penalty, this argument is not particularly strong.

6   A deliberate or reckless deception is not necessarily a dishonest one (*Goldman* (1997)).

7   It has been held that 'menaces' is an ordinary word. The jury generally require no direction with respect to it (*Lawrence* (1972)).

Question 35

Part (a)

Critically evaluate the *Ghosh* test of dishonesty.

Part (b)

Swoop was walking along the empty pier at Mudpool when she found a $50 note. She was delighted and decided to celebrate by having a meal at 'El Caro', a posh restaurant on the front. Sitting back, having consumed her meal, she overheard an American lady at an adjacent table say to her husband that she had lost $50. Swoop nevertheless decided to keep the money.

Discuss Swoop's liability.

Answer plan

Part (a)

The question requires a *critical* evaluation of the *Ghosh* test. An account of the test and its application is necessary, but not sufficient. The main criticisms of the test are based on the perceived dangers of leaving the matter of 'dishonesty' to the jury:

- the role of the jury in cases where the issue of dishonesty is raised;
- the two part test enunciated in *Ghosh*;
- the problems of leaving questions of dishonesty to the jury.

Part (b)

A relatively straightforward problem centering on the meaning of dishonesty:

- application of s 2(1)(c) of the Theft Act 1968;
- the later assumption principle in s 3(1) of the 1968 Act.

Principal authorities: *Feely* (1973); *Ghosh* (1982); *Gilks* (1972).

Answer

Part (a)

Many of the offences under the Theft Acts 1968 and 1978 require the prosecution to prove that D's 'appropriation', 'obtaining' or 'receiving', etc, was 'dishonest'.

For the purposes of theft only, s 2(1) of the 1968 Act specifies three instances of states of mind which as a matter of *law* are to be regarded as honest. The burden is on the prosecution to prove that D did not have one of the specified beliefs. If the jury have a reasonable doubt that D was dishonest – if the prosecution has failed to prove the absence of an honest belief – then the jury *must* acquit.

Section 2(1) was intended to be only a *partial* (negative) definition of dishonesty. The Criminal Law Revision Committee recognised that it would be unwise to attempt an exhaustive list of those states of mind which, in law, might be regarded as honest. The assumption in their *8th Report* seems to have been that, in cases not covered by s 2, the issue of dishonesty would be left to the jury to determine as a question of fact. In *Feely* (1973), this course was accepted as correct by the Court of Appeal. The court held that, as dishonesty was an 'ordinary' word, the jury did not require assistance from the judge as to its meaning. According to the court, the jury would be expected to decide the issue by reference to the 'current standards of ordinary decent people'.

This approach has been criticised by most academic writers as the jury are not only given the task of deciding questions of primary fact (that is, what did the accused believe or intend, etc), but are also left the responsibility of evaluating those beliefs and intentions. In a sense, where dishonesty is a 'live' issue, the jury decide the limits of liability for theft. The *Feely* approach appoints the jury to the role of 'mini-legislators'.

Some subsequent cases went even further than *Feely*. In *Gilks* (1972), for example, the judge directed the jury to consider whether the defendant *himself* thought he was acting honestly. This implies that the defendant's own standards are applied (see also *Boggeln v Williams* (1978); *McIvor* (1982); *Landy* (1981)).

In *Ghosh* (1982), the Court of Appeal held that, in determining whether the prosecution has proved that the defendant was acting dishonestly, a jury must first of all decide whether, according to the ordinary standards of reasonable and honest people, what was done was dishonest. If it was not dishonest according to those standards, the prosecution fails.

If it was dishonest by those standards, then the jury must consider whether the defendant himself realised that what he was doing was, by those standards, dishonest. It is dishonest for the defendant to act in a way which he knows ordinary people consider to be dishonest. If the defendant did not know that, the prosecution fails.

This means that a person is not dishonest if what he did was in accordance with the jury's understanding of ordinary standards or he mistakenly believed that what he did was in accordance with those standards.[1]

The first part of the test corresponds to the *Feely* principle. And, of course, the *Ghosh* test preserves the principle that the issue of dishonesty is a matter of fact for the jury and not the judge.[2]

There are a number of dangers with this approach. There may be considerable variation in standards from one jury to the next. The jury may consist of people who have quite low standards. They may believe, for example, that it is not dishonest to help oneself to the property of an employer. This would mean that some people's property rights would be less well protected than others.[3]

The second limb of *Ghosh* presents further problems. Fortunately, it does not go as far as *Gilks*. The defendant is not his own legislator. He is not to be judged by his own standards. However, it does mean that a person who has a low opinion (whether mistaken or not) of the general morality of the community will escape liability for theft. The person who has taken his employer's property and genuinely believes that 'everybody thinks it is all right to steal from their employer' is not dishonest according to *Ghosh*. Again, this means that the proprietary rights of some individuals or groups are, potentially at least, accorded less protection in law than others.

Although much of the criticism regarding *Ghosh* warns that the jury may apply terribly low standards, there is also the danger that they might apply excessively high standards. In crimes of dishonesty other than theft, the issue of dishonesty is exclusively one for the jury – s 2 applies only to theft. Thus, for example, the jury might conclude that a defendant who practised a deception to obtain money to which he mistakenly believed he was entitled was dishonest.[4]

Also, it is debatable whether juries find the test easy to understand. (They must acquit unless they think that the defendant believed that ordinary, reasonable and honest people (like themselves?) would think that what he did, believed and intended was dishonest!)

The task of the jury is made a little easier by the fact that, if it is accepted that what D did was dishonest according to ordinary standards, the judge need direct the jury only by reference to the second limb (*Thompson* (1988)).

But, if D raises the issue of dishonesty by claiming, for example, that he thought what he was doing was not dishonest according to ordinary standards, the judge should direct the jury in accordance with *Ghosh*, even if the judge believes that D was patently dishonest (*Price* (1989); *Green* (1992); *Clarke* (1996)).

It is submitted that the definition of dishonesty should be a matter of law for the judge, applied, in the ordinary way, by the jury to the facts as they believe them to be. The virtue of this approach would be that the concept might then be refined and developed by analogy with the states of mind specified in s 2 – each of which implicitly recognises the proprietary rights of the owner. This would have the virtue of directing attention towards the victims property rights and the defendants attitude towards those rights. This, it is submitted, is preferable to the current approach based on the vague standards of so called 'ordinary people'.[5]

Part (b)

When Swoop discovered the money on the pier, she probably did not commit theft. By virtue of s 2(1)(c), a person does not appropriate property dishonestly if she believes that the person to whom it belongs cannot be found by taking reasonable steps.

However, she may have committed theft when, having overheard the conversation between the Americans, she decided to keep the money. By virtue of s 3(1), a person who originally came by property innocently may be guilty of stealing it on the basis of a later dishonest assumption of a right to it.

Swoop, having heard the conversation, cannot conceivably rely upon s 2(1)(c). If, however, she contends that she thought that keeping the money in those circumstances was in 'accordance with ordinary standards', then the judge would be required to direct the jury in accordance with the *Ghosh* test, explained above (*Price* (1989)).

Notes

1 In *Hyam* (1997), it was said that, where a *Ghosh* direction was necessary, the trial judge should use the exact words of Lord Lane's formula. In *Wood* (2002), D claimed that he believed property which he removed from a disused shop had been abandoned. The Court of Appeal pointed out that a *Ghosh* direction was unnecessary. If the defendant genuinely believed that the goods were abandoned, then he was not, as a matter of law, dishonest, no matter how unreasonable that belief. A *Ghosh* direction should only be given in cases where ordinary people might have differing views from a defendant as to whether what he was doing was dishonest or not.

2   In *Green* (1992), the Court of Appeal held that it is a misdirection to use a witness as a measure of the objective standard of honesty.

3   In its Consultation Paper *Legislating the Criminal Code: Fraud and Deception* (Law Com No 155), the Law Commission pointed out that:

> Traditionally, offences consist of objectively defined conduct (or circumstances, or events) and mental states (or other fault elements, such as negligence), subject to objectively defined circumstances of justification or excuse (such as self-defence or duress). In general the fact-finders' task is to determine whether the defendant's conduct falls within the legal definition of the offence, not whether they think it sufficiently blameworthy to be an offence. A requirement that the conduct in question falls short of an undefined *moral* standard is out of keeping with this approach (para 5.11).

And concluded that:

> ... juries and magistrates should not be asked to set a moral standard on which criminal liability essentially depends. As a general rule, the law should say what is forbidden, and that should be informed by moral insights. A jury or magistrates should then be asked to apply the law by coming to *factual* conclusions, not moral ones.

4   Cf theft, where a mistaken belief that one is legally entitled to the property appropriated is an honest state of mind, *as a matter of law.*

5   See Elliott, D, 'Dishonesty in theft: a dispensable concept' [1982] Crim LR 341; Griew, E, 'Dishonesty – the objections to *Feely* and *Ghosh*' [1985] Crim LR 341; Smith, JC (1996) 28 Bracton Law Journal 27; Williams, G, *Textbook of Criminal Law*, 2nd edn, 1983, pp 726–30.

Question 36

Part (a)

Samantha borrowed Rachel's personal stereo player without permission. She returned the player when the batteries were practically exhausted. Rachel would not have consented to Samantha's borrowing of the player.

Assume that the batteries are not rechargeable and that Samantha knows that.

Discuss Samantha's criminal liability.

Part (b)

Mark took Henry's cat. He hoped and believed that Henry would assume the cat had strayed and that he would offer a reward to anyone finding it. He intended to return the cat to Henry after a few days, even if no reward was offered.

Discuss Mark's criminal liability.

Would your answer differ if Mark had planned to let the cat go free were no offer of reward made for its return?

Part (c)

Dick took Fob's watch and pawned it. He intended to redeem and return it to Fob the following week.

Discuss Dick's criminal liability.

Answer plan

A three part problem question involving similar issues and dealing with the offences of theft (s 1) and abstraction of electricity (s 13). The most important issues involve s 6(1) (extended meaning of intention to permanently deprive) and s 4 (property) and, in particular:

- the circumstances in which a borrowing is 'equivalent to an outright taking';
- the meaning and application of the phrase 'an intention to treat the thing as his own to dispose of regardless of the other's rights';
- the meaning of 'property';
- the parting of property under a condition as to its return (s 6(2)).

Answer

Part (a): theft

It is proposed to consider, first, Samantha's liability for theft, contrary to s 1 of the Theft Act 1968. The punishment for theft is a term of imprisonment not exceeding seven years (s 7 of the 1968 Act, as substituted by s 26 of the Criminal Justice Act 1991).

As Samantha only intended to borrow the stereo, she cannot be convicted of stealing it. Theft requires an 'intention to permanently deprive'. Nor can she be charged with stealing the 'use' or 'enjoyment' of the player. Theft is the dishonest appropriation of *property* belonging to another with the intention of permanently depriving the other of it. The use or enjoyment of a thing is not 'property'.

It is, however, *arguable* that she is guilty of stealing the batteries, despite the fact that she did not intend to keep them. Section 6 of the 1968 Act provides that, if certain conditions are satisfied, a person may be *regarded* as having appropriated the property with the necessary intent even though, *in a literal sense*, he did not intend to permanently deprive.

The necessary conditions are that the accused appropriated the property, intending to borrow it for a period and in circumstances *equivalent* to an outright taking.

When might these conditions apply?

In *Duru* (1976), the Court of Appeal held that if D borrows a thing intending to return it in a *substantially* different state, then he is to be regarded as having the necessary intent.[1] In *Lloyd* (1985), on the other hand, Lord Lane CJ stated that a mere borrowing is never enough to constitute the necessary *mens rea* unless the intention is to return the thing in such a changed state that it can be said that *all* its goodness or virtue has gone.

In this case, the batteries are returned with 'practically all' the virtue drained from them. Is this equivalent to an 'outright taking'?

Clarkson and Keating assume that in cases where only some of the virtue is drained from a thing, the question of whether this is to be regarded as amounting to an intention to permanently deprive is a question of fact.[2] Professors Smith and Hogan, on the other hand, contend that to extend the principle to include cases where D did not intend to drain *all* the virtue would create difficulties in drawing the line between theft and mere borrowings.[3] It is submitted that, in principle, this is the better approach. To conclude otherwise would mean that the mere use of property might, in certain cases, amount to theft. On this basis, Samantha is not guilty of theft.

Abstraction of electricity

Samantha cannot be convicted of 'stealing' the electricity in the batteries. Electricity is not 'intangible property' within s 4 of the 1968 Act (*Low v Blease* (1975)).

It would appear, however, that Samantha has committed the offence under s 13 of the Act. This prohibits the dishonest use of electricity. The punishment is a term of imprisonment not exceeding five years. The offence is not restricted to the dishonest use of mains electricity. It covers dishonest abstraction from a dry battery.

The only issue remaining as far as ss 1 and 13 are concerned is the question of Samantha's dishonesty.

Samantha may have believed, albeit wrongly, that Rachel would have consented to her using the player and the batteries. If that were the case, then, for the purposes of *theft* of the batteries (discussed above), she was not, as a matter of *law*, dishonest (see s 2(1)(b)).

If, however, she did not believe that, but raises evidence that she believed that what she did would not generally be regard as dishonest, then the judge should direct the jury (in accordance with what is known as 'the *Ghosh* tests' (*Roberts* (1987)) to consider as a matter of *fact* whether she was dishonest.

In *Ghosh* (1982), the Court of Appeal held that, in determining whether the prosecution have proved that the defendant was acting dishonestly, a jury must first of all decide whether *according to the standards of reasonable and honest people* what was done was dishonest. If it was not dishonest according to those standards, the prosecution fails.

If it was dishonest by those standards, then the jury must consider whether the prosecution have proved that *the defendant himself realised that what he was doing was, by the above standards, dishonest*. It is dishonest for the defendant to act in a way which he knows ordinary people consider to be dishonest. If the defendant did not know that, the prosecution fails.

Section 2 of the Act does not apply to the issue of dishonesty for the purposes of the offence under s 13. Consequently, as far as that offence is concerned, the issue of her dishonesty is exclusively a question of fact for the jury, directed as above.

Part (b)

Theft

Might Mark be convicted of stealing the cat? He performed the *actus reus* of theft when he took it.[4]

Mark's dishonesty is not in doubt.

The issue is whether it can be said that *at the time of appropriation* he intended to permanently deprive Henry of the cat. He planned to return the cat in return for a reward, which he predicted Henry would offer.

Section 6(1) states that a person may be regarded as intending to permanently deprive if *without meaning the other to lose the thing itself* he intends to *treat the thing as his own to dispose of regardless of the other's rights*.

Did Mark intend to treat the cat as his own to dispose of?

It is submitted that he did not. Mark did not treat the cat *as his own*. Mark did not intend to represent to Henry that he, Mark, was the owner of the cat (see *Holloway* (1849)). Nor did he intend to dispose of the 'thing' *regardless of the other's rights*.[5]

Mark, lacking the necessary intent, is not guilty of stealing the cat.

Alternative facts

It is submitted that, even if his plan had been to get rid of the cat had no reward been offered, he would still have lacked the necessary intent for theft. It could not be said that he *intended* to dispose of the thing as his own regardless of the other's rights. He believed a reward would be offered.[6]

In *Warner* (1970), it was said that s 6(1) should not be interpreted as 'watering down' the requirement of an intention to permanently deprive in s 1. *Recklessness* is not sufficient.

Part (c)

Theft

Again, the issue here is whether it can be said that Dick intended to permanently deprive Fob of his watch.

Section 6(2) provides that a person who parts with property under a condition as to its return that he may not be able to perform is to be regarded as treating the property as his own to dispose of.

The pawning of another's property falls within this section.

It is necessary, however, to consider Dick's intentions. Only if he *intended* to part with the property under a condition which he might not have been able to perform would he be regarded as having *intended* to treat it as his own. Thus, if Dick believed that he would be able to redeem the pledge, he cannot be regarded as having had the necessary intent for theft.

Notes

1 The decision centred on the 'ordinary' meaning of an 'intention to permanently deprive', but the Court of Appeal explained that they could have arrived at the same result by applying s 6(1). See also *Mitchell* (1993). Both of these decisions were overruled by the House of Lords in *Preddy* (1996), in respect of another point.

2 Clarkson, CMV and Keating, HM, *Criminal Law: Text and Materials*, 4th edn, 1988, p 788.

3 Smith, JC and Hogan, B, *Criminal Law*, 8th edn, 1996, p 558.

4 Although 'wild' animals are generally not protected by the law of theft – they are not 'property' (s 4(4)) – a domestic pet, being a tame animal, is capable of being stolen.

5 Cf *Scott* (1987), where D took items from a shop. He returned the next day with the items and asked for a refund. He was convicted of theft. Scott intended to treat the items *as his own*.

6 This situation is analogous to cases like *Easom* (1971), where it was held that a 'conditional intention' to steal is not sufficient.

Question 37

Grundy was the manager of the Red Lion Public House. Contrary to his contractual obligations and without the knowledge of his customers, he sold them whisky he had bought from a local off licence. He kept the profit made from the sale of the whisky. When he was arrested in the public house, he had two bottles of whisky that he had bought from the off licence.

Discuss Grundy's criminal liability.

Answer plan

This question raises questions of liability for theft contrary to s 1 of the Theft Act 1968; obtaining property by deception contrary to s 15 of the Act; going equipped contrary to s 25; and false accounting contrary to s 17.

The principal issues are:

- the causal link between the obtaining and the deception;
- the meaning and application of s 5(3).

Answer

Obtaining property

It is proposed to consider Grundy's liability for the offence of dishonestly obtaining property (that is, the money from whisky buying customers) by deception contrary to s 15 of the Theft Act 1968. The maximum punishment is 10 years' imprisonment. The principal issue for consideration is whether Grundy practised an operative deception within the meaning of s 15.

By virtue of s 15(4), a deception may be made by conduct, that is, on the basis of an implied representation. In this case, it would appear that Grundy impliedly represented that the whisky he offered was his employer's (*Doukas* (1978)).

However, it must also be shown that there was an obtaining *by* deception. In other words, the deception must be an operative cause of the obtaining. If P would have acted in the same way, even if he had known that D's representation was false, then D is not guilty of obtaining (*Edwards* (1978)). Thus, only if the customers would not have parted with the money had they known the truth can Grundy be convicted of the s 15 offence.

In *Rashid* (1977), a British rail waiter substituted his own tomatoes for the railway tomato sandwiches. The Court of Appeal, allowing Rashid's appeal against conviction for the offence of going equipped contrary to s 25 of the 1968 Act stated that he could not be guilty of the offence as passengers would be quite indifferent as to the origin of the sandwiches.[1]

In *Doukas* (1978), the Court of Appeal distinguished *Rashid*. A hotel waiter found in the hotel with bottles of wine which he intended to sell to make a personal profit was convicted of going equipped. Doukas appealed against the decision of the judge to allow the case to go to the jury. His appeal was dismissed. The Court of Appeal held that there was sufficient evidence of an operative deception to go to the jury. In the opinion of Lord Lane, no customer, to whom the true situation was made clear, would willingly make himself a party to an obvious fraud by the waiter upon his employer.

In *Cooke* (1986), the House of Lords held that the question whether there has been an operative deception is one for the jury in the light of all the evidence and in particular that concerning 'the attitude and understanding' of the customers.

Thus, if the jury conclude that the customers of the Red Lion would have been prepared to buy the whisky even if they had known what Grundy was up to, he must be acquitted. Alternatively, if the evidence reveals that the customers would not have bought the whisky had they known of the 'fiddle', the jury should convict unless Grundy mistakenly believed that the customers would not have minded. A deception for the purposes of s 15 must be made 'deliberately or recklessly' (s 15(4)).

Going equipped

Grundy may also be charged with the offence of going equipped contrary to s 25 of the Theft Act 1968.

Section 25(1) and 25(2) provides that a person is guilty of an offence punishable with a maximum of three years' imprisonment if, when not at his place of abode, he has with him any article for use in the course of or in connection with any burglary, theft, or cheat. By virtue of s 25(5), 'cheat' is an offence under s 15.

Clearly, in the light of the discussion above, to be guilty of going equipped to 'cheat', it must be shown that Grundy intended to practise an operative deception. The question here is not whether anyone was actually deceived (*Whiteside and Antoniou* (1989)), but whether a hypothetical reasonably honest customer would have bought the whisky if he had known the truth (*Cooke* (1986)). Might he be convicted of going equipped to 'steal'?

Theft

The difficulty in convicting Grundy of theft of the money or the secret profit made from the sale of the whisky consists of showing that he appropriated property *'belonging to another'*.

By virtue of s 5(3) of the Theft Act 1968, property is to be regarded as belonging to another where it is received on account of another and the recipient is under an obligation to retain and deal with the property or its proceeds in a particular way.

However, in *Attorney General's Reference (No 1 of 1985)* (1986), the Court of Appeal held that an employee who makes a secret profit from his position does not receive the money 'on account of another' and is not under an obligation to 'retain and deal with the property' within the meaning of s 5(3).

Further, although s 5(1) states that property is to be regarded as belonging to any person who has *'any* proprietary right or interest in it', the Court of Appeal held that, even if an employee holds a secret profit on constructive trust for his employer, this does not amount to a proprietary interest for the purposes of s 5(1).[2]

False accounting

Section 17 of the Theft Act 1968 provides that where a person dishonestly and with a view to gain or intent to cause loss falsifies any account or any record or document made for any accounting purpose, he commits an offence punishable with a maximum of seven years' imprisonment.

A person is not guilty of the s 17 offence unless there is a duty to account (*Shama* (1990)).

This is determined by reference to the terms of the contract of employment. If Grundy was under a contractual duty to account for *all sales and receipts*, his omission to account for the money received for the whisky would amount to a falsification of an account (*Lee Cheung Wing and Lam Man Yau* (1992); s 17(2)).

In addition, the prosecution must prove that Grundy was 'dishonest' and that he falsified the account with a 'view to gain' or 'intent to cause loss' to another. A 'gain' includes a gain by keeping what one has (s 34(2)(a)) and, therefore, there may be a view to gain where the falsification of the account *follows* the making of a personal profit (and see *Lee Cheung Wing*).

But, if Grundy did not know that he was obliged to account for the personal profit made from sales of the whisky, he could not be convicted of the offence under s 17. There would not, in those circumstances, be a dishonest *view* to gain.

If Grundy raises evidence that he thought that what he was doing was not dishonest, the judge must direct the jury with respect to the meaning of the term (*Price* (1989); *O'Connell* (1992)).

In *Ghosh* (1982), the Court of Appeal held that, in determining whether the prosecution has proved that the defendant was acting dishonestly, the jury must first of all decide whether, according to the ordinary standards of reasonable and honest people, what was done was dishonest. If it was not dishonest according to those standards, the prosecution fails.

If it was dishonest by those standards, then the jury must consider whether the defendant himself realised that what he was doing was, by those standards, dishonest. It is dishonest for the defendant to act in a way which he knows ordinary people consider to be dishonest. If the defendant did not know that, the prosecution fails.

Notes

1   *Rashid* is criticised by Professors Smith and Hogan. They contend that the origins of the sandwiches could not be a matter of indifference to the customer. They maintain that, although he may not consciously think about whether a seller is authorised to sell, the customer proceeds on the assumption that he is and would not willingly participate in a fraud against the employer: *Criminal Law*, 8th edn, 1996, p 566.

2   Doubt is cast on the decision in the *Attorney General's Reference* by that of the Court of Appeal in *Shadrokh-Cigari* (1988). The Court of Appeal held that an equitable interest arising under a constructive trust was a 'proprietary right or interest' under s 5(1). And, in *Attorney General of Hong Kong v Reid* (1994), the Privy Council held that bribes accepted by a New Zealand Deputy Crown Prosecutor during the course of his career were held on constructive trust for the benefit of the person to whom his duties were owed.

Question 38

Frank asked Ike if he could borrow his car. Frank said he needed the car to take his friend Nanook to the railway station (a distance of five miles). In fact, although Frank intended to take his friend to the station, he did not tell Ike that he intended to keep the car for the entire day and use it to visit his friend, Ray, who lived in a town 30 miles away. Ike let him borrow the car on condition that it was returned within an hour. Frank took Nanook to the railway station. Whilst leaving the station car park, Frank collided with a low wall, damaging it, smashing a headlight and denting the front wing of the car. Frank then drove to Ray's house and suggested that they go to the races. Frank said that Ike had let him borrow the car for the day. Although Ray suspected that Ike had not consented to Frank's borrowing the car – he knew that Ike had refused to lend the car to Frank in the past – he asked no questions and got in the car. As they approached the race track, Moon, a six year old child, ran out in front of the car. Frank slammed on the brakes. The car stopped short of Moon, who was uninjured, but Ray, who was not wearing a seat belt, lurched forward. His head struck the car window and he sustained a slight injury to his forehead. Ray got out of the car, saying that he no longer felt like going to the races and intended to take a bus home. Frank told Ray that he would meet him later. He was about to drive off when Doreen, a large cat which had been sleeping on a windowsill, fell and landed on the car causing an enormous dent to the bonnet.

Later that evening, Frank returned the car to Ike.

Discuss the criminal liability of Frank and Ray.

Answer plan

This question concerns the offences of 'taking a motor vehicle or other conveyance without authority' contrary to s 12(1) of the Theft Act 1968 and 'aggravated vehicle-taking' contrary to s 12A of the same Act. Liability for criminal damage contrary to s 1(1) of the Criminal Damage Act 1971, and the offences of 'dangerous driving' and 'careless driving' contrary to ss 2 and 3, respectively, of the Road Traffic Act 1988 are discussed in outline.

Note that s 12(1) creates two offences. If the conditions of liability are satisfied, Frank is guilty of the primary offence of taking a conveyance. Ray, on the other hand, may be liable for the secondary offence in s 12(1) of allowing himself to be carried in the taken vehicle.

One of the principal issues raised relates to whether or not Frank, having induced Ike to part with the car by misrepresenting why he wanted it, took the vehicle without consent. The major issue affecting Ray's liability concerns the *mens rea* requirement for the secondary offence. The facts of the question state that he 'suspected' the vehicle was taken without consent. Whether or not that is sufficient for liability is discussed below.

The question raises a number of issues concerning some of the aggravating circumstances in s 12A(2). In particular, the question of whether fault is required with respect to the aggravating circumstances is discussed.

Principal authorities are: *Whittaker v Campbell* (1984); *Peart* (1970); *McKnight v Davies* (1974); *Caldwell* (1982).

Answer

Frank

Section 12 of the Theft Act 1968, as amended by s 37(1) of the Criminal Justice Act 1988, provides that a person is guilty of an offence punishable, on summary conviction, with a fine not exceeding level 5 on the standard scale, imprisonment for up to six months or both, if, without having the consent of the owner or other lawful authority, he takes any conveyance for his own or another's use or, knowing that any conveyance has been taken without such authority, drives it or allows himself to be carried in or on it.

The section creates two offences: the primary offence consists of taking a conveyance and the secondary offence of driving or allowing oneself to be carried in a taken conveyance.

For both offences, the prosecution must prove that the conveyance was taken without the consent of the owner or other lawful authority and, in *Whittaker v Campbell* (1984), the Divisional Court held that consent obtained by means of a deception is nevertheless a valid consent for the purposes of the offence under s 12(1). The Court of Appeal reached a similar conclusion in the case of *Peart* (1970). D had obtained the consent of the owner of a van in Newcastle to lend it to him by pretending that he needed it for an urgent appointment in Alnwick – a town not too far from Newcastle. He knew that the owner would not have lent him the van if he had known of his real intention. Nonetheless, it was held that the taking was with the owner's consent. The Court of Appeal, however, restricted themselves to considering whether there had been a taking without consent when, in Newcastle, Peart initially took possession of the van. For technical reasons concerning the grounds of appeal, the court did not consider whether there had been a fresh taking without consent when he deviated from the route to Alnwick and made for Burnley. In the later case of *McKnight v Davies* (1974), the Divisional Court held that where there is a wholly unauthorised deviation from an authorised route, there is, at that point, a 'taking without consent'. Thus, it would appear that Frank took the conveyance without consent when he left the railway station and, instead of returning the car to Ike, made for Ray's.

Next, it is necessary to consider Frank's liability for the offence of 'aggravated vehicle-taking'. Section 1 of the Aggravated Vehicle-Taking Act 1992 inserts a new s 12A after s 12 of the 1968 Act. This provides that a person is guilty of aggravated vehicle-taking if he commits an offence under s 12(1) and after the vehicle was taken and before it was recovered, one of a number of aggravating circumstances or events occurred.

Although damage to the vehicle is an aggravating circumstance, there can be no liability for the aggravated offence with respect to the damage to the car caused when leaving the car park of the railway station because, as explained above, that occurred *before* Frank had committed the *actus reus* of the basic offence.[1] He may, however, be guilty of the offence of criminal damage contrary to s 1(1) of the Criminal Damage Act 1971. The maximum punishment for this offence is 10 years' imprisonment (s 4(2)). The prosecution would have to prove that he was at least reckless with respect to causing the damage to the car. This would require proof that his act of driving the car created an obvious and serious risk of damage and he had either not given any thought to the possibility of there being such a risk or he recognised that there was some risk of damage involved and unjustifiably took that risk (*Caldwell* (1982)).

In addition, when colliding with the wall, Frank may have committed the summary offence of 'careless driving' contrary to s 3 of the Road Traffic Act 1988, as substituted by s 2 of the Road Traffic Act 1991, punishable with a fine at level 4.

It must be proved that he drove 'without due care and attention'. This involves an objective standard; *viz,* a failure to exercise the degree of care and attention that a reasonable and prudent driver would exercise in the circumstances (*Simpson v Peat* (1952); *Scott v Warren* (1974)). All the factual circumstances must be considered by the magistrates and, although a failure to observe the provisions of the Highway Code may be relied upon as evidence of carelessness, such failure is not conclusive (s 38(7) of the 1988 Act).

Frank may have committed the offence of aggravated vehicle-taking later when approaching the race track. In addition to damage caused to the vehicle, s 12A(2) of the 1968 Act specifies a number of other aggravating circumstances. These include the fact that the vehicle was driven dangerously on a road or other public place.[2]

Dangerous driving is defined in s 12A(7) as driving in a way which falls far below what would be expected of a competent and careful driver and it would be obvious to a competent and careful driver that driving the vehicle in that way would be dangerous. This provision is based on the definition of 'dangerous driving' in s 2 of the Road Traffic Act 1988, as substituted by s 1 of the Road Traffic Act 1991. Section 2(A)(3) of the 1988 Act provides that 'dangerous' refers to danger either of injury to any person or of serious damage to property.[3] The test is, again, an objective one for the magistrates or jury, who should consider all the relevant evidence.

A further specified aggravating circumstance is that, owing to the driving of the vehicle, an accident occurred by which injury was caused to any person. No fault with respect to the manner of driving is required (*Marsh* (1997)). It is sufficient to prove that the driving was a factual cause of the injury and, consequently, Frank will be liable irrespective of whether an injury was foreseeable and despite the fact that the injury would have been avoided had Ray worn a seat belt.[4]

Furthermore, with respect to the dent caused by the cat, it is sufficient to prove that the basic offence was committed and that damage was caused to the vehicle whilst the defendant was in the vehicle or in its vicinity. For this form of aggravation also, no fault is necessary. Nor is it necessary to show a causal relationship between the taking and the damage.

The maximum penalty on indictment for the aggravated offence is two years' imprisonment. In addition, by virtue of s 3(1) of the 1992 Act, disqualification from driving for not less than 12 months must be ordered unless there are special reasons for not disqualifying.

Ray

Ray may be liable for the secondary offence of allowing oneself to be carried in a conveyance taken without consent. The prosecution must prove that he knew that the car had been taken without Ike's consent. The facts of the question state that he suspected that Frank had taken the car without Ike's permission, but did not enquire and cannot be said to actually have known of the lack of consent. Generally, however, where knowledge is an ingredient of liability, 'wilful blindness' will suffice (*Sleep* (1861); *Ross v Moss* (1965)). This means that a person knows a relevant circumstance exists when he is virtually certain that it does or has no substantial doubt that it does and deliberately refrains from enquiring.

Provided the prosecution can prove the necessary *mens rea* for the basic offence, Ray may also be convicted of the aggravated offence. Liability extends to any person who commits the basic offence under s 12(1) of the Theft Act 1968, whether primary or secondary and the same aggravated circumstances apply.

In Ray's case, however, it is not clear whether the injury sustained in the car would amount to an aggravating circumstance. Although the statute provides that an injury caused to '*any* person' will suffice, it would indeed be surprising if this were held to apply where the only person injured was the defendant himself. Provided, however, that Ray was still 'in the immediate vicinity' of the vehicle (s 12A(3)(b)) when Doreen fell on the bonnet, then he may be convicted of the aggravated offence. As mentioned above, no fault on the part of the defendant is required with respect to the damage, and it would appear that his apparent withdrawal from the venture has no effect on his liability.[5]

Notes

1   Section 12(A)(3) of the Aggravated Vehicle-Taking Act 1992 provides that it is for defendant to prove (on the balance of probabilities) that the damage or other aggravating circumstance occurred before he committed the basic offence.

2   Although the facts of the question say nothing about the manner of Frank's driving, it is necessary to discuss liability for offences involving dangerous driving as he *may* have committed one of those offences.

3   Dangerous driving is punishable with a maximum of two years' imprisonment and, unless there are special reasons, disqualification from driving for not less than 12 months.

4   If Parliament had intended that the driving be merely a factual cause of the injury, the formula 'while it was being driven, an accident involving the vehicle occurred by which injury was caused to any person' would have been preferable.

5   Note also that s 27 of the Transport Act 1981 made the wearing of seat belts in motor vehicles compulsory.

Question 39

John took his video recorder to be repaired by Fred, a video repairman. John explained that the video recorder would neither record nor play video tapes. Fred agreed to examine the recorder. He told John that he would telephone him later when he had discovered the fault. Later that afternoon, Fred phoned John and told him that the heads needed to be replaced at a total cost of £100. In fact, all that was required was a slight adjustment to the existing heads.

John agreed to the fitting of the new heads.

Fred fitted the new heads and then went to collect his car which was being serviced at a local garage. His car was ready. The total cost of the service was £75. He paid for the service by cheque backed by a cheque guarantee card, valid up to £100. Fred had no funds in his account and his bank had instructed him not to use his cheque book and cheque card.

John returned later to collect his video recorder. He paid the £100 in cash.

John asked Fred to carry the video recorder to his car for him. John falsely stated that he had a bad back. Fred was reluctant to assist him as he was very busy. He instructed his employee, Dupe, to take the recorder to John's car which was parked about a mile from the shop.

Discuss the criminal liability of Fred and John.

Answer plan

This question concerns a number of offences involving deception – obtaining property by deception contrary to s 15 of the Theft Act 1968; obtaining a pecuniary advantage by deception contrary to s 16 of the same Act; and obtaining services by deception contrary to s 1 of the Theft Act 1978.

The principal issues are:

- the representations made when using cheques and cheque cards;
- the meaning and application of 'dishonesty' in cases of obtaining;
- the obtaining of gratuitous services;
- the meaning and application of 'property belonging to another' for the purposes of s 15.

The principal authorities are: *King and Stockwell* (1987); *Gomez* (1992); *Charles* (1977).

Answer

Fred

Obtaining property by deception – s 15 of the Theft Act 1968

Firstly, it is proposed to consider Fred's liability under s 15 of the Theft Act 1968 for the offence of obtaining property, that is, the £100, by deception. This offence is punishable with a maximum of 10 years' imprisonment.

According to s 15(4), any false representation of fact, made deliberately or recklessly, amounts to a deception. Provided, therefore, that Fred knew that his statement that the heads needed replacement was false, or he was aware that it might have been false, he practised a deception. On the other hand, if Fred genuinely believed that the heads did need to be replaced, he practised no deception (*Jeff and Bassett* (1966)).

Assuming Fred practised a deception, it must be proved that he obtained the money by virtue of it. The deception must be a cause of the obtaining. In *King and Stockwell* (1987), the appellants persuaded a lady to hire them to cut down her trees. They represented, falsely, that the trees were in such a dangerous state that cutting them down was necessary. The appellants argued that had money been paid pursuant to this agreement, it would have been paid because the agreed work had been performed and not as a result of the deception. The argument was rejected. The court held that, in such cases, the issue whether the deception is an operative cause of the obtaining is to be left to the common sense of the jury.

Provided the above requirements are satisfied and that Fred had a dishonest intention to permanently deprive John of the money, he may be convicted of the offence under s 15.

If Fred is guilty of the s 15 offence then he may, in addition, be convicted of stealing the money, contrary to s 1(1) of the 1968 Act. In *Gomez* (1992), the House of Lords held, by a majority, that an appropriation of property belonging to another can occur even if the owner consents to what D does and even if ownership in the property transfers to D and, therefore, the fact that John gave Fred the money does not preclude a conviction for theft.

Obtaining a pecuniary advantage by deception – s 16 of the Theft Act 1968

The maximum penalty for this offence is a term of imprisonment not exceeding five years.

By virtue of s 16(2)(c) of the 1968 Act, a pecuniary advantage is obtained where D is given the opportunity to earn remuneration or greater remuneration in an office or employment. In *Callender* (1992), the Court of Appeal held that 'employment' was wide enough to include contracts made with independent contractors.

Provided, therefore, that Fred practised a deliberate or reckless deception (discussed above) and that he was dishonest, he may be convicted of the s 16 offence (see *Clarke* (1996)).

He may also have committed this offence when he paid using his cheque and card for the repairs to his car. By virtue of s 16(2)(b), a pecuniary advantage is obtained where D is allowed to borrow by way of overdraft.

In *Charles* (1977), the House of Lords held that a person who draws a cheque supported by a cheque card impliedly represents that he has authority from the issuing bank to use the card so as to create a contractual relationship between bank and payee; if he does not have that authority – that is, if the cheque would not be met but for the use of the card – a deception is practised. This rule applies even where the payee did not consider whether the drawer of the cheque was exceeding his authority.[1]

Provided the conditions on the cheque card are satisfied, the bank will honour the cheque. In Fred's case, this will result in his account being overdrawn. In *Waites* (1982), the Court of Appeal held that in these circumstances a person has been 'allowed to borrow by way of overdraft' – even though the drawer has been expressly forbidden to write any more cheques! (See also *Bevan* (1986).)

Both *Waites* and *Charles* make it clear that for liability under s 16(2)(b) it is not necessary that the person deceived suffers financial loss nor that the pecuniary advantage is obtained from that person. Provided that Fred was aware that he lacked the authority and assuming he was dishonest, he is guilty of the offence under s 16(2)(b).

Evasion of liability by deception – s 2(1) of the Theft Act 1978

The offence under s 2(1)(b) of the Theft Act 1978 requires *an intention to make permanent default* of an existing liability and, clearly, Fred incurs no liability for this offence. For the same reason, he cannot be convicted of the offence under s 3 of the 1978 Act (see *Allen* (1985)).

Obtaining property by deception – s 15 of the Theft Act 1968

Was Fred guilty of the s 15 offence in respect of the car?

The facts raise two issues:

(a) Did the car *belong to another* at the time of the obtaining?
   For the purposes of s 15, property belongs to any person having possession or control of it or having any proprietary right or interest in it (s 5(1); s 34(1)).
   In these circumstances, the repairer has what is known as a 'lien' over the car. The repairer has the right to retain the car until payment is made. Thus, although Fred owns the car, it belongs to the garage for the purposes of s 15.
(b) Was the obtaining dishonest?

In *Ravenshad* (1990), the Court of Appeal stated that where D has practised a deliberate deception, it may not always be necessary to give a direction on the issue of dishonesty. This is incorrect. The issues of deception and dishonesty are separate issues (*Goldman* (1997)). Where D raises evidence that he may have believed that he was acting honestly according to ordinary standards, then dishonesty is a 'live' issue (*Price* (1989)) and the jury should be directed along the lines required by the Court of Appeal in *Ghosh* (1982) to consider whether Fred was dishonest.

In *Ghosh* (1982), the Court of Appeal held that D is not dishonest if what he did was, in the opinion of the jury, not dishonest according to the ordinary standards of reasonable and honest people or he mistakenly believed that it was not dishonest according to those standards.

As Fred presumably had no intention to cause any loss to the garage – if the conditions on the guarantee card were satisfied, the cheque would be met – the jury might conclude that he was not dishonest vis à vis *the repairer* and, therefore, did not dishonestly obtain the car. If, on the other hand, the jury conclude that Fred was dishonest, then he is not only guilty of obtaining the car by deception contrary to s 15, but also of stealing it contrary to s 1. The car 'belonged to another' (see s 5, above) and the fact that the garage proprietor allowed D to drive off with the vehicle does not preclude a conviction for theft (see *Gomez*, above).

John

Obtaining services by deception – s 1 of the Theft Act 1978

Although John practised a deception by falsely representing that he was unfit to carry the video recorder and although Fred, by virtue of that deception, 'caused some act to be done', that is, he instructed his employee, Dupe, to carry the recorder to John's car, there was no obtaining of services contrary to s 1 as the benefit was not conferred 'on the understanding that it [had] been or [would] be paid for'. Section 1 does not apply to gratuitous services.

Note

1   The decision in *Charles* has been criticised on two grounds. First, it is submitted that it is not accurate to suggest that card holders act as agents for the issuing bank. Secondly, the decision appears to overlook the requirement of a causal link between the obtaining and the deception. Although P stated in evidence that he would not have accepted the cheques had he known D's lack of authority, he also said that he accepted cheques with a guarantee card because in those circumstances the bank takes the risk. Thus, he had no real interest in whether D had authority to use the card. How can it be said that D obtained *by* deception if, in effect, P was indifferent as to the truth of the apparent representation?

The decision in *Charles* means that an operative deception is practised even if the garage proprietor did not care whether Fred had authority. Only in the unlikely event that the jury are not convinced that the proprietor would have refused the cheque, had he known that Fred had no authority to use the card, can it be said that there was no obtaining *by* deception.

Question 40

Chump caught a rabbit on Adolf's land. He took it to his houseboat. Flash, who had been observing Chump, followed him. Whilst Chump had a nap, Flash, intending to take the rabbit, boarded the houseboat. Flash was about to leave with the rabbit when Chump started to wake up. Flash picked up Chump's walking stick, hit Chump over the head with it and left with the rabbit.

Discuss the criminal liability of the parties.

Answer plan

This question raises issues of theft contrary to s 1 of the Theft Act 1968, burglary contrary to s 9(1)(a) and s 9(1)(b) of the Act, and aggravated burglary contrary to s 10. Minor questions of liability for criminal damage and the offence of 'going equipped' are raised.

Flash's liability for 'aggravated assaults' is fairly 'open' – that is, we are not told the extent of the injuries sustained nor his *mens rea* at the relevant time. Thus, a full discussion of the ingredients of liability for each of the various offences – under ss 18, 20 and 47 of the Offences Against the Person Act 1861 – is required.

The principal issues are:

- the meaning and application of s 4(4) of the 1968 Act – theft of 'wild animals';
- liability under s 9(1) – burglary;
- the meaning and application of the expression 'has with him' in s 10 – aggravated burglary – and s 25 – going equipped;
- the ingredients of liability for aggravated assaults.

Answer

Theft

Whilst Chump may be guilty of an offence of poaching under the Game Acts and Poaching Acts (see Sched 1 to the Theft Act 1968), he is not guilty of theft.

The common law rule that wild creatures could not be stolen because they were not regarded as property is preserved by s 4(4) of the Act. This provides that a person cannot steal a wild creature unless it has been reduced into possession by or on behalf of another person and possession of it has not since been lost or abandoned. The owner of the land on which the animal is found is protected by the criminal law relating to poaching, but not by the law of theft.

Neither may Chump be charged with criminal damage contrary to s 1 of the Criminal Damage Act 1971. The definition of 'property' in s 10 of the 1971 Act is very similar in this respect to the definition in s 4(4) of the 1968 Act.

As, however, the rabbit *has been reduced into, and remains in, the possession* of Chump, it is capable of being stolen from him. Therefore, as the facts indicate that Flash had a dishonest intention to permanently deprive, he is guilty of stealing the rabbit from Chump.

The maximum punishment for theft is seven years' imprisonment (s 7 of the 1968 Act as amended by s 26 of the Criminal Justice Act 1991).

Burglary

By virtue of s 9(1)(a) of the Theft Act 1968, a person is guilty of burglary if he enters any building as a trespasser intending to commit one of a number of offences including theft and, by virtue of s 9(3), Chump's houseboat – an 'inhabited vessel' – is a building for the purposes of this offence.

As a matter of civil law, a person enters as a trespasser if he enters without the possessor's consent. For the purposes of burglary, the prosecution must prove, in addition, that, at the time of entry, the accused knew that he was entering without permission or was reckless with respect to that fact (*Collins* (1973)).

As Flash knew of the facts that made his entry a trespass, he entered with the appropriate *mens rea*.

The penalty for burglary in respect of a dwelling is a term of imprisonment not exceeding 14 years (s 9(3)(a)).

He may also be convicted of two counts of burglary contrary to s 9(1)(b). This sub-section provides that a person is guilty of burglary if, *having entered* any building as a trespasser, he steals anything in the building or inflicts or attempts to inflict grievous bodily harm on any person in the building.

The ingredients of liability – that D entered as a trespasser and that, at the time of the theft, he knew or was reckless as to the facts which made his entry a trespass – were present when he appropriated the rabbit.

He also may have committed burglary under s 9(1)(b) when he struck Chump on the head. However, the facts of the problem are 'open'. Neither the extent of any injuries suffered by Chump nor Flash's *mens rea* is disclosed.

Assuming that the injuries amounted to 'grievous bodily harm'[1]

In *Jenkins* (1983), the Court of Appeal appeared to accept that, for the purposes of s 9(1)(b) of the Theft Act 1968, the infliction of grievous bodily harm need not, in itself, amount to an offence of any kind.[2] The better view, it is submitted, is that the serious offence of burglary requires a *mens rea* beyond that relating to the trespassory entry and that the prosecution are required to prove that D's conduct amounted to an offence under either s 18 or s 20 of the Offences Against the Person Act 1861.

The s 18 offence – causing grievous bodily harm with intent – carries a maximum penalty of life imprisonment. The *mens rea* requirement is an intention to cause grievous bodily harm. If grievous bodily harm was his aim or purpose or he foresaw that grievous bodily harm was a virtually certain result of his conduct, then he intended it (*Woollin* (1998)).

For the offence under s 20 – which carries a maximum punishment of five years' imprisonment – the prosecution must prove that Flash foresaw the risk of causing some harm, albeit not serious harm (*Savage*; *Parmenter* (1991)).[3]

Assuming the injuries amounted to 'actual bodily harm'

If the injuries sustained are not serious, Flash may be guilty of the lesser offence of assault occasioning actual bodily harm contrary to s 47 of the Offences Against the Person Act 1861. The maximum punishment for this offence is five years' imprisonment.

'Actual bodily harm' means 'any hurt or injury calculated to interfere with the health or comfort of the victim' provided it is more than transient or trifling (*Miller* (1954)). There is no need for a physically discernible injury (*Reigate Justices ex p Counsell* (1983)).

It is unnecessary to prove that the accused intended or was reckless with respect to causing actual bodily harm (*Savage*; *Parmenter*). The offence is committed where, as in this case, D intentionally (or recklessly) applies unlawful force to another, V, who, as a consequence, suffers harm, as defined above.

Assault occasioning actual bodily harm is not a specified offence for burglary under s 9(1)(b).

Aggravated burglary

Finally, it is proposed to consider whether Flash committed the offence of aggravated burglary, contrary to s 10 of the Theft Act 1968.

Section 10 provides that it is an offence, punishable with a maximum of life imprisonment (s 10(2)), if a person commits any burglary and at the time has with him, among other things, any 'weapon of offence'.

If Flash intended to use the stick to cause injury to or incapacitate Chump, then it was a 'weapon of offence' (s 10(1)(b)).

However, to be guilty of the offence under s 10, the accused must have the article with him at the time of committing the burglary. Where the accused is charged with burglary contrary to s 9(1)(a), this is the time of the trespassory entry. Where the charge is burglary contrary to s 9(1)(b), the relevant time is the time of commission of the specified offence.

Clearly, Flash did not commit aggravated burglary at the moment of entry. Did he commit aggravated burglary when he struck Chump?

Smith and Hogan suggest that, by analogy with decisions concerning s 1 of the Prevention of Crime Act 1953 (possession of an offensive weapon), 'has with him' should be interpreted to imply a degree of continuous possession (see, for example, *Ohlson v Hylton* (1975)). In *Kelly* (1992), however, the Court of Appeal held that s 1 of the 1953 Act and s 10 of the 1968 Act are directed at entirely different mischiefs. Potts J, delivering the judgment of the court, stated that, whereas the former is directed at the carrying of a weapon with intent to use it if the occasion arises, the latter is directed at the actual use of articles which aggravate the offence of simple burglary.

Similarly, in *Minor* (1988), the Divisional Court held that, for the offence of going equipped contrary to s 25 of the 1968 Act, it was sufficient that D had the article with him prior to the commission of a burglary, theft or cheat. If this decision is correct, then Flash may be convicted of going equipped with the stick, provided he intended to use it to cause Chump grievous bodily harm.[4] He was not at his place of abode and he had (although only for a matter of moments) the article for use in the course of a burglary.[5]

Notes

1   This was defined by the House of Lords in *Smith* (1959) as 'really serious bodily harm'. In *Saunders* (1985), the Court of Appeal held that the adverb 'really' is superfluous. The question whether Chump's injuries amounted to grievous bodily harm is for the jury. See also *Birmingham* (2002).

2   If this were accepted, it would mean that the prosecution would not have to prove that the accused inflicted grievous bodily harm with the *mens rea* necessary for a conviction under either s 18 or s 20 of the Offences Against the Person Act 1861. (In 1984, the House of Lords allowed Jenkins' appeal on another ground and made no comment on this issue.)

3   If Flash intended grievous bodily harm, but the injuries sustained were less serious, then he may be convicted of an attempt to cause grievous bodily harm contrary to s 1(1) of the Criminal Attempts Act 1981. An attempt to cause grievous bodily harm is also a specified offence for the purposes of burglary contrary to s 9(1)(b) of the Theft Act 1968.

4   In *Ellames* (1976), the Court of Appeal held that the intention to use the article must relate to the future. Presumably, therefore, there can be no liability for the offence under s 25 in relation to the theft of the rabbit.

5   Professor Card has criticised the decision in *Minor*. He suggests that 'it cannot be said in common sense terms that D has the thing with him, nor that he was going equipped for stealing, etc' (which is the description of the offence given by the marginal note to the section); Card, R, *Cross and Jones: Criminal Law*, 12th edn, 1992, p 337.

Question 41

George agreed to paint Liam's flat for £500. He gave George an advance of £50. Having painted the flat, George was given a roll of notes by Liam's wife, Margaret, in payment. George put the money in his pocket without counting it. When he got home, he discovered that Margaret had given him £500. George decided to keep the excess. Later that evening, Liam, having discovered his wife's mistake, visited George to request the return of the £50. George was not at home but his wife, Lucy, who was aware that George had been overpaid, persuaded Liam that her husband had been given £450 by Margaret.

Discuss the criminal liability of George and Lucy.

Answer plan

This problem is fairly intricate. It involves liability for theft contrary to s 1 of the Theft Act 1968; obtaining property by deception contrary to s 15 of the 1968 Act; and evasion of liability by deception contrary to s 2(1) of the Theft Act 1978.

As there are issues relating to the liability of Lucy as an accessory, George's liability should be discussed first.

Note that the facts of the problem are 'open' with respect to the question of George's dishonesty.

The most important issues are:

- the meaning and application of 'dishonesty' for the purposes of theft;
- property got by another's mistake – s 5(4) of the 1968 Act;
- accessorial liability;
- was assistance given at the time of the theft?;
- enabling another to retain as a basis of liability for s 15 of the 1968 Act;
- evasion of liability under s 2(1)(b) of the 1978 Act.

Answer

George – theft contrary to s 1 of the Theft Act 1968

Theft is defined as the:

> ... dishonest appropriation of property belonging to another with the intention of permanently depriving the other of it.

George did not commit theft when Liam's wife handed over the money. Clearly, as he was unaware of the extra £50, he did not dishonestly appropriate it. He may have been guilty of theft, however, when, on discovering that he had been overpaid in error, he decided to keep the excess. Although he originally came by the property innocently, appropriation is defined to include any later assumption of a right to property by 'keeping or dealing with it as owner' (s 3(1)). Therefore, George, by keeping the £50, appropriated it.

Did he, however, appropriate 'property *belonging to another*'?

Section 5(1) provides that:

... property shall be regarded as belonging to any person having possession or control of it or having in it any proprietary right or interest ...

Section 5(4) provides that where a person gets property by another's mistake, *and* is under a legal obligation to make restoration (in whole or in part) of the property, then the property (or part) shall be regarded as belonging to the person entitled to restoration.

Where D is overpaid in error, although, as a matter of civil law, the ownership in the money passes to him, he is under a quasi-contractual legal obligation to make restoration (*Moynes v Coopper* (1956); *Davis* (1989)). Therefore, for the purposes of theft, the £50 belonged to another.[1]

It may be unnecessary for the prosecution to rely on s 5(4) to attribute a 'notional' proprietary interest to Liam or his wife. In *Chase Manhattan Bank NA v Israel-British Bank (London) Ltd* (1981), it was held that where an action will lie to recover money or other property paid or transferred under a mistake of fact, the payer or transferor retains an equitable proprietary interest. Applying this rule to the law of theft, the Criminal Division of the Court of Appeal in *Shadrokh-Cigari* (1988) held that the property paid in such circumstances is property belonging to another within s 5(1).[2]

Therefore, either by virtue of s 5(4) or the rule in *Chase Manhattan*, George may be convicted of stealing the £50 provided the remaining conditions of theft are satisfied.

Section 5(4) provides that an intention not to make restoration is to be regarded as an intention to permanently deprive. Thus, the only point remaining which requires consideration is whether George was dishonest in keeping the excess.

Section 2(1) of the 1968 Act provides that certain beliefs are, *as a matter of law*, honest beliefs. Where one of these beliefs is alleged, the judge must instruct the jury that the defendant is to be acquitted if he had or may have had one of the defined states of mind. The reasonableness of the belief is not legally relevant. The only issue is whether it was genuinely held but, of course, the unreasonableness of a belief is some evidence that it was not genuinely held (*Holden* (1991)).

When George discovered the extra £50, he may have believed that it was a bonus or tip, in which case his decision to keep it would have been an honest one, by virtue of s 2(1)(b). Alternatively, he may have been aware that Liam or Margaret made a mistake but believed that, despite the mistake, he was legally entitled to keep the money, in which case, he would be able to take advantage of s 2(1)(a). This provides that a person is not dishonest if he believes, albeit mistakenly, that he has, in law, the right to deprive the other of the property.

If George was aware that he had no legal right to retain the money, but alleges that he believed he was morally entitled to retain it, then, according to the Court of Appeal in *Price* (1989) and *O'Connell* (1992), the issue of his dishonesty should be left to the jury, instructed in accordance with the principles expounded in *Ghosh* (1982).

The jury must decide whether, according to the ordinary standards of decent and honest people, keeping the extra money was dishonest. If it was not dishonest by those standards, the prosecution fails.

If, on the other hand, the jury decide that it was dishonest according to those standards, then they should consider whether George realised that keeping the money was, by the above standards, dishonest. If he did not realise that, then the prosecution fails.

Accessorial liability of Lucy

Provided George was dishonest and is guilty of theft, his wife Lucy may be guilty as an accomplice to the theft. By virtue of s 8 of the Accessories and Abettors Act 1861, a person who aids, abets, counsels or procures the commission of an offence is liable to be tried and punished for that offence as a principal offender.

Lucy may have aided the commission of the theft.

Although accessorial liability attaches only where assistance is given *before* the conclusion of the offence (*King's Case* (1817)), it could be argued that where, as in this case, the appropriation consists of '*keeping* or *dealing* with the property as owner', the act of theft is a continuing one, in which case, the question whether George was still in the course of committing the offence is, presumably, a question of fact for the jury.[3]

The fact that George was unaware of Lucy's assistance is, it is submitted, immaterial.[4]

With respect to the *mens rea*, the prosecution must prove that Lucy intended to assist and that she knew the essential matters, that is, the circumstances which must be proved in order to constitute the offence (*Johnson v Youden* (1950)). The facts of the problem clearly support this conclusion. She had been informed that her husband had been overpaid and was aware that this was in error.

In addition, it must be shown that Lucy was either aware that George was acting with *mens rea*, that is, that he was dishonest as discussed above or, if she did not know that, she was aware that he may have been acting dishonestly (*Carter v Richardson* (1976)).

Handling – s 22 of the Theft Act 1968

If the theft was concluded prior to Lucy's involvement, then, as explained above, there can be no accessorial liability. In those circumstances, however, Lucy – assuming she *knows* or *believes* the money to be stolen – could be convicted of handling stolen goods contrary to s 22 of the Theft Act 1968. Lucy assisted George to retain the stolen money by persuading Liam that no money was owing (see *Kanwar* (1982)).

Conspiracy

There is no question of liability for conspiracy (even if George and Lucy had dishonestly agreed to keep the money). By virtue of s 2(2) of the Criminal Law Act 1977, a person is not guilty of statutory conspiracy if the only other person with whom he or she agrees is his or her spouse. The same rule applies to common law conspiracy to defraud (*Mawji* (1957)).

Obtaining property by deception – s 15 of the Theft Act 1968

Lucy may be guilty of obtaining property by deception contrary to s 15(1) of the Theft Act 1968.

Clearly, she practised a deliberate deception when she falsely told Liam that George had received £450 (see s 15(4)). And, although Lucy does not by deception obtain property for herself, there is, by virtue of s 15(2), an obtaining of property for the purposes of this offence where the accused, by any deception, dishonestly 'enables another to ... retain'.

The property obtained must, at the time of the obtaining, belong to another. By virtue of s 34(1), the definition of 'belonging to another' in s 5(1) applies to s 15. However, s 5(4) does not apply and, therefore, the prosecution will have to rely upon the principle expressed in the *Chase Manhattan* case (above).

In addition, the prosecution must prove that Lucy was dishonest. The partial definition in s 2 does not apply to s 15. The judge must direct the jury in accordance with *Ghosh* (above). For a charge brought under s 15, he need not expressly direct them that a claim of legal right is a defence as, according to the Court of Appeal in *Woolven* (1983), it is incorporated within the *Ghosh* rules.[5]

Evasion of liability by deception – s 2(1) of the Theft Act 1978

Finally, Lucy may be guilty of evading liability by deception contrary to s 2(1) of the Theft Act 1978.[6]

Section 2(1)(b) provides that a person commits an offence where, by deception, he dishonestly induces a creditor to wait for payment or to forgo payment of an existing legally enforceable liability to make a payment. In addition, D must either intend to make permanent default of an existing liability of his own or intend to let another, X, make permanent default of a liability owed by X (*Attewell-Hughes* (1991)).

It covers the situation where a debtor, by telling lies, persuades the creditor that there never has been a debt.

Provided Lucy was dishonest, and that she knew that George wished to avoid the debt, she is guilty of this offence. She has, by deception, induced Liam to forgo payment of an existing liability, that is, £50, and did so with intent to let another, that is, George, make permanent default.

It is immaterial whether the money is owed to Liam or Margaret as the offence is committed where the creditor or *a person claiming payment on behalf of the creditor* is induced by a deception to forgo payment.

If, however, Lucy did not know that George wished to default, then she did not *intend to let* him make permanent default and, therefore, would not be guilty of the offence under s 2(1)(b).

Notes

1   It is not clear whose money was used to pay George, but, as far as George's liability is concerned, it is immaterial whether it belonged to Liam or Margaret. See also *Hale* (1978).

2   Cf *Westdeutsche v Islington London Borough Council* (1996), in which the House of Lords held that receipt of money by another's mistake might not always give rise to a trust.

3   In *Atakpu and Abrahams* (1994), Mr Justice Ward stated:

On a strict reading of *Gomez*, any dishonest assumption of the rights of the owner made with the necessary intention constitutes theft and that leaves little room for a continuous course of action. We would not wish that to be the law. Such restrictions and rigidity may lead to technical anomalies and injustice. We would prefer to leave it for the common sense of the jury to decide that the appropriation can continue for so long as the thief can sensibly be regarded as in the act of stealing.

4   The Court of Appeal in *Attorney General's Reference (No 1 of 1975)* (1977) stated that D may 'procure' the commission of an offence even though the principal is unaware of D's involvement. The court stated, *obiter*, that the other forms of accessorial liability will *almost inevitably* involve the knowledge of the principal. Lord Widgery said that he found it difficult to think of a case of aiding, abetting or counselling when the parties have not discussed the offence which they have in mind. However, the court did not expressly state that the knowledge and/or agreement of the principal is a prerequisite of liability for the aider. Lord Widgery also stated that the words 'aid, abet', etc, should be given their ordinary meaning. It is submitted that the ordinary meaning of the word 'aid' does not imply consensus.

5   In *McAleer* (2002), the Court of Appeal held that where D claims that he believed he was acting honestly because of a claim of right, a full *Ghosh* direction may not be necessary, but the judge must make it clear that they must acquit if D might have believed he was entitled to the property.

6   There is no liability under 2(1)(a) as there is no remission of liability when the creditor is deceived into believing that no debt exists.

Question 42

Tony, the tenant of 23 Railway Cuttings:

(a) removed the lead from the roof;

(b) dug up a rose bush in the garden and gave it to his uncle, Sidney;

(c) offered to sell the living room fireplace to his friend, Hattie. She declined the offer;

(d) picked mushrooms from a neighbouring field intending to sell them to Luigi, the owner of a local restaurant;

(e) agreed that his girlfriend, Lolita, could take a cherry tree growing in the garden when she visited the following day.

Tony knew that his landlord would not have approved of any of the alterations or planned alterations to the house or garden.

Discuss the criminal liability of the parties.

Answer plan

This question involves consideration of the meaning of 'property' for the purposes of the Theft Act 1968 and, in particular, the situations in which a person may be guilty of theft contrary to s 1 where they appropriate things forming part of the land.

The following points need to be discussed:

- theft of 'things forming part of the land';
- an 'offer to sell' as appropriation;
- conspiracy where one party is 'exempt';
- attempting the impossible;
- the wider meaning of property for the purposes of criminal damage.

The principal authorities are: s 4(2) of the Theft Act 1968; s 1 of the Criminal Attempts Act 1981; s 1 of the Criminal Law Act 1977.

Answer

The situations in which a person may be convicted of theft where they have appropriated 'something forming part of the land' are defined in s 4(2)(b) and s 4(2)(c) of the Theft Act 1968.[1] Section 4(2)(c) is somewhat narrower than s 4(2)(b). Whereas the non-possessor can be guilty of stealing *anything* forming part of the land, a tenant can be guilty only where he appropriates a *fixture* or *structure*.

Parts (a) and (b)

Tony by virtue of s 4(2)(c) may be convicted of stealing the lead contrary to s 1 of the Theft Act 1968, but he is not guilty of stealing the rose bush. Consequently, his Uncle Sidney cannot be guilty of handling stolen goods contrary to s 22 of the 1968 Act. The goods are not stolen.

Part (c)

With respect to the fireplace, s 4(2)(c) of the Theft Act 1968, unlike s 4(2)(b), does not require that the fixture be severed to amount to an appropriation of property; in *Pitham and Hehl* (1976), the Court of Appeal held that an offer to sell is an assumption of the owner's right to sell and hence an appropriation. Thus, provided, as the facts imply, Tony had a dishonest intention to permanently deprive, he may be convicted of theft.

Pitham has been criticised by leading academics. Professor Williams argues that the purported exercise of a power is not an assumption of a right of the owner. He points out that a person who purports to sell property belonging to another does not commit a civil wrong against the owner if there is no subsequent taking of possession and, thus, there is no reason why he should be convicted of stealing it.[2]

Tony may be guilty of attempting dishonestly to obtain property, *viz*, the money for the fireplace, by deception contrary to s 1(1) of the Criminal Attempts Act 1981.

Section 1(1) provides that if, with intent to commit an offence an indictable offence, a person does an act which is more than merely preparatory to the commission of the offence, he is guilty of attempting to commit the offence.

The question whether an act is 'more than merely preparatory' is a question of fact (s 4(3)). Thus, where there is evidence on the basis of which a jury could reasonably conclude that the accused had gone beyond mere preparation, the judge must leave the issue to the jury (*Gullefer* (1990)). It is submitted that, in this case, there is clear evidence that Tony has done an act that is more than merely preparatory.

The above analysis is based on the assumption that the accused intended to practise a deception. Where a person offers goods for sale, he impliedly represents that he has a right to sell those goods (see *Edwards* (1978)) – but the facts of the problem are unclear as to whether Tony intentionally practised such a deception. He may have made it clear to Hattie that he had no right to sell the fireplace or he may have assumed that she knew he had no right to sell it in which case there would be no liability for attempting to obtain by deception.

What would the position be if Tony had intentionally made a false representation, either impliedly or expressly, that he had a right to sell the fireplace but Hattie had known that the representation was false?

Section 1(2) of the Criminal Attempts Act provides that a person may be guilty of attempting to commit an offence even though the facts are such that the commission of the offence is impossible. This is reinforced by s 1(3), which provides that D is to be judged according to his intentions and understanding of the facts.

In *Shivpuri* (1987), the House of Lords, interpreting these two provisions, held that in such cases it must be proved, first, that the accused had an intention to commit the crime in question and, secondly, that the conduct of the accused would have been more than merely preparatory to the commission of the offence if the facts had been as D believed them to be.

Thus, if Tony intentionally represented, falsely, that the fireplace was his to sell, he would be guilty of an attempt, even if Hattie knew that he had no right to sell it.

Part (d)

Although, in general, the person who picks wild mushrooms or flowers from wild plants growing on another's land is, by virtue of s 4(3) of the Theft Act 1968, excepted from the provisions of 4(2)(b), the exception does not apply where it is done for reward or sale or other commercial purpose.

Professor Smith argues that an isolated small scale case of picking might be held not to amount to a 'commercial' purpose. The wording of the sub-section implies that sales must be 'commercial' and suggests, therefore, that the protection of the sub-section would be unavailable to Tony only if he had been making a business of dealing in the mushrooms.[3]

Part (e)

Tony and Lolita may be guilty of statutory conspiracy to steal contrary to s 1(1) of the Criminal Law Act 1977.

The relevant part of the section provides that a person is guilty of conspiracy if he agrees with another that a course of conduct shall be pursued which, if carried out, would necessarily amount to the commission of an offence by one of the parties to the agreement.

There is no requirement that both parties are capable of committing the agreed offence as principal. Tony and Lolita made an agreement to dig up the tree which, if carried out, would amount to the commission of an offence by one of them (Lolita) and that constitutes a conspiracy. The fact that s 4(2) would exempt Tony from liability as a perpetrator does not exempt him from liability for conspiracy, and the exemptions to liability for *conspiracy* in s 2 of the 1977 Act are not relevant.[4]

The above analysis is based on the assumption that Lolita had a dishonest intent. If, however, she mistakenly believed that Tony had the authority to allow her to remove the tree, then her intended taking of the tree would not be 'dishonest' (s 2(1)(a) of the Theft Act 1968). Thus, as both parties to the agreement must have *mens rea*, there would be no conspiracy (s 1(1) and s 1(2) of the 1977 Act).

Criminal damage

The definition of 'property' for the purpose of criminal damage is contained in s 10 of the Criminal Damage Act 1971. It is broadly similar to the definition in s 4 of the Theft Act 1968, except that criminal damage can be committed in respect of land or a building.

Thus, Tony may be convicted of criminal damage contrary to s 1(1) of the 1971 Act for damaging the roof and digging up the rose bush.

The *mens rea* requirement, which appears to be satisfied in both cases, is intention or *Caldwell*-type recklessness with respect to the risk of damage.

As he knew his landlord did not approve of alterations, he cannot take advantage of the defence of 'lawful excuse' in s 5(2)(a) of the 1971 Act.

As far as their liability for conspiracy is concerned, s 5(2)(a) of the 1971 Act provides that D has a lawful excuse if he damages property with the consent of a person who D mistakenly believed was entitled to consent. Thus, there would be no conspiracy if Lolita mistakenly believed that Tony was entitled to authorise the removal of the cherry tree,[5] as no offence has been committed if the agreement has been carried out in accordance with *their* intentions.

Finally, the mushrooms cannot be the subject matter of criminal damage (s 10(1)(b) of the 1971 Act).

Notes

1   The relevant provisions are:
   - s 4(2)(b), which provides that a person may be convicted of theft if, when not in possession of the land, he appropriates anything forming part of the land by severing it or causing it to be severed; and
   - s 4(2)(c), which provides that a person in possession under a tenancy may be convicted of theft if he appropriates any fixture or structure let to be used with the land.

2   Professor Williams argues that it is 'jurisprudentially preposterous' to say that a person may be guilty of theft merely by making an offer. He contends that the error in the reasoning of the Court of Appeal lies in their failure to distinguish between the rights of an owner, such as the right to possession, and the powers of an owner, including the power to sell. An assumption of the rights of an owner is clearly an appropriation. Williams, G, *Textbook of Criminal Law*, 2nd edn, 1983, pp 763–66.

3   Smith, JC, *The Law of Theft*, 6th edn, 1989, p 55.

4   See also *Whitchurch* (1890) and *Duguid* (1906); *Sockett* (1908) is authority for the proposition that Tony might have been guilty as an accomplice had Lolita carried out the agreement.

5   It is immaterial whether this belief is justified or not so long as it is honestly held (s 5(3); *Jaggard v Dickinson* (1981)).

Question 43

The acquisition of an indefeasible title to property is capable of amounting to a dishonest appropriation of property belonging to another for the purposes of s 1(1) of the Theft Act 1968.

Explain and discuss.

Answer plan

This question calls for an analysis of the recent series of cases concerning liability for theft where D receives property by way of gift. If a person of full capacity makes a gift to another, then in the absence of fraud or coercion, full ownership in the property transfers to the recipient. As the *actus reus* of theft involves the 'appropriation of property belonging to another', it would seem to follow that the recipient could not be guilty of theft even if his behaviour in accepting the gift was, for some reason, morally reprehensible. That was the conclusion reached by the Court of Appeal in *Mazo* (1997), but not by the House of Lords in *Hinks* (2000). Other relevant authorities include:

- *Hopkins and Kendrick* (1997);
- *Lawrence* (1982);
- *Gomez* (1993);
- *R v Morris, Anderton v Burnside* (1983).

Answer

In 1996, Karen Hinks became friendly with John Dolphin, a man of limited intelligence, and between April and November 1996, accompanied him to his building society where he withdrew practically all his savings, a total of £60,000, and gave her the money. She then deposited the money in her account. Hinks was charged with theft, contrary to s 1(1) of the Theft Act 1968, in respect of the sums of money deposited in her account. At her trial, a consultant psychiatrist described Dolphin as naïve and trusting, but nonetheless capable of appreciating the concept of ownership and of divesting himself of property.

The defence submitted that the sums of money were gifts from Mr Dolphin and that, the ownership in the money having passed to Hinks, there was no case to answer. Counsel argued that there is no 'appropriation of property belonging to another' if, in the absence of fraud or coercion, the owner, with full capacity, consents to or authorises the transfer of property. The submission was rejected by the judge. The judge directed the jury that, even if the gifts were valid, the appellant was guilty of theft provided that her conduct fell short of the standards of ordinary and decent people and the appellant realised this. Appropriation, the judge said, included 'a straightforward taking or transfer of ... property', whether by gift or otherwise.

The jury returned a unanimous verdict of guilty.

Hinks, relying in part on the decision of the Court of Appeal in *Mazo* (1997), appealed against her conviction on the grounds, *inter alia*, that the recipient of a valid gift could not be guilty of theft.

The gifts cases

Mazo had received gifts from S, an elderly lady whose mental faculties were deteriorating. It was held that the receipt of valid gifts made *inter vivos* could not amount to theft even if the recipient was dishonest. As the trial judge had not directed the jury to consider whether S had the capacity to make the gifts, the defendant's conviction was quashed. A taking with consent would amount to theft only where the recipient did not get an indefeasible title.

However, the decision of the Court of Appeal in *Hopkins and Kendrick* (1997) cast doubt on *Mazo*.

Hopkins and Kendrick were managers of a residential home for the elderly. The victim, Mrs Clare, who was 99 years of age and virtually blind, had moved into the home in 1991. Her affairs were looked after by her daughter until the daughter's death in November 1992, whereupon the appellants took control of them. A large number of cheques were drawn on her account and, after obtaining power of attorney, they liquidated her financial assets, transferring the proceeds into a building society account. The account was set up in the names of the victim and the two appellants, but only one signature was necessary for the drawing of a cheque. The appellants cashed a number of cheques. The appellants contended that they had acted throughout on her instructions and that some of the payments were for the benefit of the victim and others were gifts from her. The appellants were charged with conspiracy to steal and were convicted.

The appellants appealed on the grounds that, following *Mazo*, the judge should have directed the jury that if the donor had capacity to make the gifts or to consent to the transfer of property, there was no appropriation and hence no theft. The Court of Appeal dismissed the appeal, holding that the submission was 'bold and surprising' and in conflict with the decisions in *Lawrence* (1982) and *Gomez* (1993) (discussed below).

Despite this, the court considered it necessary to distinguish *Mazo*. There was clear evidence in *Hopkins and Kendrick* that the victim lacked the capacity to make a gift.

Ebsworth J said:

> The judge, in summing up, in our view, made it wholly clear to the jury, for the purposes of the law, what the evidence was in relation to the level of mental capacity. There is nothing in the summing up, and nothing in the evidence, as it appears from the summing up, which could have resulted in a jury being confused as to whether Mrs Clare was somebody who is just 'not

quite up to it', with reduced mental capacity, which was what was said of S, or lacking the capacity to manage her affairs. There is, both for reasons of a strict reading of the law and, in our judgment, on the way in which it was put to the jury, no basis upon which there was either a misdirection or anything which could have rendered the verdict of the jury unsafe.

Professor Smith points out:

An instruction to convict only if [the victim] lacked the capacity to manage her own affairs was ... unnecessary if *Mazo* was wrong.[1]

The approach in *Mazo* has much in its favour. It removes a potential inconsistency between the civil law and the criminal law. Professor Smith comments:

If the gifts in these cases were valid in the civil law – neither void nor voidable for fraud, duress, undue influence or any other reason – the donees acquired an absolute, indefeasible title to the property. If it were seized from them by the police, they, not the donors or anyone else, would be entitled to recover it. They would have an action in conversion against the police – or the donor, if the police returned the property to her. It is submitted then that the question in both *Mazo* and *Hopkins and Kendrick*, in the absence of proof of deception, duress or undue influence, was whether P was competent to make the disposition she did.[2]

Hinks – the decision of the Court of Appeal

The Court of Appeal in *Hinks* (2000) preferred the approach in *Hopkins and Kendrick* to that in *Mazo* and dismissed the appeal. Rose LJ thought that Professor Smith's analysis was flawed and stated that 'civil unlawfulness is not a constituent of the offence of theft'. His Lordship concluded that an appropriation may occur even though the owner has consented to the property being taken. It followed that the receipt of a gift was capable of amounting to an appropriation and that the state of mind of the donor was irrelevant. Rose LJ observed that it was important not to conflate the two distinct ingredients of appropriation and dishonesty. Belief or lack of belief that the owner consented to the appropriation was relevant to dishonesty, but not to the issue of whether there had been an appropriation of property belonging to another.

Hinks appealed to the House of Lords, the Court of Appeal having certified that a question of law of general public importance was involved in its decision, *viz*:

Whether the acquisition of an indefeasible title to property is capable of amounting to an appropriation of property belonging to another for the purposes of s 1(1) of the Theft Act 1968.

Hinks – the decision of the House of Lords

The House of Lords (Lord Hutton and Lord Hobhouse dissenting) dismissed the appeal. It was immaterial whether the gifts to the appellant were valid or not. Appropriation is a neutral concept and thus a person could appropriate property belonging to another even though that other person had made an indefeasible gift of it.

Lord Steyn, speaking for the majority, reviewed the previous decisions of the House of Lords concerning the issue of consent and appropriation – *Lawrence; R v Morris; Anderton v Burnside* (1983) and *Gomez* – and concluded that the decisions in *Lawrence* and *Gomez* were binding upon the House.

Lawrence – the first case to deal with the issue – involved an Italian student, Mr Occhi, who arrived at Victoria station and asked Lawrence, a taxi driver, to take him to an address in Ladbroke Grove. The appellant told the student that the fare would be expensive. Mr Occhi got into the taxi and offered £1. Lawrence took the money tendered but said that it was not enough and, with Mr Occhi's permission, removed a further £6 from his open wallet. He then took Mr Occhi to his destination. The proper fare for the journey was approximately 50 pence. Lawrence appealed against his conviction 'of theft of the approximate sum of £6'. He contended that as he had taken the money with the consent of the student, he had not stolen it. The House of Lords, dismissing his appeal, held that s 1(1) was not to be construed as though it contained the words 'without the consent of the owner'.

In *Morris*, the appellants had taken goods from the shelf in a supermarket, removed the correct price label and attached a lower one. One was arrested after he had passed through the checkout paying the lower price; the other was arrested at the checkout before he had paid for the goods. The House of Lords concluded that both were properly convicted of theft. Lord Roskill said that the combination of switching the labels and removing the items from the shelf amounted to an appropriation. At that point, there was a usurpation or 'assumption of the rights of an owner' within s 3(1) of the Theft Act 1968.

Lord Roskill observed, at p 293:

> If, however, one postulates an honest customer taking goods from a shelf to put in his or her trolley to take to the check-point there to pay the proper price, I am unable to see that any of these actions involves any assumption by the shopper of the rights of the supermarket.

And that:

> In the context of s 3(1) an appropriation in my view involves not an act expressly or impliedly authorised by the owner but an act by way of adverse interference with or usurpation of those rights.

In *Gomez*, D1, an assistant manager of a shop, obtained authority from his manager, P, to supply goods to D2 in return for two cheques. D1 knew that the cheques were worthless. The House (Lord Lowry dissenting) held that although P had authorised the transaction, there was an appropriation of property belonging to another and allowed the prosecution appeal. Lord Keith, speaking for the majority, stated that although the actual decision in *Morris* was correct, it was unnecessary and erroneous to suggest that an authorised act could never amount to an appropriation and that *Morris* could not be regarded as overruling *Lawrence*. Lord Browne-Wilkinson considered the view expressed by Lord Roskill to be flawed, as it introduced the mental state of the owner into the concept of appropriation. In his opinion, the word 'appropriation' related purely to the act done by the accused.

The Court of Appeal in *Mazo* concluded that *Gomez* was restricted to cases where the consent of the owner was induced by fraud, deception or a false representation. A taking with consent only amounted to theft where the recipient did not get an indefeasible title. But Lord Steyn in *Hinks* considered that although the certified question in *Gomez* referred to situations where the consent had been induced by fraud, the majority judgments did not differentiate between cases involving deceit and those which did not.

Lord Steyn added that the tension between the civil and criminal law was not so important as to justify a narrowing of the definition of appropriation. Such a course would unjustifiably restrict the scope of the law of theft. Nor was he persuaded by counsel's submission that the decision would lead to 'absurd and grotesque' results. The requirement that the appropriation was dishonest would provide adequate protection against injustice.

Dishonesty

Section 2(1) of the Theft Act 1968 defines three states of mind which are, as a matter of law, not dishonest. The list is not exhaustive. Where the statute is silent, the issue of dishonesty is a question of fact for the jury and, in such cases, the jury should be instructed that a defendant is dishonest if what he did fell short of the ordinary standards of reasonable and honest people and he realised that (*Ghosh* (1982)).

Lord Hutton, whilst agreeing with the majority response to the certified question, thought that the direction on the issue of Hinks' dishonesty was materially defective. The instructions had failed to address the issue of capacity as it related to this element of theft and thus there was the danger the jury might have convicted simply on the basis that the behaviour of the defendant was morally reprehensible.

Belief that the owner would have consented

Section 2(1)(b) of the Theft Act 1968 provides that an appropriation is not to be regarded as dishonest if it is done in the belief that the owner would have consented had he known of the appropriation and the circumstances of it. Clearly, the sub-section is intended to apply to situations where the alleged thief *mistakenly* believed he would have had the owner's consent, but it would be remarkable if it did not also apply to the situation where the recipient of property knew that he, in fact, did have the owner's consent to appropriate the property.

Indeed, in *Lawrence*, Viscount Dilhorne had said that if the appellant had believed that Mr Occhi had known that the fare was excessive and nonetheless agreed to pay it, the element of dishonesty would not have been established.

Lord Hutton observed that a person's appropriation should not be regarded as dishonest if the other person actually gives the property to him and that, in cases involving gifts, issues of capacity and deceit are relevant to this element of theft. Provided Mr Dolphin had capacity to make the gifts and Ms Hinks had practised neither fraud nor coercion, the appropriation was not dishonest, irrespective of how deplorable her conduct may have been.

Belief in a legal right to deprive

In his dissenting speech, Lord Hobhouse referred to s 2(1)(a) of the Theft Act, which provides that a person is not dishonest if he appropriates property in the belief that he has a legal right to deprive the other of it and pointed out that in the case of a valid gift, the recipient's knowledge that he has such a right must inevitably be relevant to the question of whether he is guilty of theft.

The majority declined to consider the judge's directions on the issue of dishonesty. It had not formed part of the certified question and Lord Steyn felt that the House was not properly informed as to how the issue had been dealt with at trial. Nonetheless, his Lordship considered a number of hypothetical situations involving the transfer of an indefeasible title to property in which the transferor acted under a misapprehension of which the recipient was aware. His Lordship remarked, at p 843, that:

> ... a jury could *possibly* find that the acceptance took place in the belief that the transferee had the right in law to deprive the other of it within the meaning of s 2(1)(a) of the 1968 Act. (Emphasis added.)

Does this mean that a defendant who fails to appreciate that he is in law entitled to the property transferred to him might be guilty of theft?

It surely cannot be correct that, whilst a defendant who mistakenly believes that he has a legal right to property that he appropriates is exonerated, a defendant who mistakenly believes that he has no legal right to a gift is guilty of stealing, provided the jury conclude that his acceptance of the gift was morally reprehensible.

Property belonging to another

Lord Hobhouse noted, at p 854, that although the House of Lords and the Court of Appeal have warned on a number of occasions against introducing complex questions of civil law into the law of theft:

> [T]he truth is that theft is a crime which relates to civil property and, inevitably, property concepts from the civil law have to be used and questions answered by reference to that law.

Section 1(1) of the Theft Act 1968 requires that the property belonged to another at the time of the appropriation and s 5 of the Act defines and qualifies the expression 'belonging to another' by reference to a number of civil law concepts. Thus, in some cases of theft, it will be necessary to have recourse to the civil law to determine whether the relevant property belonged to the alleged victim or the defendant. If the transferor has validly transferred ownership and possession to the defendant and retains no equitable or restitutionary rights, no keeping or dealing with the property by the defendant can amount to theft, irrespective of whether he is dishonest and whether he is regarded as appropriating it.

Conclusion

Hinks is the fourth case in which the House has considered whether an act of appropriation requires an unlawful assumption of the rights of an owner and it is the third in which it has concluded that it does not. Despite the strength of the arguments to the contrary and despite the intention of the framers of the Theft Act 1968, every acquisition of property amounts to an appropriation. A person appropriates property when he accepts a gift.[3]

Notes

1   See the commentary on the decision in the *Criminal Law Review*, 1997, p 360.

2   *The Law of Theft*, 8th edn, 1997, p 19.

3   Lord Steyn believed that eliminating the need for an explanation of the civil law in respect of appropriation was 'a great advantage in an overly complex corner of the law'. Civil unlawfulness, it seems, is not a constituent of this element of

theft. But if Lords Hutton and Hobhouse are correct, and it is submitted that they are, the judge may have to explain the relevant civil law issues to the jury when instructing them to consider whether the appropriation was dishonest and whether the property belonged to another at the time of the appropriation.

Question 44

Dodger was a pickpocket. He entered a branch of the MidWest bank and waited for a customer to make a large withdrawal of cash. Mrs Pendlebury entered the bank and withdrew £500. She put the money in an envelope and put the envelope into her bag. Whilst she was distracted, Dodger picked the envelope from her bag. Mrs Pendlebury realised what had happened and screamed for assistance. Dodger dropped the money and ran out of the bank. Trevor, an employee of the bank, tried to block Dodger's escape. Dodger pushed Trevor who fell and suffered slight bruising. Dodger hailed a taxi and asked the taxi driver to take him to the station. When they arrived at the station, Dodger asked if he could pay by cheque. The taxi driver reluctantly agreed. Dodger 'paid' the fare with a stolen cheque.

   Discuss Dodger's criminal liability.

Answer plan

This question involves a number of offences contrary to the 1968 and 1978 Theft Acts. Although it does not raise any particularly difficult issues, it is important to be methodical about answering this question. It is advisable in a question of this type for your answer to mirror the sequence of events.

   Particular issues to be considered are:

- burglary: did D 'enter the bank as a trespasser'?;
- robbery: was force used in order to steal?;
- assaults: only minor injuries are suffered and therefore only liability under s 47 of the Offences Against the Person Act 1861 needs to be considered;
- obtaining services by deception: was there a causal link?;
- evasion of liability by deception: representations made when drawing cheques;
- making off without payment: does a person make off if he leaves with permission? Is payment made 'as expected or required' when a stolen cheque is given?

Answer

Burglary (s 9(1)(a))

Dodger may be convicted of burglary contrary to s 9(1)(a) of the Theft Act 1968. This provides that a person commits burglary if he enters a building as a trespasser with intent to commit one of a number of specified offences, including theft (s 9(2)).

A person enters as a trespasser if he enters without consent or permission. Although there is an implied permission to enter a bank, this is restricted to particular lawful purposes. As Dodger entered the building intending to steal, he entered in excess of the implied permission (*Jones and Smith* (1976)) and, as he knew of the facts that made his entry trespassory, he entered with the appropriate *mens rea* (*Collins* (1973)).

Dodger did not intend to steal specific property from a particular individual when he entered the bank. This, however, does not present a problem. A person may be convicted of burglary contrary to s 9(1)(a) if he intended to steal something in the building, even though, at the time of entry, he had no specific item in mind. In *Attorney General's References (Nos 1 and 2 of 1979)* (1979), it was held that an intention to steal, conditional on there being money in the building, would suffice for burglary. The indictment should be framed in general terms alleging an 'intent to steal' without reference to specific property or victim.

Theft

When Dodger took the money from Mrs Pendlebury's bag, he committed theft contrary to s 1 of the Theft Act 1968. In *Corcoran v Anderton* (1980), two youths snatched a bag from a woman. The Divisional Court held that the appropriation took place at the moment they snatched it from her grasp.

The fact that Dodger did not manage to keep possession of the money makes no difference to his liability. Theft requires an intention to permanently deprive; there is no requirement of permanent deprivation in fact.

Burglary (s 9(1)(b))

At this point, he also committed burglary contrary to s 9(1)(b) of the 1968 Act.

This provides that a person is guilty of burglary if, having entered a building as a trespasser, he commits one of a number of specified offences, including theft.

It must be shown that the defendant entered as a trespasser (see discussion of this point, above) and that *at the time of the theft* he knew or was at least reckless with respect to the facts that made his entry trespassory (*Collins*).

Robbery

Robbery under s 8 of the Theft Act 1968 requires the use or threat of force on any person in order to steal. There is no evidence in this case that he used force on Mrs Pendlebury when he stole the envelope from her bag. And, although for the purposes of robbery the force may be used on *any* person and not necessarily the person from whom the property was stolen, the force used against Trevor, it is submitted, would not suffice for robbery. Section 8 requires that the force is used 'immediately before or at the time of the theft' and 'in order to steal'. Dodger applied force to Trevor *after* the theft and did so in order to escape and not to steal (see *James* (1997)).

In *Hale* (1978), it was said that an appropriation is a continuing act and that a person may be guilty of robbery when he uses force as he makes off with the property. The Court of Appeal held that the question whether the theft has come to an end is one for the jury (see also *Atakpu and Abrahams* (1994)). In *Hale*, however, the defendants still had possession of the property as they made their getaway. In the case of Dodger, the theft clearly came to an end when he dropped the envelope.

Assaults

Dodger may be convicted of an assault occasioning actual bodily harm contrary to s 47 of the Offences Against the Person Act 1861. The section requires that the defendant committed an assault or a battery which resulted in actual bodily harm (*DPP v Little* (1991)).

When Dodger pushed Trevor in order to escape, he committed a battery. A battery is the intentional or reckless infliction of unlawful personal force on any person (*Faulkner v Talbot* (1981)).

'Actual bodily harm' was defined in *Miller* (1954) to include any hurt or injury which interferes with the health or comfort of the victim and this would include even minor bruising.

Although the *actus reus* of the offence under s 47 requires that actual bodily harm be occasioned, the House of Lords held in *Savage* (1991) that, as far as the *mens rea* for the offence is concerned, it is not necessary to prove that the accused intended or foresaw actual bodily harm; all that is required is intention or recklessness with respect to the application of force.

Recklessness in this context bears a 'subjective' meaning – '*Cunningham*-type' recklessness is required (*Spratt* (1991)).

Thus, as he intentionally applied force to Trevor, and Trevor suffered actual bodily harm as a result, Dodger may be convicted of the offence under s 47, punishable with a maximum of five years' imprisonment.[1]

There is no liability under either s 18 or s 20 of the 1861 Act. To amount to a 'wound', the inner and outer skin must be broken (*JCC v Eisenhower* (1984)) – a bruise is not a wound – and, presumably, no jury would consider the injuries suffered by Trevor to be serious.

Obtaining services by deception

Dodger may be guilty of the offence of 'obtaining services by deception' contrary to s 1 of the Theft Act 1978.

If, when he hired the taxi, Dodger intended to use the stolen cheque to pay the fare, then he practised a deception which induced the taxi driver to 'confer a benefit by doing some act ... on the understanding that the benefit ... will be paid for'.[2]

(A deception is a false statement made deliberately or recklessly (s 15(4) of the Theft Act 1968)). A person hiring a taxi impliedly represents that he intends to pay the appropriate fare at the destination and, thus, if he intends to avoid payment, he practises a deception.)

Evasion of liability

When he induced the taxi driver to accept the cheque, Dodger evaded liability by deception contrary to s 2(1)(b) of the Theft Act 1978. He practised a deception which induced the taxi driver to wait for payment of an existing liability.

In *Gilmartin* (1983), it was held that the giver of a cheque impliedly represents that it will be honoured. Dodger knew the cheque would not be met and, consequently, he practised a deception. Section 2(3) provides that, for the purposes of 2(1)(b), a person induced to take a cheque in payment is not to be regarded as having been paid, but as being induced to wait for payment.

As Dodger intended to make permanent default, he is guilty of the s 2(1)(b) offence.[3]

Making off without payment

Whether Dodger might be convicted of 'making off without payment' contrary to s 3 of the Theft Act 1978 is not clear.

It remains to be authoritatively decided whether a person can be said to have 'made off without having paid as required or expected' if he left with the consent of the creditor, that consent having been obtained by deception.

A circuit judge at Lincoln Crown Court held that there is no 'making off' if the creditor consents to the defendant's leaving in circumstances such as those in the present problem (*Hammond* (1982)). It was said that a person who takes a cheque without a cheque card is aware of the risk of non-payment and, as he allows D to leave, it cannot be said that D 'makes off'.

It is submitted that this interpretation of the section is wrong. The section is aimed at the bilking customer – it should not matter whether D leaves with stealth or openly, with or without the apparent consent of P.

If this latter view is correct, Dodger committed the s 3 offence on leaving the taxi. A stolen cheque does not operate as a conditional discharge of his liability to pay. Dodger made off *without having paid as expected or required*.

Going equipped

Section 25 of the Theft Act 1968 provides that a person is guilty of an offence if:

- when not at his place of abode;
- he has with him any article;
- for use in the course of or in connection with any burglary, theft or cheat.

By virtue of s 25(5), a 'cheat' is an offence under s 15 of the 1968 Act.

Although Dodger has not actually used the stolen cheque for a specified offence, he may be convicted of the s 25 offence if it could be proved that he *intended* to use it to obtain property if and when the opportunity arose (*Ellames* (1976)).

Notes

The facts raise no issue of dishonesty and so this element has not been discussed. However, it is, of course, an ingredient of the *mens rea* for each of the Theft Acts offences (except s 25 of the 1968 Act). If the issue is raised, the prosecution must prove beyond reasonable doubt that the appropriation, obtaining or evasion was dishonest.

1   But note that, as a matter of prosecuting policy, according to the Crown Prosecution Service, the appropriate charge will be:

[Common assault] contrary to s 39 where the injuries amount to no more than ... (among other things) ... minor bruising [Code for Crown Prosecutors, June 1994, para 2:4].

2   If his decision to avoid payment was only made when he reached the destination, then the vital causal link between the deception and the obtaining would be lacking (see, for example, *Collis-Smith* (1971)).

3   There was no remission of the liability nor did the taxi driver agree to extinguish the debt and, therefore, there can be no liability under s 2(1)(a) of the 1978 Act.

Question 45

George was an assistant in a shop selling video recorders. One day, Arnold visited him at the shop and told him that, unless George gave him a video recorder, he would get his (that is, Arnold's) brother, Malcolm, to go round to George's house and beat up his wife when she returned from her mother's. George took a video recorder from the shelf and gave it to Arnold.

Arnold swapped the video recorder with his friend, Barry, for a compact disc player which Barry had lawfully purchased. Barry knew that the video recorder was stolen, but did not reveal his knowledge to Arnold.

Barry sold the video recorder for £280 to Charlie, a *bona fide* purchaser. Charlie gave Barry a cheque in payment.

Later that evening, Charlie learned how Arnold had come by the video recorder. Although he knew he was not entitled to, Charlie sold the video recorder for £300 to Eric, a *bona fide* purchaser. Charlie deposited the money in an account jointly held by him and his wife, Maureen.

Arnold, who had become bored with the compact disc player, sold it to David. David was aware of the circumstances by which Arnold had come by the disc player.

Discuss the liability of George, Arnold, Barry, Charlie, Maureen and David.

Answer plan

This problem centres on the law relating to handling stolen goods, an offence contrary to s 22 of the Theft Act 1968. It also raises issues concerning:

- theft (s 1);
- robbery (s 8);
- blackmail (s 21);
- procuring the execution of a valuable security (s 20(2));
- obtaining a money transfer by deception (s 15A);
- dishonestly retaining a wrongful credit (s 24A); and
- attempt (s 1 of the Criminal Attempts Act 1981).

Answer

George

Theft

George may be charged with theft contrary to s 1 of the Theft Act 1968. He may, however, be able to take advantage of the defence of duress. There is an evidential burden on the accused in respect of the defence, but the burden of disproving it lies with the prosecution (*Gill* (1963)).

It is available where the defendant was, or may have been, compelled to commit an offence because he had good cause to fear that, if he did not do so, he would be killed or would suffer serious injury and a sober person of reasonable firmness sharing the characteristics of the accused would have responded in a similar fashion (*Graham* (1982); *Howe* (1987)).[1] In *Ortiz* (1986), the Court of Appeal held that threats to seriously injure one's spouse might amount to duress.

The major difficulty that George may have in successfully pleading the defence relates to the immediacy, or lack thereof, of the threat. In *Hudson* (1971), the Court of Appeal held that if the prosecution prove that the defendant failed to avail himself of a reasonable opportunity to render the threat ineffective – by, for example, reporting the matter to the police – the defence cannot be relied upon. The question is one for the jury who, in deciding whether an opportunity was reasonably open to the defendant, should have regard to all the circumstances and to any risks to which he might be exposing himself or his wife (see also *Cole* (1994)).

If George's plea is successful, then he will be absolved of criminal liability. If not, then the threats ought to be regarded as a factor in mitigation.

Arnold

Handling

If George's plea of duress is unsuccessful, then, conceivably, Arnold was guilty of handling stolen goods contrary to s 22(1) of the 1968 Act. However, a receiver is guilty of handling only if he dishonestly received them otherwise than in the course of the stealing. The stipulation is a reference to the offence of theft by virtue of which the goods originally became stolen.

Was the theft complete at the time Arnold received the video recorder?

In *Pitham and Hehl*, it was held that theft is an instantaneous occurrence complete at the moment the goods are first appropriated. This decision is unlikely to be followed as it would mean that the phrase 'in the course of the stealing' was of no effect. It is submitted that a better approach is to be found in the decisions of the Court of Appeal in *Atakpu and Abrahams* (1994) and *Hale* (1978), in which it was held that an appropriation continues as long as the thief is 'on the job' – a question for the jury.

Theft

Irrespective of whether he is guilty of handling, Arnold is guilty of theft contrary to s 1 of the Act. He dishonestly appropriated property belonging to another with the intention of permanently depriving the other of it.

Robbery

Although Arnold has stolen and employed threats in order to steal, he cannot be guilty of robbery contrary to s 8 of the Theft Act 1968, because he did not 'put or seek to put any person in fear of being then and there subjected to force'. George was not in fear of being subject to force. Neither was his wife. She was not present at the time the threats were made (*Taylor* (1996)).

Blackmail

Arnold may, however, be guilty of blackmail contrary to s 21 of the Theft Act 1968. The *actus reus* consists of a 'demand with menaces'.

He made a 'demand' when he instructed George to give him a recorder.

'Menaces' includes threats of any action detrimental or unpleasant to the person addressed, provided that it would have moved an ordinary person of normal stability and courage to accede unwillingly to the demand (*Thorne* (1937); *Clear* (1968)).

The question whether a threat amounts to a menace is one for the jury. One might reasonably expect them to conclude that a threat to beat up a man's wife would move him to accede unwillingly to a demand to hand over property.

It is immaterial that the threat related to action to be taken by Malcolm and not Arnold, the person making the threat (s 21(2)). Nor does it matter that the victim of the blackmail, George, was not the individual at whom the threatened action was directed.

The requirement that the demand was made with a 'view to gain' in terms of property is satisfied (s 34(2)(a)).

Whether or not the demand with menaces was unwarranted is a question of *mens rea*. There is nothing in the facts to suggest that Arnold believed that he had reasonable grounds for making the demand and that the menaces were a proper means of reinforcing the demand, and, therefore, it would appear that he is guilty of blackmail (and see *Harvey* (1981)).

Attempt to obtain property by deception

In *Edwards* (1978), the Court of Appeal held that where a person purports to sell property, he impliedly represents that he has a right to sell it. Provided Arnold thought that Barry believed the goods belonged to him, Arnold may be convicted of attempting to obtain property by deception contrary to s 1(1) of the Criminal Attempts Act 1981 (see s 1(2) and (3)).

Barry

Theft and handling

Barry is guilty of theft of the video recorder contrary to s 1 and handling stolen goods contrary to s 22 of the Theft Act 1968.

Obtaining by deception

Despite his deception, Barry is not guilty of obtaining property by deception contrary to s 15(1) of the Act because the 'thing in action' represented by the cheque is property which belonged to D from the moment it came into being. It was never 'property belonging to another' (*Preddy* (1996)). Nor could he be convicted of dishonestly obtaining the cheque itself (*Clark* (2001)). In addition, in *Williams* (2001), it was held that as the presentation of the cheque caused a dimunition of the victim's credit balance in his bank account, it amounted to an appropriation of the victim's property and thus D may be convicted of stealing it.

But, provided the cheque has been presented and honoured, a 'money transfer' as defined in s 15A – that is, a debit of an amount of money made to one account and a credit to another, the credit resulting from the debit – has been obtained by deception.

The penalty for obtaining a money transfer is a term of imprisonment not exceeding 10 years (s 15A).

Procuring the execution of a valuable security

He was also guilty of this offence which was complete on the signing of the cheque. The maximum penalty for this offence is seven years' imprisonment (s 20(2)).

Charlie

Theft

Charlie, as he was *bona fide,* was not guilty of theft when he took possession of the video recorder. Nor, on discovering that it was stolen, was he guilty of theft by 'keeping or dealing with it as owner'. Section 3(2) provides an exception to the later assumption in s 3(1). The sub-section protects – from a conviction for theft – the innocent purchaser of stolen goods who later discovers they are stolen and decides to keep them or otherwise dispose of them.

Also, as he had no *mens rea* when he took possession, he cannot be convicted of handling by receiving. Nor, when he sold it, did he commit handling. In *Bloxham* (1983), it was held that a person who sells stolen goods on his own behalf does not undertake nor assist in the realisation or disposal by or for the benefit of another. The House of Lords held that a person who sells an article does not assist the buyer to dispose of it, since the buyer does not dispose of it nor does the seller undertake the realisation or disposal for the benefit of another as he sells it for his own benefit. The buyer benefits from the purchase, but not from the realisation.

However, Charlie may be convicted of obtaining property, *viz,* £300 cash by deception, by representing that the goods were his to sell (see the discussion of *Edwards* (above)). Section 3(2) does not affect the principles of civil law concerning ownership, nor does it provide protection from the offence in s 15(1).

As one of the outcomes of the House of Lords' decision is that all instances of obtaining property by deception except those involving land are also instances of theft, Charlie may be convicted of stealing the money.[2]

Maureen

Dishonestly retaining a wrongful credit

A 'wrongful credit' (that is, one deriving from a theft) has been made to an account in respect of which she has an interest. If she knows or believes that the property is stolen and has dishonestly failed to take reasonable steps to cancel the credit, she is guilty of an offence contrary to s 24A. So too is Charlie.

A person guilty of an offence under this section is liable to imprisonment for a term not exceeding 10 years.

David

By virtue of s 24(2), the compact disc player amounted to 'stolen goods', since it directly represented the goods originally stolen (the video recorder) in the hands of the thief (Arnold) as the proceeds of a disposition of them. As he was aware of the circumstances – and provided he is dishonest – he is guilty of handling by receiving.

Notes

1   The characteristics of the defendant which may be attributed to the reasonable person include age and sex; and, if appropriate, serious physical disability or recognised psychiatric conditions such as post-traumatic stress disorder; but:

> ... the mere fact that the accused is more pliable, vulnerable, timid or susceptible to threats than a normal person are not characteristics with which it is legitimate to invest the reasonable/ordinary person for the purpose of considering the objective test [*per* Stuart-Smith LJ in *Bowen* (1996)].

See also *Hegarty* (1994); *Horne* (1994); *Hurst* (1995) and *Flatt* (1996). Cf *Emery* (1993).

2   It is possible that Charlie thought that, despite everything, selling the recorder was not dishonest; in which case, it is a matter for the jury directed in accordance with *Ghosh* (1982).

Question 46

Part (a)

Albert approached Mrs Bennett as she was walking in the park with her six month old baby, Edgar. Albert threatened to hurt Edgar unless Mrs Bennett handed over some money. Mrs Bennett took £50 from her purse and gave it to Albert.

Discuss Albert's criminal liability.

Part (b)

Michael was owed £30 by Thomas. When Michael asked for the return of the money owing, Thomas told him that he was unable to pay until the end of the month. Angered by this, Michael told Thomas that unless he hand over his watch in satisfaction of the debt he would beat him up. Reluctantly, Thomas handed over the watch.

Discuss Michael's criminal liability.

Answer plan

The principal issues are:

- robbery contrary to s 8 of the Theft Act 1968;
- blackmail contrary to s 21;
- the meaning of 'puts or seeks to put any person in fear of being then and there subjected to force' in s 8;
- the meaning of 'menaces' in s 21;
- the difference between the meaning of 'dishonesty' for the purposes of theft and 'unwarranted' for the purposes of blackmail.

Answer

Part (a)

Theft

Albert has committed theft of the £50 contrary to s 1 of the Theft Act 1968, an offence carrying a maximum of seven years' imprisonment (s 7, as amended by s 26 of the Criminal Justice Act 1991). Although Mrs Bennett gave him the money, it was obviously not intended as a gift and, thus, it can be said that he 'appropriated property belonging to another'; the facts imply that he had the *mens rea* for theft.

Robbery

A person is guilty of robbery contrary to s 8 if he steals and, immediately before or at the time of doing so, and in order to do so, he uses force on any person or puts or seeks to put any person in fear of being then and there subjected to force. The offence is punishable with life imprisonment (s 8(2)).

However, although for the purposes of robbery, threats of force used on *any* person in order to steal will suffice, s 8 requires that the accused puts or seeks to put that person *in fear of being then and there subject to force*. This requirement is not satisfied in the current problem. Albert did not put nor seek to put Mrs Bennett in fear of being subject to force because the threat was to hurt Edgar. Neither did he put, nor presumably seek to put, Edgar in fear of being subject to force, as Edgar was, of course, unaware of Albert's threats (see *Taylor* (1996)).

For similar reasons, Albert may not be convicted of common assault contrary to s 39 of the Criminal Justice Act 1988 nor assault with intent to rob contrary to s 8(2) of the Theft Act 1968. A person is guilty of an assault if he intentionally or recklessly causes another to apprehend immediate and unlawful personal violence. In other words, the victim must anticipate the application of immediate and unlawful force to his body. For the reasons explained above, neither Mrs Bennett nor Edgar apprehended such force (*Fagan v Metropolitan Police Commissioner* (1969)).

Blackmail

Section 21 of the Theft Act 1968 provides that a person is guilty of blackmail if, with a view to gain for himself or another or with intent to cause loss to another, he makes any unwarranted demand with menaces. Blackmail is an offence triable only on indictment and punishable with imprisonment for a maximum of 14 years (s 21(3)).

Albert has made a demand for £50.

A 'menace' includes threats of any action detrimental to or unpleasant to the person addressed. It is not restricted to threats of violence directed at the victim of the demand (*Thorne v Motor Trade Association* (1937)). Provided the threat is of such a nature and extent that the ordinary person of normal stability and courage would be influenced to accede unwillingly to the demand, the threat amounts to a menace (*Clear* (1968)).

Albert's threat to hurt Edgar would appear to amount to a menace. It is an issue for the jury, but one might reasonably expect them to conclude that a threat to hurt a baby would move a mother to accede unwillingly to a demand to hand over money.

A blackmail demand must be made with a view to gain or intent to cause loss in terms of money or other property (s 34(2)(a)). In this case, Albert made the demand with a view to gain money.

Provided the prosecution can prove that Albert either did not believe that he had reasonable grounds for making the demand or that he did not believe that the menaces were a proper means of reinforcing the demand – and, from the facts, there appears to be no reason to doubt this – Albert's demand with menaces was 'unwarranted' and he may be convicted of blackmail (see below for a fuller discussion of the meaning of 'unwarranted').

Part (b)

Theft

Michael has committed the *actus reus* of theft; that is, he has 'appropriated property belonging to another'.

If, however, he genuinely, albeit mistakenly, believed that he was legally entitled to take the watch in satisfaction of the debt then, in accordance with s 2(1)(a) of the Theft Act 1968, his appropriation was not dishonest and therefore he did not commit theft. Furthermore, if Michael believed he had the legal right to deprive, he cannot be convicted of either theft or robbery even if he knew that he had no legal right to use nor threaten force (*Robinson* (1977)).

Section 2(1)(a) is limited to the situation where the accused believes he has a *legal* right to deprive another of property. If Michael knew that he had no legal right to the watch but considered himself to be *morally* entitled to take it, then the question of his dishonesty falls to the jury directed in accordance with the test expounded by the Court of Appeal in *Ghosh* (1982).

According to the Court of Appeal, the jury should be instructed, first, to determine what the accused's beliefs and intentions were and then, having done so, to decide whether what the accused did was dishonest according to the ordinary standards of reasonable and honest people. If they were not dishonest according to those standards, the prosecution fails.

However, if the accused's actions were dishonest according to the ordinary standards of reasonable and honest people, the jury must consider whether the accused realised that what he did was dishonest according to those standards. If the accused did not realise that, then he was not dishonest and the prosecution fails.

If the jury conclude that Michael was not dishonest, then he is neither guilty of theft nor robbery. On the other hand, if the court concludes that he was dishonest, he will be guilty of theft and, as he put Thomas in fear of being subjected to force, in order to steal, he will also be guilty of robbery.

Blackmail

Michael made a demand with menaces (as explained above) when he threatened to beat up Thomas unless he paid the money owing.

In addition, he acted with a view to gain. In *Parkes* (1973), it was held that the repayment of a debt is a gain. Whether he is guilty of blackmail will, therefore, depend upon whether his demand with menaces was 'unwarranted'.

This is a question of *mens rea*. The onus is on the prosecution to prove *either* that Michael did not believe that he had reasonable grounds for making the demand for the return of the money *or* that he did not believe that the use of the threat to beat Thomas was a proper means of reinforcing the demand.

Michael might have believed he had reasonable grounds for making the demand but, unless he also believed that the threat employed was morally and socially acceptable, he will be guilty of blackmail. The test is subjective, but the word 'proper' refers to general standards. A person believes a threat to be 'proper' not merely by believing that it is in accordance with his own standards. The test is whether he believes that the use of the threat would be regarded as proper by people generally.[1]

In *Harvey* (1981), the Court of Appeal held that, in general, where the accused knew that the act threatened was unlawful, it will not be possible for him to contend that he thought it was proper. Therefore, it is unlikely that Michael's demand with menaces was 'warranted' and, thus, he may be convicted of blackmail (see also *Harrison* (2001)).

Note

1   But see *Lambert* (1972), where it was accepted that menaces were warranted if D believed that by his own standards what he threatened was proper.

Question 47

Plug went into a supermarket intending to do some shopping and to steal some goods if the opportunity presented itself. Plug put a bottle of sherry in the trolley provided by the supermarket intending to conceal it in a large inside pocket of his coat pocket at a later stage and remove it from the shop without paying for it. Continuing with his shopping, Plug took a bottle of wine from its shelf. He intended to pay for the wine. He then decided to return the sherry to the shelf as he had no opportunity to put it in his pocket and he did not want to buy it. At the checkout, the shop assistant rang up the price marked on the bottle of wine. At that point, Plug realised that the wine had been underpriced, but he chose to say nothing. In addition, the assistant gave Plug too much change. Plug did not notice the excess until after he had left the supermarket.

Answer plan

The principal issues are:

- burglary contrary to s 9(1)(a) and (b) of the Theft Act 1968;
- theft contrary to s 1(1);
- obtaining property by deception contrary to s 15;
- 'property got by another's mistake' – s 5(4).

The principal authorities are: *Gomez* (1993); *Jones and Smith* (1976); *Collins* (1973).

Answer

Burglary

By virtue of s 9(1)(a) of the Theft Act 1968, a person is guilty of burglary if he enters a building as a trespasser intending to commit one of a number of specified offences and, by virtue of s 9(2), these include theft contrary to s 1 of the Act.[1]

The *actus reus* of burglary contrary to s 9(1)(a) consists of entering a building as a trespasser, and a person enters as a trespasser if he enters without the consent or permission of the occupier. Furthermore, it was decided in *Jones and Smith* (1976) that a person is a trespasser for the purposes of s 9 if he enters premises in excess of the permission that has been given to him, provided that he knows that he is entering in excess of the (implied) permission or, at least, is reckless with respect to that fact (see *Collins* (1973)).

As Professor Williams has pointed out, the decision implies that a person who enters a building intending to commit one of the specified offences is a trespasser at the moment of entry; thus, a person who enters a supermarket intending to steal items within the shop is a burglar. The shopkeeper's invitation to enter the premises does not extend to those who enter for the purpose of stealing.[2]

It is unclear, however, whether an entry is trespassory if, as in Plug's case, a person enters partly for lawful purposes, that is, to do their shopping and partly for unlawful purposes, that is, to steal. Assuming that an entry for mixed lawful and unlawful purposes is trespassory, then he is guilty of burglary. The fact that he did not, at the time of entry, intend to steal specific items does not preclude a conviction for burglary (*Walkington* (1979); *Attorney General's References (Nos 1 and 2 of 1979)* (1980)).

Theft

Section 1 of the Theft Act 1968 provides that a person is guilty of theft if he dishonestly appropriates property belonging to another with the intention of permanently depriving the other of it. The maximum penalty for theft is a term of imprisonment not exceeding seven years (s 7 of the Theft Act, as substituted by s 26 of the Criminal Justice Act 1991).

Sherry

Whether Plug was guilty of theft when he removed the bottle of sherry from the shelf depends upon whether he could be said to have appropriated it.

Appropriation involves an 'assumption of the rights of an owner' (s 3(1)) and, according to Lord Roskill in *Morris* (1983), a person does not assume the rights of an owner where he does an act expressly or impliedly authorised by the owner.

Lord Roskill approved the decision of the Divisional Court in *Eddy v Niman* (1981), where D, a shopper, intending to steal, had put items in the basket provided by the supermarket. The Divisional Court held that, despite D's secret dishonest intention, there was no theft at that stage as D had acted within the scope of the authority granted to shoppers. The Divisional Court was of the opinion that it is only where D *does some act inconsistent with the rights of the owner or usurps a right of the owner* that he can be said to appropriate the items.

However, in *Gomez* (1993), the House of Lords decided that, whilst an act by way of adverse interference with or usurpation of the rights of an owner does amount to an appropriation, the concept is not limited to such acts and, thus, a person who removes goods from a supermarket shelf appropriates them and they will be guilty of theft provided the *mens rea* elements can be satisfied. In Plug's case, they clearly can. He intended to permanently deprive the supermarket of the sherry and, at the time he appropriated the goods, he was dishonest (see discussion of this concept, below). The fact that he returned the sherry is of no consequence. He was guilty of theft at the time he removed it from the shelf.[3]

Furthermore, Plug may also be guilty of burglary contrary to s 9(1)(b). This provides that a person is guilty of burglary if, having entered a building as a trespasser, a person steals anything therein. The prosecution would have to prove that the entry was trespassory and that Plug knew that or was reckless with respect to that at the time he appropriated the sherry (see the discussion above; *Jones and Smith; Collins*).

The wine

Although Plug 'appropriated' the wine when he took it from the shelf, he did not steal it. At that moment, he lacked the dishonest intent to steal and, it is submitted, there was no theft when he took possession of the bottle after the cashier had rung up the wrong price. In *Dip Kaur* (1981), it was held that a mistake as to price does not render a contract void. The ownership in the goods transfers to the buyer who, therefore, cannot be said to appropriate property *belonging to another* when he pays for and takes possession of the goods.

Doubt was cast on the decision in *Kaur* by Lord Roskill in *Morris*. His Lordship did not fully explain why he considered *Kaur* to be wrongly decided, but said that he did not consider fine points of civil law regarding void and voidable contracts to be relevant issues as far as theft was concerned. In *Hinks* (2000), the House of Lords adopted a similar point of view. Speaking for the majority, Lord Steyn said that there were great advantages, in a theft trial, in not having to explain 'complex' civil law concepts to the jury.

It is respectfully submitted that this approach is misguided. It is not possible to avoid recourse to the civil law when the facts raise the issue of whether the property belonged to another at the time of the alleged appropriation. In *Walker* (1984), the Court of Appeal allowed D's appeal against conviction for theft where the trial judge had failed to direct the jury with respect to the relevant issues of civil law contained in the Sale of Goods Act 1979.

In addition, although the point was not argued in *Kaur*, Plug may contend that taking incorrectly priced goods is not dishonest.

If Plug mistakenly believed that he had a right in law to take the wine at the price indicated, then, as a matter of law, he was not dishonest (s 2(1)(a)). Alternatively, even if he knew that he had no legal right to the wine at the wrong price, he may raise evidence that he believed that it was not dishonest by ordinary standards to take advantage of a pricing error made by a supermarket. If so, the judge should direct the jury in accordance with what is known as the '*Ghosh* tests' to consider, as a matter of fact, whether he was dishonest (*Roberts* (1987)).

In *Ghosh* (1982), the Court of Appeal held that, when determining whether the prosecution has proved that the defendant was acting dishonestly, the jury must first of all decide whether *according to the standards of reasonable and honest people* what was done was dishonest. If it was not dishonest according to those standards, the prosecution fails.

If it was dishonest according to those standards, then the jury must consider whether the prosecution have proved that the defendant himself realised that what he was doing was, *by the above standards*, dishonest. If the defendant did not know that, the prosecution fails.[4]

Obtaining property by deception

Did Plug obtain the wine by deception?

The Divisional Court in *Kaur* held that D, in that case, had used no deception to obtain the goods. In general, silence constitutes neither fraud nor deception and the answer to the question posed above is, therefore, 'no'.[5]

Theft of the change

Plug did not steal the excess change when he was given it by the cashier. At that time, he was unaware of the excess and, therefore, he did not dishonestly appropriate it. However, he may be guilty of theft at a later stage when, on becoming aware of the shop assistant's mistake, he decided to keep the excess change. First, s 3(1) provides that, even if the original taking was innocent, a later assumption of a right to property by keeping or dealing with it as owner will amount to an appropriation. Secondly, although, as a matter of common law, the ownership in the money passed to Plug on delivery, the excess change is regarded, for the purposes of theft, as belonging to the supermarket. The conditions in s 5(4) apply: the money was 'got by another's mistake' and Plug is 'under a [quasi-contractual] obligation to make restoration'.

Again, Plug may contend that keeping excess change is not dishonest. The issues relating to the question of dishonesty are discussed above.

Notes

1   The penalty for burglary in a building other than a dwelling place is a term of imprisonment not exceeding 10 years (s 9(3)(a), as substituted by s 26(2) of the Criminal Justice Act 1991).

2   Williams, G, *Textbook of Criminal Law*, 2nd edn, 1983, p 848.

3   The question certified for the decision of the House of Lords in *Gomez* was as follows:

When theft is alleged and that which is alleged to be stolen passes to the defendant with the consent of the owner, but that consent has been obtained by a false representation, has: (a) an appropriation within the meaning of s 1(1) of the Theft Act 1968 taken place; or (b) must such a passing of property necessarily involve an element of adverse interference with or usurpation of some right of an owner?

It is therefore arguable that the *ratio* of the majority is restricted to the situation where the defendant practises a deception to obtain possession or ownership of the article.

Gomez was applied in *Atakpu* and *Abrahams* (1994), but, in that case too, the property was obtained by virtue of false representations made by the defendants.

In *Hinks*, however, Lord Steyn said that although the certified question in *Gomez* referred to the situation where consent has been obtained by fraud, the majority judgments did not 'differentiate between cases of consent induced by fraud and in any other circumstances. The *ratio* involves a proposition of general application'.

4   It was decided in *Hyam* (1997) that, where a direction on dishonesty is necessary, the exact words used in *Ghosh* should be followed.

5   *DPP v Ray* (1974) is distinguishable from the present facts. In that case, the restaurant customer was taken to impliedly represent, on ordering a meal, that he intended to pay for it, a representation which he continued to make throughout. A shopper, on the other hand, does not impliedly represent the accuracy of the prices displayed on goods for sale. Nor, if he remains silent, does he do anything positive to induce a false belief in the accuracy of the price.

Question 48

Simon checked in at the Shilton Hotel. He produced a forged membership card of the Golden Travel Club. Membership of the club entitled clients of the hotel to a 20% discount off the price of a room. In addition, club guests receive a complimentary bottle of wine in their rooms. He decided that, before going to his room, he would have a drink in the hotel lounge. He entered the lounge, but found it to be empty. He noticed that the bar till was open. He went behind the bar, intending to take any cash he found in the till. The till was empty, so he left the lounge. He went to his room and consumed the wine. The following morning, he checked out of the hotel. He paid the discounted price for the room. He then went to the hairdressers to have his hair cut. He paid for his haircut with a stolen credit card.

Discuss Simon's criminal liability.

Answer plan

This question requires consideration of a number of offences found in the Theft Acts 1968 and 1978 (principally, those involving deception).

The principal issues to be considered are:

- the requirement of a 'causal link' in deception offences;
- does a person 'make off' if they have (fraudulently obtained) consent to depart;
- burglary and conditional intent;
- evasion of liability – s 2 of the Theft Act 1968.

Answer

Evasion of liability

It would appear that, when Simon checked into the hotel presenting a forged club card, he committed the offence of 'evasion of liability by deception' contrary to s 2(1)(c) of the Theft Act 1978. The maximum penalty for this offence is a term of imprisonment not exceeding five years (s 4(2)(a)).

Section 2(1)(c) is not restricted to the evasion of an existing liability. It also covers the situation where, as in this case, the accused practises a deception to obtain an abatement of a prospective liability.

Section 5(1) of the Theft Act 1978 provides that 'deception' bears the same meaning for the purposes of s 2 as it does for s 15 of the Theft Act 1968, that is, a deliberate or reckless deception by words or conduct as to fact or law.

Simon represented by his conduct (the presentation of the card) that he was a member of a club entitled to a discount. He obtained the abatement of liability by virtue of that deception. Therefore, provided that Simon was dishonest at the time he checked in, he is guilty of the offence in question.[1]

Obtaining services

In addition, it would seem that Simon has, by deception, dishonestly obtained services from another contrary to s 1(1) of the Theft Act 1978. The maximum punishment for this offence is also five years' imprisonment.

The comments made above regarding the issues of 'deception' and 'dishonesty' apply equally to the offence now under discussion.

Simon was permitted to enjoy the services of the hotel on the understanding that they would be paid for, albeit at a reduced rate and, thus, there was an 'obtaining of services from another'.[2]

Obtaining property

With respect to the free bottle of wine, Simon may be charged with the offence of obtaining property by deception contrary to s 15 of the Theft Act 1968. The maximum punishment is 10 years' imprisonment.

Simon has, by the false representation that he was a member of the Golden Travel Club, induced the hotel to make him a gift of the wine. By virtue of s 15(2), he has obtained property, that is, the ownership of the wine by deception and, provided he was dishonest, he is guilty of the offence. In addition, he may be convicted of stealing the wine contrary to s 1 of the Theft Act 1968. In *Gomez* (1992), the House of Lords held, by a majority, that an appropriation of property belonging to another can occur even if the owner consents to what D does and even if ownership in the property transfers to P.

Burglary

Did Simon commit burglary contrary to s 9 of the Theft Act 1968 when he went behind the bar intending to steal any cash he found in the till?

According to s 9(1)(a), a person is guilty of burglary if he enters any building or part of a building as a trespasser with intent to commit one of a number of specified offences.[3] These include theft of anything in the building or part of the building (s 9(2)).

Trespass, in the law of tort, refers to presence on property without legal right. In general, presence on the property without the consent of the possessor is a trespass. Thus, a person enters a building or part of a building as a trespasser if he enters without permission and, if permission to enter is limited to certain parts of the premises, there is a trespassory entry when that permission is exceeded. Whether the area behind the bar constituted a separate 'part' of the building from which Simon was excluded is a matter for the jury (*Walkington* (1979)). If they are satisfied that the hotel management had impliedly prohibited customers from that area and that Simon knew of (or was reckless in respect of) that prohibition, then he may be convicted of burglary (*Collins* (1973)).

The fact that Simon intended to steal 'any cash that he found' does not preclude a conviction for burglary. In *Attorney General's References (Nos 1 and 2 of 1979)* (1980), it was held that where D is charged with entry into a building or part of a building with intent to steal, and the indictment does not allege an intent to steal a specific object, he can be convicted if, at the time of entry, he intended to steal *something* in the building or part of the building. This applies even though he merely intended to steal anything that he may find worth stealing and even though there was, as in this case, nothing that he regarded as being worth stealing.

Evasion of liability

When Simon checked out, continuing the deception that he was entitled to a discount, he committed the offence under s 2(1)(b) of the Theft Act 1978.[4]

The receptionist was induced to forbear from demanding the full price by Simon's continuing representation that he was entitled to a discount and he intended to make permanent default in *part* on the still existing liability to make a payment.

The maximum punishment is five years' imprisonment (s 4(2)(a)).

Making off without payment

Whether Simon may be convicted of the offence of 'making off without payment' contrary to s 3 of the Theft Act 1978 is more controversial. It remains to be authoritatively decided whether a person can be said to have 'made off without having paid as *required* or expected' if he leaves with the consent of the creditor, the consent having been obtained by a continuing deception. In *Hammond* (1982), a circuit judge held that there is no 'making off' if a creditor consents to D leaving.

It is submitted that this interpretation of the section is wrong. The section is aimed at the bilking customer – it should not matter whether D leaves with stealth or openly, with or without the apparent consent of the creditor.

The punishment for contravention of s 3 is a term of imprisonment not exceeding two years (s 4(2)(b)).

The hairdressers

Provided Simon intended to use the stolen credit card prior to having his hair cut, he committed the offence of obtaining services by deception contrary to s 1 of the 1978 Act. In *Lambie* (1982), it was held that the user of a credit card impliedly represents that he has authority to use it.

In addition, whether or not he intended to use the card from the outset, he is guilty of the offence of evasion of liability contrary to s 2(1)(a) of the Act. By tendering a stolen credit card in 'payment' for the haircut, he, by deception, secured the remission of an existing liability to make a payment (*Jackson* (1983)).

Going equipped for stealing

It would appear from the facts of the problem that Simon was guilty of this offence contrary to s 25(1) of the 1968 Act. The Golden Travel Club Card was an article that he had with him for use in connection with a 'cheat' (an offence under s 15 of the Act). The credit card would also be an article for the purposes of s 25 if he intended to use it to obtain property if the opportunity arose (*Ellames* (1974)).

Notes

1   Although there is nothing in the facts of the problem to raise the issue of dishonesty, there are some general observations that may be made in respect of this element of the *mens rea*. First, dishonesty is a question of fact for the jury. Secondly, the partial negative definition of dishonesty in s 2 of the Theft Act 1968 does not apply to the various offences of deception. Finally, it is only where there is evidence that the accused was not dishonest on the basis of the tests in *Ghosh* (1968) that the judge must leave the issue to the jury. As the facts do not raise any issues of dishonesty, it has been assumed throughout that Simon was dishonest.

2   Section 1(2) provides that there is an obtaining of services from another where the other is induced to confer a benefit by doing some act, or causing or permitting some act to be done, on the understanding that the benefit has been or will be paid for.

3   Where, as in this case, the building entered is not a dwelling, the maximum punishment is 10 years' imprisonment. For a discussion of the meaning of 'dwelling', see Smith, JC, *The Law of Theft*, 7th edn, 1993, p 183.

4   According to this sub-section:

> ... a person commits an offence where by any deception he dishonestly and with intent to make permanent default, in whole or in part, on any existing liability to make a payment induces a creditor to forgo payment.

Question 49

Part (a)

Stanley, a schizophrenic, received what he believed were instructions from 'God' to destroy all 'places of sin'. Stanley explained to 'God' that it was a crime in England to destroy property. 'God' reassured Stanley that, if he did as he was instructed, no human life would be endangered and informed him that, unless Stanley set about the task immediately, the towns of England would be destroyed in alphabetical order. Stanley, who lived in Accrington, responded straightaway. He went out and threw a petrol bomb through the window of a betting shop. The shop was completely destroyed. Although there were a number of people in neighbouring buildings, no one was injured.

Discuss Stanley's criminal liability.

Part (b)

Optic lived at No 11 Acacia Avenue. One night, he arrived home drunk. By mistake, he attempted to get into No 13. As his key failed to open the door, he assumed that the lock was broken. He went to the back of the house and, to gain entry, smashed the window of the back door.

Discuss Optic's criminal liability.

Would your answer differ if No 11 had been the house of one of Optic's friends with whom Optic had been spending a few days?

Answer plan

Although both parts of this question contain elements of liability for criminal damage, they deal with quite different issues. The first part focuses on the defence of insanity. The second part involves analysis of the contrasting treatment of, on the one hand, drunken mistakes going to the *mens rea* and, on the other, drunken mistakes going to a 'defence' of 'lawful excuse'.

The principal issues are:

- the meaning of 'recklessness';
- the meaning and application of 'lawful excuse' in s 5(2)(b) of the Criminal Damage Act 1971 – protection of property;
- the defence of insanity – nature and quality of act; insane delusions;
- drunkenness and 'Caldwell recklessness';
- the meaning and application of 'lawful excuse' in s 5(2)(a) – belief in consent; mistake induced by drunkenness and s 5(2)(a).

The principal authorities are: *Caldwell* (1982); *Jaggard v Dickinson* (1981); *Sullivan* (1984).

Answer

Part (a)

Stanley may be charged with criminal damage contrary to s 1(1) of the Criminal Damage Act 1971 ('simple damage') and damaging property being reckless as to whether the life of another would be endangered contrary to s 1(2) ('dangerous damage'). Where an offence is committed by fire, then it is charged as arson (s 1(3)), punishable with life imprisonment (s 4(1)).

Clearly, Stanley committed the *actus reus* of both offences ('property' includes land – s 10(1) of the 1971 Act).

In the case of simple damage, the *mens rea* is satisfied on proof of an intention to damage/destroy property belonging to another or recklessness with respect to that. The facts of the problem indicate that he intended to destroy the building.

Section 5(2)(b) of the 1971 Act provides that a person has a lawful excuse for the purposes of 'simple damage' if he destroyed property to protect other property which he believed to be in need of immediate protection. (This 'defence' does not apply to 'dangerous damage.) In *Hunt* (1977), however, the Court of Appeal held that whether property was in need of protection involves an objective question – whether in fact the action taken might protect property.[1]

Undoubtedly, the court would take the view that destroying a betting shop could not protect Accrington and, thus, Stanley committed 'simple damage' (subject to the defence of insanity discussed below).

For 'dangerous damage', the prosecution would have to prove that he was at least reckless with respect to the prospect of the life of another being endangered.[2] This requires proof that: (a) by setting fire to the betting shop,

Stanley created an obvious risk that life would be endangered; and (b) Stanley had either: (i) not given any thought to the possibility of there being any such risk; or (ii) having recognised that there was some risk, went on to take it (*Caldwell* (1982)).

Whether a risk is 'obvious' is determined by reference to whether the reasonable prudent person would have appreciated it as such. It is immaterial that D failed to appreciate the risk. This rule applies even if D was incapable, for whatever reason, of appreciating the risk. The first part of the definition is entirely objective (*Elliott v C* (1983)).

Let us assume that, in this case, the risk of life being endangered was 'obvious', as defined. That is not the end of the matter. The prosecution must prove, in addition, that Stanley had one of the 'states of mind' ((b)(i) or (b)(ii), above). The facts state that Stanley considered the risk of human life being endangered and acted on the assurance of 'God' that it would not be. Thus, Stanley lacked both of the alternative 'states of mind' required by the second limb of the test. He falls within the so called 'loophole' in the *Caldwell* test (see *Reid* (1992)).[3]

Insanity

According to the *M'Naghten Rules* (1843), a person is legally insane if at the time he committed the act he was suffering from:

(1) a defect of reason caused by disease of the mind;
(2) (a)   as not to know the nature and quality of his act; or
    (b)   if he did know that, he did not know that what he was doing was wrong.

There is a presumption of sanity in English law. The burden of proving insanity is, therefore, on Stanley. He must prove his case on a balance of probabilities (*M'Naghten Rules*; *Bratty v Attorney General for Northern Ireland* (1963)).

Whether a condition amounts to insanity is a question of law (*Bratty v Attorney General for Northern Ireland*).

In *Sullivan* (1984), Lord Diplock explained that disease of the mind in the rules refers to an impairment of the faculties of reason, memory and understanding. It is unnecessary to show that the brain is diseased – the disorder may be functional.

The condition from which Stanley suffered is clearly capable in law of amounting to a disease of the mind.

The judges in the *M'Naghten* case said that, in cases of insane delusion, the defendant is to be considered in the same situation as to responsibility as if the facts were as he perceived them to be. His delusion that 'God' was going to destroy other property unless he destroyed the places of sin falls within this rule. If the facts had been as he believed, he would have had a lawful excuse. He believed that the property was in immediate need of protection (see s 5(2)(b)(i)) and that the means adopted were reasonable, and, therefore, the proper verdict on a charge of simple damage is 'not guilty by reason of insanity'.

As explained above, Stanley apparently lacked the *mens rea* for 'dangerous damage'. However, again, he is entitled only to a qualified acquittal. Where the defendant has put his state of mind in issue, the judge may rule that he has raised the defence of insanity (*Bratty v Attorney General for Northern Ireland*; *Sullivan* (1984)).[4]

As Stanley understood his act to be legally wrong, the case for insanity must be based on the 'nature and quality' limb. This refers to whether Stanley knew what he was doing. It has not been authoritatively decided whether this would apply to the situation where D dismisses a risk that the reasonable man would recognise as 'obvious', but, it is submitted, the foreseeable consequences of an act are an element of the nature and quality of the act – and this interpretation is supported by the rule regarding insane delusions.

Where a defendant is found not guilty by reason of insanity, the judge must make one of a number of orders including a hospital order with or without restrictions on discharge (s 5 of the Criminal Procedure (Insanity) Act 1964, as substituted by Sched 1 to the Criminal Procedure (Insanity and Unfitness to Plead) Act 1991).

Part (b)

Optic may be guilty of 'simple damage' as defined in s 1(1) of the Criminal Damage Act 1971 (see above). He has damaged property, that is, the window belonging to another.

Clearly, he did not *intend* to damage property *belonging to another*, but he may have been reckless. If, in the light of all the evidence, the jury conclude that the risk that the property might belong to another was 'obvious' (as explained above), then Optic will be liable if he failed to give any thought to the risk that the property belonged to another. The fact that he thought it was his does not necessarily mean that he put his mind to the *risk* of it belonging to another.[5]

If he thought about the risk but, because he was drunk, concluded, wrongly, that there was no risk, then, although he was not reckless,[6] he may nonetheless be convicted of 'simple damage'. Where D is alleged to have 'recklessly damaged property belonging to another', the offence is one of 'basic intent' (*Caldwell*) and lack of *mens rea* caused by drunkenness is no defence to a crime of basic intent (*Majewski* (1977)).

Alternative facts

In this situation, Optic will have a 'lawful excuse' if he believed that the person *whom he believed to be entitled* to consent to the damage (that is, his friend) would have consented to the damage (s 5(2)(a) of the 1971 Act).[7]

In similar circumstances, the Divisional Court, in *Jaggard v Dickinson* (1981) held that D could rely on her intoxication to explain her mistaken belief. The court considered that the *Majewski* rule was inapplicable. This was not a case where the D's 'drunken mistake' went to the *mens rea*.

The Divisional Court were influenced by the fact that s 5(3) provides that, for the purposes of s 5(2), it is immaterial whether the belief is justified or not so long as it is genuinely held.

Notes

1   This decision ignores the clear subjective terms in which the sub-section is expressed. The use of the expression *'in order to protect property'* implies a subjective test. *Hunt* was followed, however, in the cases of *Ashford and Smith* (1988) and *Hill and Hall* (1989) (see also *Blake v DPP* (1993)).

2   It is not necessary to prove that life was in fact endangered (*Sangha* (1988); *Parker* (1993)).

3   In *Reid*, Lord Browne-Wilkinson appeared to suggest that the loophole applies in situations where 'despite D being aware of the risk and deciding to take it, he does so because of a *reasonable* misunderstanding' (p 696f).

There are two objections to this:

(a) If D takes a risk of which he is aware, he is reckless. As explained above, the lacuna in *Caldwell* applies where D has considered whether there is a risk and concluded there is *none*.

(b) There is no justification for narrowing the lacuna to the situation where D *reasonably* concludes there is no risk. As Lord Goff pointed out, both limbs of the *Caldwell* test of recklessness are tests of *mens rea* and that a *bona fide* mistaken belief that there was no risk will excuse. The reasonableness of the mistake is merely evidence that it was genuinely held (p 690f–h).

4   According to Lord Denning in *Bratty* (1963), the prosecution may adduce evidence of insanity when the defendant puts his state of mind in issue. Professor Williams argues that this is not limited to cases of automatism and would apply where the defendant, as in this case, alleges a mistake of fact: Williams, G, *Textbook of Criminal Law*, 2nd edn, 1983, p 664.

5   In *Pigg* (1982), the Court of Appeal held that *Caldwell* recklessness applies to the circumstances of an offence as well as the consequences.

The prosecution may give evidence that Optic was drunk in support of their case that he had not thought about the risk or that he had consciously taken a risk that he would not have had he been sober (*Griffiths* (1989); *Clarke* (1990)).

6   See the explanation of the 'Caldwell loophole' in Part (a) and note 3, above.
7   The defendant has an evidential burden in relation to a s 5(2) defence (Gannon
     (1988)).

Question 50

Part (a)

George telephoned Paul and said that, if Paul did not destroy some
compromising photographs of George with Patti, he would set fire to Paul's
shop. In fact, Paul's telephone was faulty with the result that he did not
hear the message.

Discuss George's criminal liability.

Part (b)

John, a farmer, noticed that a large dog, Martha, belonging to Stuart, was
attacking his sheep. He asked Ringo, who was shooting grouse in a
neighbouring field, if he would lend him his shotgun. Ringo refused. John
wrenched the gun from Ringo's grasp and pushed Ringo to the ground.
John shot and killed Martha.

Discuss John's criminal liability.

Answer plan

The first part of the question is concerned with the offences of blackmail
contrary to s 21 of the Theft Act 1968 and threats of damage to property
contrary to s 2 of the Criminal Damage Act 1971. The second part concerns
issues of liability for criminal damage and, to a minor extent, battery.

Part (a)

The principal issues are:

- whether a 'demand with menaces' is 'made' for the purposes of blackmail
  if the intended recipient does not hear it (s 21 of the Theft Act 1968);
- the meaning and application of 'view to gain' or 'intent to cause loss' in
  s 21;
- whether a 'threat of damage' is 'made' if the intended recipient does not
  hear it (s 2 of the Criminal Damage Act 1971).

Part (b)

The principal issues are:

- the meaning and application of 'lawful excuse' in s 5(2)(b) of the Criminal Damage Act 1971;
- the availability of the defence of 'duress of circumstances'.

Principal authorities: *Treacy v DPP* (1971); *Clear* (1968); *Harvey* (1981); *Hunt* (1977); *Martin* (1989); *Conway* (1989).

Answer

Part (a)

Blackmail

George may be guilty of blackmail contrary to s 21 of the Theft Act 1968, an offence punishable with a term of imprisonment not exceeding 14 years (s 21(3)).

The *actus reus* of blackmail is a 'demand with menaces'.

In *Treacy v DPP* (1971), the House of Lords held by a majority that a demand contained in a letter is made when it is posted irrespective of whether it arrives or is read by the person to whom it is addressed. Lord Diplock was influenced by the fact that the person who makes an uncommunicated demand is no less wicked nor less in need of deterrence than the person whose demand is received.

The same may be said of the person who makes an oral communication which is not heard and, thus, it is submitted, George made a demand, *viz*, that Paul give him the photographs.

A threat of any action detrimental to or unpleasant to the person addressed is capable of amounting to a menace so long as the threat is of sufficient intensity that it would move the ordinary person of normal stability and courage to accede unwillingly to the demand (*Thorne v Motor Trade Association* (1937); *Clear* (1968)). Thus, it is unnecessary to know how Paul would have reacted to the threat to demolish his shop. The question – and it is one for the jury – is whether the *ordinary person* would be influenced by the threat.

The demand must be made with a 'view to gain' *or* 'intent to cause loss' in terms of money or other property (s 34(2)(a)). In this case, George intended to cause Paul the loss of property, that is, the photographs.

The prosecution must prove that the 'demand with menaces' was unwarranted. This is a question of *mens rea*. Section 21(1) provides that D's demand with menaces is unwarranted unless D made it in the belief: (a) that he had reasonable grounds for making the belief; and (b) that the use of the menaces was a proper means of reinforcing the demand.

The facts of the problem suggest that George's demand with menaces was unwarranted. Even if he believed that he had reasonable grounds for demanding the photographs, it is improbable that he believed the use of the menaces was a proper means of reinforcing the demand. If George knew that what he threatened to do was unlawful, his demand with menaces was unwarranted (*Harvey* (1981)).

Threats to destroy property

It is an offence contrary to s 2 of the Criminal Damage Act 1971 to threaten to destroy or damage property belonging to another intending that the person threatened would fear that the threat would be carried out.

The offence is not limited to written threats and, although there is no direct authority on the point, it is submitted that, by analogy to blackmail, a threat is made even if it is not received.[1]

Part (b)

Criminal damage

John may be charged with criminal damage contrary to s 1(1) of the Criminal Damage Act 1971, an offence which, by virtue of s 4, is punishable with a maximum of 10 years' imprisonment.

The offence is committed where D intentionally or recklessly damages property belonging to another.

Tame animals or animals reduced into possession amount to 'property' for the purposes of this offence (s 10(1)(a)). The killing of an animal constitutes destruction of property. Thus, clearly John committed the *actus reus* of the offence. Similarly, his *mens rea* is not in doubt – John intentionally destroyed property belonging to another.

Section 1(1) provides, however, that no offence is committed if D had a 'lawful excuse'. Section 5(2)(b) provides that D has a lawful excuse if he destroyed the property in order to protect property belonging to himself which he believed to be in immediate need of protection.

For the reasons explained above, the sheep are 'property' belonging to John.

Although the defence in s 5(2)(b) is expressed in 'subjective' terms, the Court of Appeal in *Hunt* (1977) held that the defence will be denied if it is proved that what was done could not amount, objectively, to something done in protection of property.

In this case, the objective requirement is satisfied. If, as the facts imply, John believed that his sheep were in immediate need of protection and he believed that shooting the dog was a reasonable means of protecting his property, then he has a 'lawful excuse'. It is immaterial whether those beliefs were justified. All that matters is that they were genuinely held (s 5(3)).

Battery

John may be charged with the battery of Ringo.

Battery is a summary offence. It is committed where a person intentionally or recklessly inflicts unlawful personal violence upon another (*Rolfe* (1952)). The slightest degree of force will suffice (*Cole v Turner* (1704); *Collins v Wilcock* (1984)). The maximum punishment is a fine not exceeding level 5 on the standard scale and/or a term of imprisonment not exceeding six months or both (s 39 of the Criminal Justice Act 1988).

It is clear from the facts that John intentionally applied force. The issue is whether he did so 'unlawfully'.

Section 5(2) of the Criminal Damage Act 1971 only provides a defence of 'lawful excuse' to a charge of criminal damage. It does not apply to other offences. It would appear that there is no other defence of which John may take advantage.

The recognised defence of 'duress of circumstances' applies where D can be said to be acting reasonably and proportionately in order to avoid a threat of death or serious injury to himself or another person (*Martin* (1989)). And, although there is some weak authority for the proposition that a defence of necessity might be available in cases where a lesser danger threatens (see, for example, *Conway* (1989), *per* Woolf LJ), there is no modern authority in which a threat of damage to property has been recognised as providing an excuse or justification for an offence against the person.

Note

1   In *Cakmak* (2002), when considering the ingredients of an offence of threatening to destroy or damage property belong to another contrary to s 2(a) of the Criminal Damage Act 1971, there were three main issues: (i) whether, objectively, a threat had been made to another; (ii) whether the words and actions amounted to a threat to destroy or damage property in law and whether in fact such a threat had been made; and (iii) a question of *mens rea*, whether the defendants intended that the person threatened would fear that the threat would be carried out.

INDEX